Naturalized Bioethics

Naturalized Bioethics represents a revolutionary change in how health care ethics is practiced. It calls for bioethicists to give up their dependence on utilitarianism and other ideal moral theories and instead to move toward a self-reflexive, socially inquisitive, politically critical, and inclusive ethics. Wary of idealizations that bypass social realities, the naturalism in ethics that is developed in this volume is empirically nourished and acutely aware that ethical theory is the practice of particular people in particular times, places, cultures, and professional environments. The essays in this collection examine the variety of embodied experiences of individual people. They situate the bioethicist within the clinical or research context, take seriously the web of relationships in which all human beings are nested, and explore a number of the many different kinds of power relations that inform health care encounters.

Naturalized Bioethics aims to help bioethicists, doctors, nurses, allied health professionals, disability studies scholars, medical researchers, and other health professionals address the ethical issues surrounding health care.

Hilde Lindemann is Professor of Philosophy at Michigan State University. A former editor of *Hypatia* and the *Hastings Center Report*, she is the author of a number of books, including *An Invitation to Feminist Ethics* and *Damaged Identities, Narrative Repair*.

Marian Verkerk is Professor of the Ethics of Care at the University Medical Center, Groningen, in the Netherlands, where she is also Head of the Department of Medical Ethics, Health Law, and Medical Humanities and Director of the Center for the Ethics of Care.

Margaret Urban Walker is Lincoln Professor of Ethics and Professor of Philosophy at Arizona State University. Her work on moral epistemology and moral psychology includes *Moral Repair: Reconstructing Moral Relations after Wrongdoing; Moral Contexts*; and *Moral Understandings: A Feminist Study in Ethics*, now in its second edition.

Naturalized Bioethics

Toward Responsible Knowing and Practice

Edited by

HILDE LINDEMANN
Michigan State University

MARIAN VERKERK
University of Groningen

MARGARET URBAN WALKER
Arizona State University

CAMBRIDGE
UNIVERSITY PRESS

CAMBRIDGE UNIVERSITY PRESS
Cambridge, New York, Melbourne, Madrid, Cape Town, Singapore, São Paulo, Delhi

Cambridge University Press
32 Avenue of the Americas, New York, NY 10013–2473, USA

www.cambridge.org
Information on this title: www.cambridge.org/9780521719407

First published 2009

Printed in the United States of America

A catalog record for this publication is available from the British Library

Library of Congress Cataloging in Publication Data
Naturalized bioethics : toward responsible knowing and practice / edited by
    Hilde Lindemann, Marian Verkerk, Margaret Urban Walker.
        p. ; cm.
    Includes bibliographical references and index.
    ISBN 978-0-521-89524-8 (hardback) – ISBN 978-0-521-71940-7 (pbk.)
    1. Medical ethics.   2. Naturalism.   3. Ethics, Evolutionary.
    I. Lindemann, Hilde.   II. Verkerk, Marian.   III. Walker, Margaret Urban,
    1948– [DNLM: 1. Bioethics.   2. Ethical Theory.   WB 60 N2846 2009]
    R724.N38 2009
    174′.957 – dc22   2008014230

ISBN 978-0-521-89524-8 hardback
ISBN 978-0-521-71940-7 paperback

Contents

Contributors

Elizabeth (Libby) Bogdan-Lovis is Assistant Director of the Center for Ethics and Humanities in the Life Sciences and Co-director of the Bioethics, Humanities, and Society Program at Michigan State University. She precepts ethics modules in the College of Human Medicine. Her master's thesis adopted a critical social science perspective focusing on the political economy of childbirth management. This same approach, which examines the distribution of power and wealth and its effects on health and healing, aptly characterizes her ongoing scholarship. Her most recent work includes a coedited issue of *Social Science and Medicine* devoted to a social analysis of evidence-based medicine.

Tod Chambers is Associate Professor of Bioethics and Medical Humanities and of Medicine at Northwestern University's Feinberg School of Medicine. His areas of research include the rhetoric of bioethics and cross-cultural issues in clinical medicine. He is the author of *The Fiction of Bioethics* (Routledge, 1999) and, with Carl Elliott, is coeditor of *Prozac as a Way of Life* (University of North Carolina Press, 2003). He is presently working on a second monograph on the rhetoric of bioethics.

Raymond G. De Vries is a member of the Bioethics Program, the Department of Obstetrics and Gynecology, and the Department of Medical Education at the Medical School, University of Michigan. He is the author of *A Pleasing Birth: Midwifery and Maternity Care in the Netherlands* (Temple University Press, 2005) and coeditor of *The View from Here: Bioethics and the Social Sciences* (Blackwell, 2007). He is working on a critical social history of bioethics and is studying the regulation of science; clinical trials of genetic therapies and deep brain stimulation; international research ethics; informed consent and the "problem" of therapeutic misconception; and the social, ethical, and policy issues associated with nonmedically indicated surgical birth.

Jodi Halpern is Associate Professor of Bioethics and Medical Humanities at the University of California, Berkeley. She was in the Medical Scientist Training Program at Yale University and received her M.D. in 1989 and her Ph.D. in Philosophy in 1994, winning Yale's Porter Prize for outstanding dissertation across all disciplines. She completed her internship and residency in psychiatry at UCLA in 1993 and a Robert Wood Johnson Clinical Scholar Fellowship at UCLA in 1996. During 1997–98 she was a Rockefeller Fellow at Princeton University. The author of *From Detached Concern to Empathy: Humanizing Medical Practice* (Oxford University Press, 2001), she has a Greenwall Faculty Fellowship to study the role of emotional predictions in health care decisions about unfamiliar future health states.

Agnieszka Jaworska is Associate Professor of Philosophy at the University of California, Riverside. Her research lies at the intersection of ethical theory, medical ethics, and moral psychology. Her current project, entitled "Ethical Dilemmas at the Margins of Agency," concerns the ethics of treatment of individuals whose status as persons is thought to be compromised or uncertain, such as Alzheimer's patients, addicts, psychopaths, and young children. It is part of a larger investigation of the nature of caring as an attitude. Professor Jaworska received her B.S.E. from Princeton University and her Ph.D. from Harvard University. She was trained in clinical bioethics in the Department of Bioethics at the National Institutes of Health. She has published in *Ethics, Philosophy and Public Affairs,* and *Philosophy and Phenomenological Research.*

Eva Feder Kittay is Professor of Philosophy at SUNY, Stony Brook. She publishes on care ethics, feminist philosophy, and disability theory. Major publications include *Love's Labor: Essays on Women,*

Equality, and Dependency (Routledge, 1999) and *Metaphor: Its Cognitive Force and Linguistic Structure* (Oxford University Press, 1987); and four edited collections: *Blackwell Studies in Feminist Philosophy* (with Linda Alcoff, 2007); *The Subject of Care: Feminist Perspectives on Dependency* (with Ellen Feder; Rowman & Littlefield, 2003); *Women and Moral Theory* (with Diana Tietjens Meyers; Rowman & Littlefield, 1987); and *Frames, Fields and Contrasts* (with Adrienne Lehrer and Richard Lehrer; L. Erlbaum, 1992). She is working on two books, one tentatively titled *A Quest for a Humbler Philosophy: Thinking about Disabled Minds and Things That Matter*, and the other a collection of her essays on the ethics of care. She is the mother of two children, one of whom has significant cognitive impairments.

Mare Knibbe is a Ph.D. student in medical ethics (since 2004) at the Center for the Ethics of Care, University of Groningen, the Netherlands. She graduated in religious studies at the University of Groningen with a major in medical ethics and a minor in the psychology of religion. For her thesis on how medical and psychological perspectives serve as frameworks for moral questions in psychiatry, she received the fifth Professor Hubbeling Prize, awarded by the Faculty of Theology and Religious Studies once every three years to stimulate academic research. In her research project for the Ph.D., about ethical aspects of organ donation from living related donors, she uses a combination of qualitative research methods and care ethics.

Hilde Lindemann is Professor of Philosophy at Michigan State University. Her books include *An Invitation to Feminist Ethics* (McGraw-Hill, 2005) and, as Hilde Lindemann Nelson, *Damaged Identities, Narrative Repair* (Cornell University Press, 2001). With James Lindemann Nelson she coauthored *Alzheimer's: Answers to Hard Questions for Families* (Doubleday, 1996) and *The Patient in the Family* (Routledge, 1995), and she has also edited two previous collections: *Feminism and Families* and *Stories and Their Limits: Narrative Approaches to Bioethics* (both Routledge, 1997). She is the former editor of *Hypatia: A Journal of Feminist Philosophy*, and coeditor (with Sara Ruddick and Margaret Urban Walker) of Rowman & Littlefield's Feminist Constructions series. She has also been the general coeditor (with James Lindemann Nelson) of the

Reflective Bioethics series at Routledge. A Fellow of the Hastings Center, her ongoing research interests are in feminist bioethics, feminist ethics, the ethics of families, and the social construction of persons and their identities.

Margaret Olivia Little is Associate Professor in the Philosophy Department and Senior Research Scholar at the Kennedy Institute of Ethics at Georgetown University. Her research focuses on reproductive ethics, feminist bioethics, and metaethics. She is the coeditor (with Brad Hooker) of *Moral Particularism* (Oxford University Press, 2000) and author of *Intimate Assistance: Re-Thinking Abortion in Law and Morality* (Oxford University Press, forthcoming). A Fellow of the Hastings Center, she is currently a Visiting Scholar at the Department of Bioethics of the National Institutes of Health.

Lisa Kane Low is Assistant Professor at the University of Michigan, where she holds joint appointments in the College of Literature, Science, and the Arts; the Women's Studies Department; and the School of Nursing. She also holds a clinical position as a certified nurse midwife in the Department of Obstetrics and Gynecology. The primary focus of her research has been exploring the intersections of medicine, midwifery, culture, and social context when selecting the care practices to be used during labor and birth.

Naomi Scheman is Professor of Philosophy and of Gender, Women's, and Sexuality Studies at the University of Minnesota. She edited *Feminist Interpretations of Wittgenstein* (Penn State Press, 2002) with Peg O'Connor and has published a volume of her collected essays, *Engenderings: Constructions of Knowledge, Authority, and Privilege* (Routledge, 1993). A second volume is in preparation, tentatively entitled *Shifting Ground: Margins, Diasporas, and the Reading of Wittgenstein*. She is currently trying to argue for a connection between narrative-based ontology and community-based research and for a conception of objectivity grounded in commitments to trustworthiness and social justice.

Jackie Leach Scully is Senior Lecturer in the School of Geography, Politics and Sociology at Newcastle University, and she is also

Honorary Senior Lecturer in the Faculty of Medicine of the University of Sydney, Australia. Books and edited collections include *Quaker Perspectives in Moral Issues in Genetics* (Mellen, 2002), *Good and Evil* (coedited with Pink Dandelion; Ashgate, 2007), *Gekauftes Gewissen? Zur Rolle der Bioethik in Institutionen* [Buying a conscience? The role of bioethics in institutions] (coedited with Rouven Porz, Christoph Rehmann-Sutter, and Markus Zimmermann-Acklin; Mentis, 2007), and *Disability Bioethics* (Rowman & Littlefield, 2008).

Joan C. Tronto is Professor of Women's Studies and Political Science at Hunter College and the Graduate School, City University of New York. She received her Ph.D. from Princeton University. She is the author of *Moral Boundaries: A Political Argument for an Ethic of Care* (Routledge, 1993) and of numerous articles about the nature of care and gender. Recent publications have appeared in *Hypatia* and *American Political Science Review*. An expert on women in American politics and feminist political theory, she is currently completing a book on democracy and care.

Annelies van Heijst is Assistant Professor in Ethics and Care at the University of Tilburg, the Netherlands, and a trainer and supervisor of professionals in health care institutions. She published *Longing for the Fall* (1995) and *Models of Charitable Care* (2008) and received a national grant for the translation of her book *Menslievende zorg*, which will be published as *Professional Loving Care* (Peeters Publishers, 2009).

Marian Verkerk studied philosophy at the University of Utrecht, where she earned her Ph.D. in 1985. From 1988 until 2000 she was Senior Lecturer in Ethics in the Department of Philosophy at the Erasmus University, Rotterdam. Since 2001 she has been Professor of the Ethics of Care at the University Medical Center, Groningen. She is Head of the Department of Medical Ethics, Health Law, and Medical Humanities, and she is also Director of the Center for the Ethics of Care, both at the University Medical Center, Groningen. She is a member of the Health Council (the advisory board for the Dutch government). She is also a member of one of the review committees on euthanasia in the Netherlands.

Margaret Urban Walker is Lincoln Professor of Ethics and Professor of Philosophy at Arizona State University. Her work on moral epistemology and moral psychology includes *Moral Repair: Reconstructing Moral Relations after Wrongdoing* (Cambridge University Press, 2006); *Moral Contexts* (Rowman & Littlefield, 2003); and *Moral Understandings: A Feminist Study in Ethics*, 2nd edition (Oxford University Press, 2007). She is currently writing on reparation and the moral significance of truth telling.

Acknowledgments

The working group meetings that were an essential element in the development of this book were made possible by an International Research Grant from The Netherlands Organization for Scientific Research (NWO), Humanities Division. The editors of this collection extend grateful thanks to the NWO and to Annemieke Brouwers of the Center for the Ethics of Care at the University Medical Center, Groningen, for the good care she has taken of us all since the project's inception. We would also like to thank the Netherlands School for Research in Practical Philosophy, the Lincoln Center for Applied Ethics at Arizona State University, and Michigan State University.

Naturalized Bioethics

Introduction

Groningen Naturalism in Bioethics

Margaret Urban Walker

Talk of "naturalizing" ethics carries different messages to different ears. If naturalism is a trend or a theme in many areas of philosophy at the beginning of the twenty-first century, it is not one trend or theme but several that may cohere or compete.[1] Minimally, naturalism in ethics is committed to understanding moral judgment and moral agency in terms of natural facts about ourselves and our world.[2] To some moral naturalists, this commitment means that moral judgments capture (or fail to capture) facts about the world that obtain independently of human opinion or feelings. Here naturalism means a metaphysical commitment to a kind of moral realism that can take forms as diverse as Aristotelian teleology and consequentialist appeals to facts about human welfare or happiness.[3] For other naturalists, though, our capacities for moral judgment do

---

[1] Gary Gutting (2005) notes in a review of Brian Leiter's collection *The Future For Philosophy* that the volume is weighted heavily with naturalistic approaches to several areas of philosophy including ethics, but he comments that "the emphasis on naturalism does accurately represent the main thrust of current philosophy and a direction that is likely to be increasingly powerful in the future."

[2] A plethora of metaethical views, views about the nature and meaning of moral judgments, either claim naturalism or reject it. A taxonomy and explication of these views, mapping cognitivist and noncognitivist naturalism, is given by A. Miller 2003, 8. Miller reserves "naturalism" officially to cognitivist moral philosophies while conceding that some contemporary expressivist or noncognitivist views are indeed naturalist, thus exemplifying the loose and contested nature of the idea. A current overview of the field is provided by Lenman 2006.

[3] For a contemporary Aristotelian naturalism, see Hursthouse 1999; others who hold diverse realist naturalist views in metaethics include Nicholas Sturgeon, Peter Railton, Frank Jackson, and David Brink. A. Miller 2003 and Lenman 2006 discuss some of these views.

not track truths in the world independent of us but are part of the naturally given expressive and adaptive equipment of human beings: we are a norm-hungry social species whose members need to coordinate actions and attitudes and that evolutionary pressure has "designed for social life."[4] These naturalists seek the explanation of our moral capacities in facts about the human beings, who, as a naturally occurring species, without recourse to supernatural or transcendent realities, bring morality into the world with them.[5] Despite intense debate among realist and antirealist naturalists in ethics, there is widespread agreement that a scientific view of ourselves and the world is ultimately (and perhaps exclusively) authoritative, a touchstone and resource for naturalism in ethics. The idea of a naturalism in ethics that is specifically responsive to science extends to methodological or epistemological claims about the need for empirical inputs or constraints on ethical theorizing. As John Doris (2002, 4) puts it, his extended study of the impact of social psychology on ethical claims about character belongs to a project of "empirically informed ethics" that is "naturalistic in spirit": "human beings and the ethical problems they encounter are in some fairly substantial sense natural phenomena that may be illuminated by recourse to empirical methodologies with affinities to those of the sciences." A recent movement to "experimental philosophy" includes an empirically based approach to ethics that not only avails itself of findings in social and developmental psychology but occasionally involves philosophers in designing and conducting their own experiments.[6]

Independent of metaphysical and methodological debates in metaethics, many of them increasingly rarified and technical, naturalism in ethics can also mean a practical call to make ethical theorizing responsive to conditions in the world. Jonathan Glover

---

[4] The phrase is from Gibbard 1990, 26, whose noncognitivist, norm-expressivist view takes moral judgments to express an agent's acceptance of norms. Blackburn 1998 offers a form of expressivism that preserves our entitlement to say that moral claims are true but not that they report facts independent of our attitudes.

[5] Naturalistic views in this vein need not be restricted to the human social organization. See, for example, de Waal 1996 on the moral reactions and relations within other primate groups.

[6] See Nichols 2004. Other experimental philosophers include Stephen Stich and Joshua Knobe.

(2000, 6), in his remarkable reflective survey of mass violence in the twentieth century, argues that "our ethical beliefs should also be revisable in light of empirical understanding of people and what they do. If, for instance, the great atrocities teach lessons about our psychology, this should affect our picture of what kinds of actions and character traits are good or bad." As Glover's book illustrates, the lessons about human psychology, leadership, political organization, and communication can be ones derived from historical case studies. In his Romanell Lecture, Philip Kitcher, drawing on both sentimentalist and pragmatist traditions, defends a pragmatic naturalism that sees the natural situation of human beings as a social and dialogical one. Kitcher (2005) affirms Adam Smith's and David Hume's vision of our natural ability and desire to mirror each other's viewpoints and sentiments and to correct our own, but he joins this naturalistic vision to John Dewey's model of progressive adjustment and moral problem solving through a societal "conversation" that has the potential to correct itself as it goes, but always in pursuit of solutions to actual moral problems.

Yet societal conversations are not open circuits in which all have a chance to be heard under conditions of comparable respect and credibility. Contemporary projects in feminist ethics and the philosophy of race often advance yet another and specifically pointed kind of naturalism about ethics: they demand that in ethical theorizing we look at *society* in addition to science and at the dominance of some voices and the exclusion of others within societal and professional conversations about morality and ethics. De facto morality, as well as the refined theories of philosophical ethics, tends to absorb or obscure the biases, hierarchical relations, and exclusive, oppressive, or violent social arrangements that many human societies sustain and even celebrate. As Aristotle painted an enduring and beautiful portrait of the great-souled and wise man that predicated a relentless natural hierarchy throughout human society as well as the human soul, so ethical theories often deceptively abstract selectively from social realities and may idealize moral positions and powers that characterize those socially privileged. Charles Mills (1997, 92), in *The Racial Contract*, makes visible the racial ideology at the historic roots of the social contract tradition, arguing for a naturalized account of morality that identifies "*actual* historically dominant moral/political consciousness and the *actual* historically dominant moral/political ideals." A naturalized and historical understanding of the idealized social contract tradition, Mills argues, begins to identify the political, epistemological, and ontological commitments that allowed "freedom and equality" to characterize only European men.

A distinctively "feminist naturalism" has emerged in feminist ethics. As Alison Jaggar (2000, 458) describes it, feminist ethical naturalism rejects the characterization of practices of moral reason as timeless and universal, "an eternal conversation among minds whose greatness raises them far above the prejudices of their particular times and places."[7] Jaggar (2000, 462) stresses the feminist commitment to methods in ethics that are multidisciplinary and informed by empirical knowledge but that work specifically to uncover and to correct or eliminate "concepts, ideals, and methods of the Western ethical tradition" that embody bias linked to gender, ethnic, and economic inequalities and hierarchies. Feminist ethical naturalism views moral theory as a "situated discourse," a culturally specific set of texts and practices produced by individuals and communities in particular places at particular times. In parallel to naturalizing movements in epistemology and the philosophy of science, feminist naturalism rejects relativism for a naturalized moral epistemology: moral inquiry seeks to understand and apply the norms implicit in our best practices of moral thinking, while "continuously reevaluating each in the light of the others," like the mariners who rebuild their boat at sea in Otto Neurath's famous image (Jaggar 2000, 465). Feminist naturalists do not assume, however, that the *dominant* understandings of and in morality are necessarily the *best* ones; the critical project of much feminist ethics, naturalistic or not, is to show that often they are not. This boot-strapping process of internal critique and reconstruction or new construction, infused with diverse sources of empirical information, fits much of feminist ethics. The ethics of care, one of the most extensively developed variants of feminist ethical theory, tends to be naturalized and practice-driven in this sense.[8]

---

[7] Jaggar 2000 is the best succinct overview of a large literature. My own proposal for naturalizing moral theory is found in M. Walker 2000 and M. Walker 2007.

[8] Founding texts of care ethics include S. Ruddick 1989, Tronto 1993, Sevenhuijsen 1998, and Kittay 1999.

The naturalism in ethics that we espouse and explore in this volume is in the spirit of this self-reflexive, socially inquisitive, politically critical, and inclusive move toward an ethics that is empirically nourished but also acutely aware that ethical theory is the practice of particular people in particular times, places, cultures, and professional environments.[9] We endorse working partnerships between philosophical and empirical inquiries in ethics and the accountability of ethics to the reality of actual practices and people's very different relations to these practices and to each other within them. Our naturalism, however, does not privilege institutionally organized natural and social scientific knowledge but embraces also the experience of individuals in personal, social, and institutional life. Our naturalism is also wary of idealizations that bypass social realities and of purely "reflective" approaches to ethics that are apt to reflect only some, and usually the socially most privileged, points of view regarding the right, the good, and moral ideals such as autonomy, respect, beneficence, and justice. Our naturalism insists that moral inquiries reflectively and reflexively assess common moral assumptions and practices even as we inescapably stand within these practices and necessarily, at any given time, appeal to some of these assumptions. We welcome all relevant scientific data but believe that the social situations of both science and morals must be kept in view, paying attention to differences of social and institutional position, perspective, and power that determine which voices and whose interests and experiences are audible and authoritative in ethics as elsewhere.[10] This kind of pragmatic but socially aware and politically critical naturalism is relaxed in one way – that is, not primarily driven by a particular metaphysical program – but it is rigorous in demanding that moral knowledge claims, arguments, and practices be subject to reflective assessment of their personal, social, institutional, and political origins and impact.

Others too have argued for a greater role for social and social scientific analysis in bioethics. The editors of *Bioethics*, in a

---

[9] For varied approaches to naturalizing moral knowledge, see Campbell and Hunter 2000 and May et al. 1996. The historical root of the twentieth-century discussion is Quine 1969. See M. Walker 2000 for my own revisionary use of Quine.

[10] The ideal of situating particular instances of bioethical inquiry or deliberation can be operationalized. For one model closely connected to this project, see Verkerk et al. 2004. See also M. Walker 1993.

compendium of articles from that journal, count "the empirical turn" and "reflexivity" among several key trends in bioethical discourse and practice (Chadwick et al. 2007, xi–xvi). Their brief description of the empirical trend identifies the role of social scientific research in identifying public understandings of science and in examining the suitability of bioethical principles to certain kinds of societies or social groups, and their briefer comment on reflexivity counsels openness to reconsidering "methods and theoretical approaches" (see also J. Nelson 2000a; Haimes 2007; De Vries et al. 2007). We agree that these trends are central and important, but we share the view of Paul Farmer and Nicole Gastineau Campos (2007, 10), authors of one of the featured articles in that collection, that bioethics (and ethics generally) needs the "view from below." It is attention not only to culture and society but to power differentials within societies and between them, and not only to methods but to voices unheard and interests unrepresented, that is urgent.

Farmer and Campos call for "resocializing" bioethics to counter individualist readings that dominate discussion of clinical and research ethics, bringing the resources of anthropology, history, political economy, and the sociology of knowledge to a discussion that has relied heavily on philosophy, the disciplinary home of ethics. We endorse this view. It is inevitable in societies structured by inequalities of access to professional training, public voice, and social authority that professional discourses and practices will tend to embody viewpoints and interests of those socially privileged in these ways. But given the powerful effects of disciplinary and professional specialization, we argue not only for a view from below but also for varied horizontal views of disciplinary frameworks and professional practices. Differently structured inquiries (social and natural sciences, philosophy, history, literature, and criticism) and institutionally differentiated practices (research, clinical, public health, and management practices) provide revealing viewpoints on each others' embedded evaluative assumptions (see J. Nelson 2000a). Why, then, foreground the idea of "naturalizing" bioethics if critical understanding of the social dimension is of such importance to our view? Why insist on the "naturalizing" terminology, in one way so promiscuous in its applications and in another so often associated with scientific, if not reductionist, projects in ethics?

We adopt this terminology precisely because we want to resist the pull to purity in philosophical ethics that has affected the formation of bioethics and to take advantage of the shift toward naturalism in philosophical ethics by demonstrating its significance for bioethics. At the same time, we want to subvert the tendency to think of "naturalism" in ethics as the exclusive province of the sciences, when some of the most intricate problems for bioethics involve understanding precisely how the enormous prestige of science and the moral aura of professional authority shape, and sometimes distort, morally adequate understandings of relationship, communication, and practice. As philosophers, we are aware of the limits and dangers of reflective (but often unreflexive) "armchair" methods, logical manipulation of general concepts, and decontextualized argument, and so we are keen to demonstrate how ethical reflection can take other forms that can make a difference in bioethics. At the same time, we see how much ethics itself has to learn about a sophisticated and socially nuanced naturalism from successfully addressing the specific challenges of bioethics. We are not willing to surrender the powerful and increasingly discussed idea of naturalism; instead, we lay claim to our own vision of it.[11]

Perhaps the common denominator of all naturalistic or naturalizing views of ethics is the conviction that morality does not come into the world from "somewhere else," a supernatural authority or non-natural moral realm, and that our knowledge of morality's nature and authority does not require forms of reason or cognition that lie beyond everything else we count as natural knowledge of the world. This common theme may seem less interesting than its particular and sometimes competing versions, but it marks a decisive moment in Western ethics where wholly a priori methods, Platonic ideals, and theological bases are left behind or at least found less than adequately persuasive. Our brand of naturalism sets a certain direction in ethics toward a kind of *curiosity* about investigating the finer grain of ethical beliefs, habits, feelings, and forms of life. It asks how

---

[11] A lively discussion of trends and programs in ethical naturalism is found in Flanagan et al. 2008. If Flanagan is correct that different forms of ethical naturalism are now distinctive enough to warrant labels ("Duke naturalism," "Pittsburgh naturalism," "Australian naturalism," and "Michigan naturalism"), perhaps we do well to put our brand on "Groningen naturalism."

"intuitions" to which contemporary moral philosophers like to
appeal are actually shaped and by whom they are shared. It also
promises an enlivened *imagination* about the complexity and revisa-
bility of ethics when it is seen as continuous with all the rest of what we
know. It urges a heightened sense of *accountability* to scientifically
vetted findings but also to other human beings and their distinctive
experiences of our shared social and moral worlds, taking account of
our often unequal power and authority to define the standards and
determine the nature of practices that affect us all. This curiosity,
imagination, and accountability are keynotes of this volume.

WHY NATURALIZE BIOETHICS?

The project "Naturalized Bioethics" was conceived to demonstrate
the critical and creative potential of a bioethics responsive to scientific findings but also deeply grounded in attention to the personal,
social, institutional, and political world in which bioethical discourses
and practices take their particular shapes and have their effects. It is
prompted by the continued dominance of the founding paradigm of
"principlism," pioneered by Tom Beauchamp and James Childress
(2001), known to all students and practitioners of bioethics, and
honored both in its application and in the amount of resistance and
criticism that it has provoked.[12] Beauchamp and Childress enu-
merate four main midlevel moral principles as essential guides to
bioethical deliberations: autonomy, beneficence, nonmaleficence,
and justice. Much current mainstream bioethical discussion, in both
academic and institutional contexts, continues to frame questions
and answers in terms of these guiding principles; they have achieved
a wide resonance, if not a strictly uniform conception or priority
ordering. It might be the case that the dissemination and authority of
the four principles has helped to regularize bioethical discourse in
ways that have supported the professionalization of bioethics in some
societies and have provided a strong, shared research paradigm for

---

[12] One recent set of reflections on the state of Beauchamp and Childress–style
principlism is an issue of the *Journal of Medical Ethics* 29 (2003). Narrative
approaches are sometimes understood to provide one significant alternative to
principlism; see H. Nelson 1997.

the enormous growth in publication in bioethics, in both dedicated journals and more broad-based media.[13] The values enshrined in the four cardinal principles are foundational for bioethics and have been formative for it not only intellectually but professionally.

Although some critics lament the formulaic character of the principlist model of bioethical reasoning, one might complain that it remains too intuitive in its application to particular cases. The Beauchamp and Childress model can claim its flexibility as a virtue in allowing for deliberative reconciliation of multiple principled priorities. Unfortunately, it does not give much guidance on how to reconcile these priorities or how to frame questions in terms of specific kinds of relations, practices, and institutional structures. To take an example that figures prominently in this volume, suppose that autonomy means, very broadly, making one's own choices according to one's own judgments and values, and respecting autonomy means respecting the right of patients and research subjects to be informed about choices and to make their own choices about treatments and participation. This assumption is not yet enough to tell us much about how institutional environments like clinics, hospitals, or laboratories affect the perceptions of decisions makers, how the fragility of illness or the rupture of hospitalization can reorder or confuse the values and identity of patients, how significant differentials of power and dependency influence the conditions of choice, or whether understandings of benefit, risk, disability, functioning, or well-being are common or compatible among those giving and those receiving professional care or those conducting and participating in research. Bioethicists and practitioners are acutely aware of the problems these questions pose in particular cases, but it is a proper part of bioethical theory to look for generalizable features of clinical and research organizations, relationships, and roles that affect, limit, or enhance the possible realization of key values in recurring contexts.

The finer analysis of ethical notions alone, though essential, does not adequately meet this need, nor is the injunction to attend to

---

[13] The development of bioethics as a distinct but multidisciplinary field and as a profession has not been uniform. Our project was rooted primarily in two countries, the Netherlands and the United States, that have seen this kind of professionalization and academic formalization. For a comparative view of the U.S. and French scenes, see De Vries et al., in press.

"context" a sufficient guide without some theoretical guidance about which features of context are ripe with possibilities for supporting or compromising moral values. *Which* features of situations provide the *morally relevant context* is itself a question for empirically enriched ethical theory that draws on factual information of many types. One aspect of a naturalized approach to bioethics is to push back against the (necessary) ethical abstractions and idealized assumptions with an empirically enriched understanding of how particular aspects of context matter morally, forcing the issue of what ethical ideals do (or even can) mean in practice. Another aspect of the naturalized approach we emphasize is a habit of reflexive examination of the positions from which we reason ethically and theorize about ethics as a *part* of the morally relevant situation. None of us is an "ideal observer." We are *situated* observers whose observations are shaped not only by moral assumptions but by much of what we take for granted experientially, socially, institutionally, and culturally, and tacit presuppositions affect what we take moral assumptions to mean.

Ethical precepts are not self-applying; we have learned the precepts and what they mean in particular communities of judgment from their typical application within those communities to particular situations. If the application of an ethical principle seems obvious to us in a situation, it might be because that application is the most common one in contexts familiar to us, or because it is the one we have learned among and from others with whom we share a certain background or lifeway, or because it has been embedded in our professional socialization with or without comment, or because it coheres with assumptions about authority and knowledge that structure our everyday social or institutional worlds. One feature of these worlds that merits often uncomfortable but essential reflection concerns the relationships of power and authority present in many kinds of situations that bioethics has reason to address: differences in authority, vulnerability, knowledge, professional credibility, and social status that make for imbalances in many contexts both between care providers and researchers and their patients or subjects and among them. The societies that house our institutions continue to be organized and segmented in significant ways by differences of class, race and ethnicity, gender, age, religion, sexuality, physical ability, and educational and professional privilege. These differences make a difference in patterns of communication, assumptions of authority and credibility, levels of familiarity and confidence in certain environments, and possibilities of trust and mutual understanding, and they are likely to be one source of both outright ignorance and subtle misunderstanding. Naturalized ethical thought enlists our curiosity and imagination, asking us to bring the inexplicit background of assumptions into the foreground for examination and comparison with less familiar alternatives. It asks us to become accountable for our situated perspectives that harbor prejudgments and biases as well as insights and expertise. Philosopher of science Donna Haraway (1991, 190) refers to "power-sensitive conversation" as a practice of objectivity that "allows us to become answerable for what we learn how to see." On our view of naturalized bioethics, empirically enriched and power-sensitive conversation is both a topic for bioethics and a model for it.[14]

The principlist model embodies an increasingly contested picture of "applied ethics" as theory or principles already in hand that are "applied" to "cases," with the theory building and justification of principles taking place somewhere offstage. Arthur Caplan (1983) long ago called this approach an "engineering model" of bioethics, and Beauchamp and Childress (2001; also Beauchamp 1984) themselves do not endorse a mechanical application of principles. Yet it is unclear whether the principlist approach envisions robust feedback from the applications that might cause us to rethink the meanings of or priority among principles. Beauchamp and Childress (2001, 13) bow to the method of reflective equilibrium in theory construction, stating, "That four clusters of moral 'principles' are central to biomedical ethics is a conclusion the authors of this work have reached by examining *considered moral judgments* and the way *moral beliefs cohere.*" It is not clear, however, that the four principles are any longer in play in an ongoing process of reflective equilibrium; they seem to stay in place come what may. James Lindemann Nelson

---

[14] Farmer and Campos 2007, 10, quotes Howard Brody (1992, 12) that "the word *power* is essentially absent from the vocabulary that scholars of medical ethics have constructed for their discipline and that has been accepted by almost everyone who does work in the field or tries to apply medical-ethical insights to the clinical context." On a collaborative model of deliberation that tries to keep the space of deliberation open, see M. Walker 1993.

(2000a, 15), arguing for an interactive understanding of the relationship between bioethics and social science inquiry, points out that "the chief values of mainstream bioethics ... remain relatively firmly fixed despite countervailing theoretical ferment in other areas of ethics and even in the light of what seem to be rather disturbing empirical findings." Reflective equilibrium as a method of theory construction in ethics, rooted in the work of John Rawls, is perhaps the most widely accepted methodology in ethics; whether or not explicitly affirmed, it is often implicitly at work when philosophers appeal, as they so often do, to our "intuitions" in support of or in objection to moral principles and theories, even when this is not the sole appeal. In reflective equilibrium, considered judgments are brought into alignment with independently plausible principles, and principles are tested and modified by the judgments they will support in a progressive process of adjustment against a backdrop of other well-justified beliefs about the world (Rawls 1971, 48–53; Daniels 1979). Reflective equilibrium as a method of justification is "naturalistic" to this extent: one relinquishes any source of axiomatic certainties in ethics and opts for an a posteriori method that leaves moral theory, principles, and judgments revisable in light of each other and of nonmoral beliefs.

Our brief for empirical enrichment in ethics is consistent with wide reflective equilibrium as an operative form of theory construction and revision. Our conception of naturalism, however, renders reflective equilibrium very wide, with relevant beliefs encompassing natural and social scientific findings; discursive and epistemological analysis of our frames of thought in particular times and places; ethnographic perspectives on institutions and social environments; experiential and third-person narratives that capture the detail of lives and situations; literary studies of how narratives are shaped by contexts and, in turn, shape our understandings; political and organizational analyses of the constraints on dialogue, deliberation, and decision; and more. In addition, our socially critical and power-sensitive approach to naturalizing ethics asks about the terms of reflective equilibrium not only among beliefs but among *people* who are parties to, and subjects of, moral decision making and who should be intelligible and accountable to each other. In bioethical reflection, whose assumptions identify problems and whose voices carry legitimate and credible demands on solutions? Our naturalism is curious about the varieties of factual knowledge and modes of analysis that yield insights into our moral and social worlds and about the experiences and perspectives of people differently placed within these worlds with different and unequal opportunities to define terms and set agendas. We believe that a bioethics that fails to ask these questions is neither epistemically sound nor fully accountable.

GRONINGEN NATURALISM IN BIOETHICS: CORE THEMES

I have spoken of "our" naturalism. By this I mean the framework for this project as conceptualized by its editors: two bioethicists, Marian Verkerk and Hilde Lindemann, and one moral philosopher, myself, whose work has sometimes been found useful by bioethicists (see M. Walker 2003; 2007). Our work was supported by the Netherlands Organization for Scientific Research, in keeping with a commitment to "empirical ethics" in the Dutch context.[15] The volume includes contributors from the Netherlands, the United States, and the United Kingdom. Contributors were invited because of an affinity we perceived between the work they have done and the project as the editors conceived it. Our authors do not share a particular meta-ethical or normative position. If there is a single position in this volume, it is a willingness to explore the transformative possibilities and challenges inherent in taking a naturalized approach to bio-ethics in the twenty-first century. We have organized the chapters in two parts under the headings "Responsible Knowing" and "Responsible Practice," but a certain artificiality in this division will be apparent. For one thing, knowing takes place through practices, such as observation, interviewing, conversing, crediting testimony, performing research experiments, appropriating the authoritative results of others, and so forth. For another, all practices rely on some shared beliefs, and the roles of individuals in many practices of concern to bioethics are structured around the power and authority that attaches to those who possess expert knowledge and the vul-nerability to them of those who do not. In finer focus, four core

[15] Central sources for empirical ethics are Musschenga 2005 and Ashcroft 2003.

themes are visible in our studies: capturing the person in bioethics; situating the bioethicist; the web of relationships; and the reality of power. These themes traverse the chapters and connect them at multiple points.

Capturing the Person in Bioethics

Philosophical moral theories often seek to conceptualize the key morally relevant features of persons and situations in ways that give moral judgment clear and generalizable outlines; the conceptions of personhood, autonomy, value, and rationality that result may be highly idealized ones. Bioethics is ripe with opportunities to trouble in practice conceptions that are clear in theory. Jackie Scully asks us to think about the "moral character of disability," which requires going beyond justifying interventions to asking about how and why we define disability, who defines it, and what is the experience of "nonnormative embodiment" of different kinds. Scully explores the "incomprehensibility" to hearing people of a hearing-impaired couple's choice to invite the conception of congenitally hearing-impaired children, looking at both some of the educational history and the cultural formation of Deaf culture as a way to appreciate, before judging, different understandings of what is normal and whose understandings assume ethical priority. Eva Kittay challenges depictions of the severally mentally handicapped in some well-known work in contemporary philosophy, finding it factually inaccurate as well as ethically questionable both as a practice of theorizing and in its implications for those whose varied and complex cognitive disabilities it misrepresents. Hilde Lindemann probes the fracture that can occur in a person's self-possession and self-understanding under hospitalization and incapacitating illness, and hence the important interpersonal activity, not clearly defined in bioethics, of helping a person hold on to the identity and values that allow him to make choices about his future that are "his own" while recognizing that identities alter under the impact of illness. Agnieszka Jaworska complicates understandings of autonomous choice by arguing that a person may choose against her values while nonetheless exercising autonomy, if the person's choices are rooted in caring, a genuine but emotionally rooted source of self-governance. Addressing the puzzle of why people so often do not do what they have reason to think is good for them, Jodi Halpern and Margaret Little identify and explain the normative activity of "coping," maintaining a sense of security and efficacy in one's world, alongside the time-honored agential activities of practical and theoretical reason. Communicating risk effectively means tapping into individuals' fundamental attempts at integration, empathizing not just with a person but with intelligible choices the person makes in solving the specific dilemma of preserving security and agency. One response to problems of better understanding individuals in context is to suggest that we situate them through stories. Some bioethicists have found narratives – both as a form of representation of moral problems and as a way to represent persons and their lives – a suitably rich mode of depiction, but Tod Chambers looks at the myth of the "real" story that can get in the way of seeing how storytelling serves and is shaped by the particular settings in which it occurs, the ends for which it is done, and the authority or expectations of the one who tells the story or elicits it.

Several of these essays converge on an idea with profound ramifications for making sense of the well being, identity, and autonomy of individuals: the place of *home* in our lives, values, choices, and understandings. Scully uses Pierre Bourdieu's idea of a "habitus," the inexplicit but grounding habits of thinking and acting that we rarely need to make explicit unless unfamiliar others or environments demand it. She argues for a better understanding of the habitus of people who live with disabilities of various kinds. Lindemann's discussion of identity highlights the essential roles of "familiar" people and places to our keeping hold on who we are, and Jaworska's account of caring describes a way, largely at an emotional level, in which we find our lives organized around what has importance for us, even at odds with our more reflective values. Halpern and Little's framework of normative coping as the existential enterprise of "feeling secure and at home in a world with others" provides the beginning of a new account of human motivation and agency that might capture this complex and deeply personal human task of being "at home." When the "home" of the body offers misery and threatens extinction of its embodied self, professionals who care for the ill, frail, and dying face choices among aggressive treatment, comforting, and letting go. Annelies van Heijst peers, sometimes painfully, into the existential reality of carnality, suffering, and death that must be met and acknowledged by professionals in the therapeutic enterprise, lest patients be inexcusably forced to endure abandonment or invisibility as well as illness. She proposes an unsentimental ideal of "professional loving care" as a real possibility for professional training.

Situating the Bioethicist

An old game in the Sunday newspapers used to ask us to find the rabbit, or the teapot, or the umbrella in the puzzle picture. Some of our authors ask, "Where's the bioethicist?" in the clinical or research picture, and suggest that the bioethicist, as well as others, should look. Raymond De Vries, Lisa Kane Low, and Libby Bogdan-Lovis examine the medically contested issue of "nonmedically indicated surgical birth," by mapping the interactions of the desires of researchers and clinicians, women, and bioethicists in shaping scientific knowledge claims, clinical practice, and ethical standards and by shaping them differently in different national and cultural contexts. Naomi Scheman argues that research and clinical bioethics should reconsider the noncollaborative picture of unilateral epistemic authority between physicians and patients and between researchers and participants. Scheman makes a case for the autonomy of patients and participants, seen relationally and contextually, as an epistemic as well as a moral value, and she defends community-based participatory research as a paradigm of good practice, with implications for how bioethicists understand the values that guide their evaluations and advice. Jackie Scully notes the irony that while responses to impairment or disability are central to bioethics, there are few disabled bioethicists; understandings of the experience of disability that are one part of an adequate basis for ethical judgment are lacking in bioethics. Eva Kittay, in a strong critique of discussions of severely cognitively impaired individuals in the work of philosophers Peter Singer and Jeff McMahan, draws a constructive moral. She offers four maxims of good practice in bioethical theorizing – epistemic responsibility, epistemic modesty, humility, and accountability – that ask theorists in bioethics to reflect on the ethical, epistemic, and practical dimensions of their own argumentative procedures and examples. Tod Chambers thinks that bioethicists who construct and analyze narratives of patients and cases should locate those stories in "the ongoing social life of the people involved in medical ethics decisions," taking care to identify how these stories come about, and why they take the form and have the content that they do. A key idea of these essays is that the bioethicist, like everyone else who is a party to health care, research, and bioethical practices, occupies a perspective specifically situated by professional and disciplinary training, social experience, institutional roles, and cultural environment – or perhaps one should say by training, experience, and role *within* a particular national and cultural environment. There is nothing wrong with thinking "from here" – there is no other alternative open to human thinkers – but epistemic, moral, and practical problems await failures to remember that "from here" implies resources and limitations that should be reflexively assessed.

The Web of Relationships

A potent theme of feminist ethical theorizing is that we exist, survive, understand ourselves, and shape our lives *in relationship*. Joan Tronto reconceptualizes informed consent in a health care context not fundamentally as an individual's act of consent but as a grant of authority from one vulnerable person to another who is trusted to use his or her professional competence and authority responsibly in the patient's best interest. The central role of the trust relationship in Tronto's view has demanding implications for the disclosure of relevant information but also for the justice of the wider web of relationships and institutions that make up the health care system. Mare Knibbe and Marian Verkerk join social inquiry to philosophical moral psychology in their study of how parents confronted with the threatening prospect of liver transplantation for their child actively protect and regulate their ability to remain hopeful by different and sometimes opposing strategies. Their strategies involve them with health professionals in a dynamic and interdependent situation in order to maintain their chosen "economies of hope" and "divisions of hoping labor." Scheman's argument for patient and participant autonomy as an epistemic value involves a relational ontology and epistemology of knowing objects and persons in the relationships and contexts that contribute to making them what they are.

Lindemann argues that a person's identity is constructed but also maintained by ongoing interactions among persons. When identity is challenged, the task of restoring, stabilizing, or revising it is essentially *interpersonal*; it requires the cooperation and active support of others. Scully makes the related point that the arrival of a hearing-impaired child in the world is more likely to seem a catastrophe when one envisions its arrival into a hearing world and family and not into a hearing-impaired family or Deaf community. Halpern and Little's model of risk communication emphasizes a specific mode of relating in clinical health communication. "Empathizing with the dilemma" entails trying to see what so threatens another person's security that she is motivated to deny it; the empathetic stance they describe creates a "we" that accepts shared vulnerability and diminishes shame in order to foster productive rather than regressive coping. Van Heijst's concept of professional loving care at its core requires "being there" for those who suffer, a relationship not reducible to medical interventions, no matter how expert and effective; "being there" translates into practical values of teamwork and balance between the human and the technical aspects of care that can be incorporated into training for health care roles. With regard to every important value or principle at work in bioethics, one needs to ask, What relationships are presupposed in the realization of this value or the implementation of this principle, and how must the web of relationships, personal and institutional, be configured to reliably ensure this value is honored?

The Reality of Power

Joan Tronto mines the social contract tradition of political thinking to reconstruct the meaning of consent in the clinical context. In situations of "necessary care," there is an inherent power imbalance. This inequality of power cannot be changed by a ritual, but the grant of authority signified by consent can legitimate the discretionary exercise of judgment and skill by the powerful in the patient's interest. Once we think of the interaction candidly in terms of the patient's vulnerability and the caregiver's power in a context of trust, larger issues come into view, such as economic interests of providers and institutions, and the organization of the health care system, that may affect access to care and its quality. The ritual of "consenting" becomes a portal to examining the inequalities, some ineradicable and others unacceptable, that are the reality among seekers and providers of care. De Vries, Low, and Bogdan-Lovis explore how health care professionals and institutions have organizational and economic motivations that affect the delivery of care and the forms of care delivered in ways over which those receiving care have little control, while cultural discourses tend to rationalize some patterns of practice independently of evidence or by shaping the evaluation of evidence. In addition, divisions of professional labor and institutional practice – for example, in obstetrical care – have the power to shape the perceptions of nurses about the naturalness or riskiness of the birth process itself. Van Heijst reminds us that institutional context and professional training may be conducive to professional loving care or not, rendering the patient even more powerless than does the illness. Kittay reminds bioethical theorists that their theories may shape attitudes and policies whether they intend this result or not, and that, while theorists may see themselves as "following the argument where it leads," others might believe they are entitled to follow the conclusions of the argument in practice. Still, not all powers are on the side of professionals. Knibbe and Verkerk caution professionals not to assume that they are the creators and moderators of hope among parents of children who are candidates for transplant; even as the words, actions, and attitudes of professionals do matter to parents own ways of sustaining hope, parents will organize their "hoping space" in their own chosen ways. Halpern and Little explain the resilience, whether productive or regressive, of people's capacities to cope and suggest that professionals need to recognize and work with this existential need. Chambers, Scully, Jaworska, and Kittay all remind us that the power to define terms, to tell an authoritative story, to make forceful arguments, and to have one's experiences and observations taken as credibly representative is no small power, and sometimes it is a power over the lives and well-being of others. We do not think one needs a dark view of the powers inherent in bioethical theorizing and consulting, and in clinical and research practices, to see that they create responsibilities and that those with responsibilities are accountable to others who place trust in them.

Our authors took up the invitation to examine practices of responsibility in an empirically grounded, socially situated, and reflexively critical analysis. Practices of responsibility earn their moral authority when they organize human care and effort in defensible ways and support a moral and social life that those within that life find habitable and valuable. They must be found so, however, under conditions of *transparency* and *critical examination* from many positions within those practices and outside of them. We hope these essays show how illuminating responding to this demand can be.

I

RESPONSIBLE KNOWING

1

Moral Bodies

Epistemologies of Embodiment

Jackie Leach Scully

> Understanding is always against a background of what is taken for granted, just relied on.
>
> – Charles Taylor, "To Follow a Rule"

A naturalized bioethics involves taking a more skeptical look at things that mainstream bioethics tends to take for granted. As Margaret Walker writes in the Introduction to this volume, naturalized bioethics grasps that "ethical theories often deceptively abstract selectively from social realities and may idealize moral positions and powers that characterize those socially privileged" and, most significantly, that this idealization has effects on moral perceptions and judgments. As moral thinking is not disconnected from other kinds of thinking that we engage in, we need to be scrupulously self-aware – more than most of us can hope to be – to avoid importing taken-for-granted assumptions about knowledge and value into our moral thinking as well.

An early consequence of this kind of bias, as feminist bioethicists were among the first to point out, is the exclusion of the viewpoints of certain social actors from serious bioethical discussions. In general, the voices of women, ethnic or cultural minorities, the very young and the very old, the minimally educated, and others are absent or underrepresented in mainstream bioethical discourse. This exclusion occurs through two main conceptual moves: the *move of commonality*, which claims that any or all of these viewpoints are adequately represented by other spokespeople (so that a white person can "speak for" a black person, or a man for a woman) because the moral views and values of these different agents still have enough in common; and the *move of marginality*, which makes the opposite claim that in fact these viewpoints are *so* marginal as to be not only numerically insignificant but also too whacky to take seriously.

It is almost a cliché, at least within feminist and other "alternative" strands of ethical and political thinking, to note that philosophy's standard model of the moral self as a disembodied, rational decision maker functioning independently at the bargaining table overlooks important aspects of moral life. Nevertheless, only recently has bioethics taken much interest in the social context within which moral decisions are made and begun to look on empirical and experiential data as useful to normative ethical reflection. With the significant exception of feminist ethics, which has addressed the consequences of bodies being *gendered*, bioethics still does not take much account of the differences that result from variations in embodiment.

This failure is paradoxical because bodily variation, and especially the kind of variation that is classed as impairment or disability,[1] is central to bioethics. Large tracts of contemporary bioethics are really about nothing *but* bodily anomaly, in the negative sense of preventing it. Because today's genetic and reproductive technologies offer radical new ways of actually doing something about disability, mainstream bioethical literature tackles disability issues primarily in terms of working out the morally appropriate ways of using these new biomedical interventions. Bioethicists working within one or more of the various theoretical frameworks have shown an interest in the morally correct stance(s) toward such topics as euthanasia, resource allocation, prenatal testing, preimplantation genetic diagnosis, and gene therapy. Most bioethical work here takes a highly normative approach, in part because bioethics is so often asked to provide a justification for biotechnological regulatory frameworks. As a result of the Anglo-American dominance of the field, bioethics' consideration of disability issues also has a strongly libertarian flavor.

What bioethics has signally failed to address is a number of crucial questions associated with the *moral character* of disability, not just how

---

[1] Terminology of disability is a particularly fraught area, and practices differ between the United Kingdom, the United States, and other countries. I am going to follow U.K. practice in which impairment refers to the physical variant, and disability to the experience of disadvantage or discrimination that results from a person having the variant.

to react to it but also how and why we define disability in the first place, how we learn to characterize variations from bodily norms, and who "we" are in all this – which groups have the authority to make those identifications and whose descriptions of disabled experience are heard. If moral and social lives are mutually constitutive, then their influences run both ways: not only are moral values and identities expressed through our social lives, but what people (including bioethicists) perceive as good and right in the first place is structured by their social experiences and allegiances. This is relevant because there are few disabled bioethicists, and even fewer who take disability as a focus for their work, so that bioethical writing about disability is almost entirely by outsiders to the experience being written about (e.g. Buchanan 1996; John Harris 2000; J. Nelson 2000b; Davis 1997). A naturalized bioethics of disability would, at a minimum, see a problem in this situation. It would seek to grasp something of how individuals' and groups' understanding of the moral nature of disability is formed in their personal, social, economic, political, and institutional worlds. What I would call "disability ethics," in analogy to feminist ethics, is less about regulating biomedical interventions into disability and more a form of ethical analysis that is consciously and conscientiously attentive to the experience of being or having a nonnormative embodiment. Whereas feminist ethics is concerned with the effects of the gendering of bodies, disability ethics looks at the effects of bodily impairment. To do this kind of exploration means working from people's experience (or lack of experience) of disability in order to consider how it constrains their perceptions, interpretations, and judgments, especially in moral issues that have direct relevance to disability and where differences in the experience of disability might be expected to be most pertinent.

As much as a disability ethics, though, this approach implies the possibility of a disability epistemology, or epistemologies, in which we ask the question, What kind of knowledge of the situation do we have, as people with particular disabilities, even before we consciously begin to evaluate it ethically? To open up this possibility means identifying the features of disabled people's lives that are sufficiently different from those of nondisabled people's, to generate – socially, politically, economically, historically, and institutionally – a different epistemic assessment of bioethical questions. I think a naturalized bioethics would argue that only when this work has been done is it possible to pursue the *ethical* question of whether epistemic and axiological difference makes a moral choice not only comprehensible but justifiable.

Gathering these data is not a trivial matter, either substantively or methodologically. If we are talking about the relatively straightforward process of getting information from those who know something of what it is like to live with disability and conveying it to those who do not, then direct contact with disabled people is probably the most obvious shift, but it may be the least easily achieved. Written or filmed disability narratives can also be informative. Disability memoirs, such as the genre of post–spinal cord lesion memoir (for examples, see Hockenberry 1995; Linton 2005), are about the process of learning to live with an unexpected impairment – often not just of its medical and practical demands on daily life but also of the author's realization of his or her changed social status and, sometimes, changed perceptions. Such accounts provide insight not only into the everyday material barriers encountered by a disabled person but also into what it takes, practically and subjectively, to "do" disability well.

Detailing other ways in which experiences of disability inflect moral understanding will not be straightforward. Some forms of experience will be accessible to straightforward empirical sociological, ethnographic, historical, or psychological inquiry. But the exploration that is needed includes the incorporation of bodily experience and social relationships into processes of moral and other evaluations, processes that take place at levels of cognition and at developmental stages that render them hard either to articulate or to observe.

CHOOSING DEAF CHILDREN

The scenario of choosing to have a hearing-impaired child is well known (even notorious) in bioethical circles. Although it has been extensively discussed in the bioethical literature and has become a favorite in teaching bioethics, my purpose in using the story here is to illustrate how careful attention to accounts from a perspective other than the mainstream can cast quite a different light on an apparently familiar situation – to the extent of justifying an act that at first sight may seem utterly wrongheaded.

In early 2002 a flurry of popular and professional bioethical discussion followed a report in the *Washington Post* that was rapidly dubbed the "deaf designer babies" or "choosing deaf children." A lesbian couple from Washington, D.C., Sharon Duchesneau and Candace McCullough, wanted to have a child by donor insemination. Both women had a congenital hearing impairment. They opted to *increase their chances* of having a deaf child by using a sperm donor with a heritable form of deafness. (One thing it is important to emphasize here is that, despite what some later accounts claimed, Duchesneau and McCullough did not *reject* the idea of having a hearing child: they said only that they felt a deaf one would be "a special gift.") Because commercial sperm banks do not accept donors with known heritable diseases or disabilities, the couple ended up using a male friend with a genetic deafness as sperm donor, resulting so far in the birth of two children, both hearing impaired (Mundy 2002).

The women's decision was greeted with both support and heavy criticism from different commentators. I do not want to go into the details of the arguments for and against here but rather to note just one aspect of the debate: irrespective of the conclusion, almost all the arguments involved the weighing up of parental rights against individual (i.e., the child's) rights. Whereas some people said that respect for the principle of autonomy permits a high degree of parental choice (usually going on to argue that, if parents are allowed to select *against* disabilities on the basis of parental autonomy, then it is hard to argue against their right to select *for* a disability if they wish), those who were critical of the women's choice argued that the child has an overriding right not to be harmed and therefore parents have a concomitant obligation not to harm her by condemning her to a disability that could have been avoided,[2] or infringing what has been described as the child's right to "an open future" (Davis 1997).

If we look at these arguments, the theoretical framework of rights that protect strong principles of autonomy and beneficence does indeed seem capable of determining whether Duchesneau and

---

[2] Remember that Duchesneau and McCullough were only *increasing* the chances of having a hearing-impaired child, not determining it absolutely. Other techniques, such as preimplantation genetic diagnosis that incorporates a test for a well-characterized locus associated with genetic deafness, would have been much more reliable.

McCullough were expressing a justifiable preference, within the
parameters of particular ideas about the limits to parental rights over
their children. The question this approach cannot ask is why the
rightness or wrongness of the decision seemed so *obvious* to different
groups of people. For the majority of commentators, and probably
readers as well, acting on a preference for a child with a hearing
impairment (even in the rather nondeterministic way of Duchesneau
and McCullough) seemed an obvious cause of harm.[3] The issue was
really only *how much* harm, and whether that could counterbalance
the wrong of infringing the (supposedly basic) ethical principle of
parental autonomy. There were also those, predominantly but not
solely from the Deaf community or disability activist groups, for
whom a hearing impairment was simply not that kind (or any kind) of
harm. For them, acting on a preference for a disabled child seemed
both intuitively correct and rationally justifiable. Even sympathetic
commentators, who were willing to fight for the parents' right to
express the preference, generally found it incomprehensible. Given
that this is a head-to-head disagreement about a fundamental
premise, one of the oddest features of the discussion was the sheer
lack of interest in clarifying where the disagreement came from.
Bioethicists contributing to this conversation failed, on the whole, to
do what a naturalized bioethics requires them to do: ask questions
about what gives rise to moral intuitions, and whether there are
"sound epistemic reasons" for taking any one intuition as authoritative, other than the fact that we happen to share it.

This extraordinarily rich case can be approached by highlighting a
number of different aspects: for example, the fact that the story
involved a lesbian rather than a heterosexual couple,[4] the debate
within the Deaf community about whether deafness is a disability at
all, and the disproportionate degree of anxiety that this isolated case
generated in the outside and especially bioethical world. To give a
fully fleshed out account of even one of the multiple social and

---

[3] This is particular to the situation of bringing a child with an impairment into the
world. It seems likely that, had Duchesneau and McCullough wanted to adopt a
disabled child in preference to a nondisabled one, they would have been
considered especially virtuous rather than especially selfish.

[4] This aspect was not lost on some of the less restrained commentators on the lunatic
fringe of the Internet.

political contexts in which this story unrolled is well beyond the scope of this chapter. Instead, what I want to do is point to some of the distinctive features of the Deaf world of which Duchesneau and McCullough considered themselves a part, features that are not particularly hard to observe and describe but that were used to inform the discussion in only the most superficial way.

THE DEAF WORLD

> Labeling us as "disabled" demonstrates a failure to understand that we are not disabled in any way within our own community.
>
> – Ladd and John, *Deaf People as a Minority Group*

Hearing-impaired people occupy a unique position in the disabled-nondisabled taxonomy.[5] While the vast majority of hearing people, and many hearing-impaired, consider audiological deafness a disability, many culturally Deaf people and others argue that being deaf is to be a member of a sociolinguistic group rather than being disabled (Lane 1992; Jennifer Harris 1995). Culturally, Deaf people claim a community with its own history, arts, language, mores, political identification, economic background, and present context of social marginalization. Although the available evidence suggests that the majority of culturally Deaf people express no preference for either deaf or hearing children (Stern et al. 2002; Middleton et al. 2001), some like Duchesneau and McCullough clearly do.

Some History

The majority of the pioneer deaf educators[6] created residential schools with the goal of teaching the deaf to speak. It seemed to them that "the problem" of deafness was the inability to articulate thought and so exhibit the rationality necessary to be accepted as a member of civil society (see discussion in Rée 1999). The first person to take seriously the idea that people who could neither hear nor speak might

---

[5] One convention of transcribing signed communications into written words is to use a more or less word-for-sign transcription in upper case where possible (as shown in the heading to this section), which can also be glossed more freely into standard English in lower case.

[6] Accounts of their work can be found in Rée 1999 and Lane 1992.

nevertheless be communicating with each other was the French Abbé de l'Epée. He combined the grammatical structure of spoken French with some of the indigenous sign language that he noticed being used by the deaf beggars roaming mid-eighteenth-century Paris to create an artificial system of signed language that he then taught in his school, the National Institution for Deaf-Mutes. So successful was the school and his system that signed language "in the French style" was rapidly transported around Europe and on to the new world of America.

Today, the Deaf world looks on the period between 1750 and 1880 as a kind of golden age in which Deaf self-confidence and organization flourished as never before. It was marked by an apparent accommodation of the majority hearing culture to the idea that hearing-speech provides only one route to communication and citizenship and that there may be others. For a time there seemed to be a possibility of a parallel form of social presence, mediated through vision-sign alongside hearing-speech. In reality, the argument was never actually won; and at the Milan Congress of educators of the deaf in 1880, the proponents of schools that encouraged sign language (and thereby effectively spun off signing communities) were defeated by the proponents of an education that aimed at integration into the hearing world. For something like the next hundred years, schools for the deaf operated with a strong, often exclusive focus on oralism and the more or less total suppression of sign language. For many hearing-impaired children, being trained to produce acceptable speech was indubitably beneficial to their lives. In the cultural narrative of the Deaf world, however, the decline of sign language represented a lapse into darkness. Novels and memoirs dealing with that period describe how residential schools imposed a hearing-speech regime, or tried to: "Their sign system ... had now escaped from the classroom and was spreading amongst the deaf beyond the control and even the knowledge of those who could hear. The pupils at the new schools for the deaf seemed to know far more [sign language] than they had ever been taught" (Rée 1999, 199).

Deaf Cultural Transmission

Several features mark Deaf culture out from most of the linguistic and ethnic cultures to which it is compared by both Deaf and hearing commentators. Deaf culture is relatively young, really coming into existence only with the rise of deaf schools in the eighteenth and nineteenth centuries. The culture is not primarily constituted by families, because most hearing impairment is not genetic. Roughly 90 percent of hearing-impaired children have hearing parents, while in most cases the offspring of two deaf adults will be hearing. Between generations, then, the transmission of both audiological deafness and Deaf culture is disrupted. In the past, this meant that schools for the deaf or Deaf clubs acted as the primary conduits for Deaf identity (Jennifer Harris 1995), and some older deaf people in North America, Britain, and Europe still prefer to give the name of their school when asked where they are "from": the school is their point of natality into the Deaf world (Padden and Humphries 2005). More than one author has suggested that the Deaf world has a stronger sense of its group identity than the hearing world (Jennifer Harris 1995; Preston 2001). This sense is common to many socially marginalized groups, but its strength is enhanced here by a third feature: for many hearing-impaired children and adolescents the Deaf world is a *found* community. Deaf memoirs are commonly structured around a powerful narrative of "coming home" to the Deaf world after years of isolation and frustration in a hearing family environment. The strength of identification with the Deaf community is also revealed by references in the ethnographic literature to instances where Deaf identity dominated over others that would normally be considered very powerful, for example, religious affiliation. Higgins reports members of a synagogue for the deaf donating items to a bazaar at a Lutheran deaf church in preference to another synagogue for hearing Jews (Higgins 1980, 39).

Deaf culture is transmitted vertically only in the small proportion of cases where both parents have the same genetic basis for their hearing impairment. The rarity of this means that deaf children of deaf parents provide a crucial continuity of Deaf culture within their home environment and thereby the means to pass cultural knowledge on to deaf children from hearing families (Preston 2001). Within the Deaf world, the so-called deaf of deaf (deaf children of deaf parents) are sometimes considered a kind of elite (Solomon 1994).

Most commentators on the Duchesneau-McCullough case assumed that hearing impairment entails a catastrophic reduction in the sum of abilities and, by implication, also a reduction in social status and future opportunities. They focused on the difficulties faced by the deaf child in an alien hearing world. Revealingly, they never raised the possibility that a hearing child might also face difficulties growing up in a Deaf familial and social world. Yet there is good sociological as well as anecdotal evidence to suggest that the life of a hearing child within a deaf family can be problematic (see Preston 2001; Singleton and Tittle 2000; Bull 1998). Hearing children can be acutely aware of their deaf family's difference and isolation; have difficulty developing a distinct individual identity against a perceived categorical difference between hearing and deaf members of the family;[7] face issues of mixed loyalties and deferred stigmatization; or be used in an age-inappropriate way as an interpreter and "cultural mediator" (Preston 2001, 96–103; Couser 1997, 250). None of this, of course, constitutes an argument that being a deaf child in a deaf family is unproblematic, only that being a hearing child in a deaf family is *not* the "normality" it was generally assumed to be. Similarly, a better knowledge of how the Deaf world functions does not provide a justification for the Duchesneau-McCullough decision, but it does make it more plausible that people whose primary social context is the Deaf world may not find it intuitively or rationally obvious that a hearing-impaired child is worse-off than a hearing child, especially if both are being raised in a hearing-impaired family and social network.

Political Consciousness

The marginalization of signed languages and of Deaf communities is still apparent. By most indicators, hearing-impaired people are economically disadvantaged, with lower academic and professional achievement, lower average incomes, and higher rates of unemployment. The givenness of this degree of marginalization was called into question toward the end of the twentieth century, as some Deaf groups took up the insights of identity politics and the tactics of civil rights movements. It would be wrong to suggest that hearing-impaired people today form a politically homogeneous group. Whereas some

---

[7] "Paradoxically, within a community of shared identity, individual differences can emerge – identities that are not restricted to a single, all-encompassing feature" (Preston 2001, 89).

identify strongly with what they consider their Deaf community, others question whether such a thing as a Deaf community exists, while still others are happy to negotiate both Deaf and hearing worlds. The hearing-impaired world today is enlivened by disagreements over the ontological meaning of deafness (sociolinguistic group or disability?), the use of aids to hearing, the ethics of giving cochlear implants to children, the politics of signing versus speech, and the status of late-deafened people in the community, to name just a few. Nevertheless, for many the basic shared experience of being deaf in a majority hearing world cuts across other identifiers such as nationality, party politics, religion, class, or even genetic family membership.

Since the 1970s hearing-impaired people have also become aware of the usefulness of having a coherent *political* Deaf community to stake a claim to civil rights, even if they are less sure of the reality of a *cultural* community. A good part of this consciousness has developed through recent historical research that gave the Deaf community a powerful narrative of oppression (including, for example, hearing-impaired people's historical lack of legal or civic status, the suppression of Sign, the attempted eradication of inherited deafness during the eugenic fervor of mid-twentieth-century Europe and North America, and the practice of forcibly removing hearing children from their deaf parents), but also one of struggle, liberation, and self-determination. Few people outside the Deaf world have any knowledge of this history, and none of the mainstream bioethical discussion of the "deaf designer babies" referred to it. Yet it is really only against this historical context that the enormous social, political, and moral significance of the Deaf world and its continued existence to those who live in it become remotely understandable.

YOU THINK ∼ HEARING YOU

Although the use of Sign is distinctive, being culturally Deaf entails much more than simply using signed instead of spoken language. Other distinctive characteristics of the Deaf social world reflect the *prediscursive* features of lives in which most stimuli are visual or tactile rather than auditory. Perhaps the most obvious is that in a Deaf context people use a lot of physical movement and contact – to attract each other's attention, for example, or let someone know that another person has entered the room. Touching and tapping each other are generally quite acceptable, and it can be difficult for a culturally Deaf person to adjust to the hearing world, which has different rules about acceptable touch and proximity. Other characteristic practices go unnoticed because they do not stand out in the Deaf world but become obvious and stigmatizing elsewhere and demand constant monitoring in order to "pass." Lou Ann Walker describes how this exercise of self-control over ingrained behaviors contributed to the disempowerment of her Deaf family. Outside the Deaf world, she writes, "whoever it was doing the talking had a power over us. Our signs were small and timid, and our faces were almost immobile. But when we were at home alone, the five of us were transformed and the signing was large and generous" (L. Walker 1986, 108).

The analytic approach of the twentieth-century French sociologist Pierre Bourdieu, and especially his notion of habitus, offers one way of getting a purchase on how the physical and social experience of disability can actively modify moral thinking. In contrast to many philosophers of mind and cognitive scientists, Bourdieu says that human understanding is not solely about the perceptions that we are aware of and able to convert into internal representations and articulate in words, but that much of our conscious understanding emerges from a prereflexive background of meaning. Moreover, this background of meaning is carried by and expressed in the everyday practices of human living – for example, how we converse, or whether we touch each other. That is, they include behaviors that can differentiate the Deaf from the hearing world. Each social field, Bourdieu (1990a, 53, 13) suggests, generates its own system of tacit rules governing practices and behaviors, "durable, transposable dispositions ... principles which generate and organize practices and representations." The entire system of dispositions functions "as categories of perception and assessment or as classificatory principles as well as being the organizing principles of action."

Habitus is pretheoretical, prereflexive knowledge that we absorb from behavior and practices that are demonstrated, rarely articulated, by the people around us. Through the action of the habitus, the subject acquires a set of dispositions that are manifested both physically in what he called the bodily hexis – "a durable way of standing, speaking, walking, and thereby of thinking and feeling"

(Bourdieu 1990a, 69–70) – and mentally in tendencies toward patterns of perceiving and interpreting. The bodily understanding of the habitus is carried as a feel for the right behavior. Knowing what is fitting is what gives us the ability to function in a given social field without constantly thinking about it: Bourdieu described this evocatively as "knowing how to play the game."

What Bourdieu seems to be saying is that reality is cognitively structured through bodily processes that originate in the social world. There is a sense of effortlessness – no perception of reality being organized, but rather a feeling of obvious rightness – that results from being at home within a familiar habitus and indicates that the structuring of reality is not something that is conscious or volitional. An agent's action (e.g., a decision about prenatal testing for inherited hearing impairment) would in Bourdieu's eyes be a conscious decision that emerged from the dispositional constraints of habitus. The reasons an agent might give for her choice are propositional and can be articulated. But the reasons given are found compelling to the agent and others *because of* the background of dispositions, and these cannot, or can only with difficulty, be articulated propositionally. Bourdieu suggests that these understandings of the right and the good are accessible to conscious scrutiny only with enormous effort. The habitus, prereflexive and embodied, slips under the radar of the most acute critique.

That we can legitimately speak of a "Deaf habitus" is indicated by the terms used by Deaf people themselves in the ethnographic and auto-biographical literature. These accounts are full of metaphors of *being at home* that suggest a state of understanding and of being understood without needing to think about it: a place, unlike the hearing world, where Deaf people know and can follow the implicit rules of the game. In his pioneer sociology of deafness, Higgins (1980, 42, 38, 76) reported his informants' saying things like, "Most of my friends are deaf, I feel more comfortable with them. Well, we have the same feelings," or "When I saw these people ... I knew I belonged to their world. I didn't belong in the hearing world," and concludes that, "Within deaf communities ... a sense of belonging and wholeness is achieved which is not found among the hearing." Similarly, Preston (2001, 14) quotes a young deaf woman who claimed that "usually I understand why a deaf person did so and so. I can understand why they

did it. But I can't explain to hearing people. . . . I don't have an answer
for them." Unlike the hearing world, the Deaf world provides Deaf
people with a habitus in which they are at home and where obvious
things do not need to be explained. And it seems as if, at least sometimes, this manifests as understandings, patterns of thinking, that are
recognized as shared. A Deaf friend, baffled by my inability to grasp
something, signs to me YOU THINK ~ HEARING YOU. She is saying
that I think like a hearing person, not like a Deaf one, and she doesn't
mean it kindly. That there might be some noticeable differences
between Deaf and hearing *thinking* seems strange, but to at least some
hearing-impaired people the difference is obvious enough, it seems,
that it is worth having a sign for it. Alongside this, what my friend says to
me and the way she says it flags how the two groups might differ in their
ranking of particular values. In Deaf discourse, noting that someone
"thinks like a hearing person" is rarely a sign of approval, while in the
hearing world it would be hard to think of it in any other way.

The understandings of the world mediated through habitus necessarily include moral understandings. The habitus has ethical relevance at two levels: those practices that are in keeping with the
habitus will be understood as good, in the dual sense of "fitting" and
"morally good"; and ingrained habits of feeling and thought will
include understandings about the good life, responsibilities to others
and how they should be fulfilled, what sorts of acts exhibit moral
agency, and so on. It is this second sense that is most relevant to the
consideration of moral choices. Bourdieu's approach has the
advantage that its focus on specific everyday practices of bodies offers
a way of fleshing out some otherwise vague and general statements
about the social construction of moral thinking. It enables us to ask
targeted questions about how, exactly, social practices provide a
framework for epistemic and ethical understandings, about what
might be different for the bodily, social, and affective world of the
Deaf that contributes to a "Deaf habitus" in which certain practices
and values are ranked differently from in the hearing world.

FOUR FINAL POINTS

Nothing of what I have said should be taken as suggesting that a
detailed, methodical, reflective exploration of the experiences of

disabled people, whether using the conceptual framework of habitus or any other methodology, will unerringly tell us the correct ethical stance to take in issues of disability. The difficulties here are both theoretical and methodological, as the following four points show.

First, one of the claims of naturalized bioethics is that real, personal, social situations cannot be universalized: they are different from each other. Naturalized bioethics says that situations that philosophers have claimed to see as "identical in their universal descriptive properties" (Hare 1981, 21) are actually not identical in morally significant ways, and it is the job of bioethicists to find out what these nonidentities are and investigate their effects on moral evaluation. It has been my claim here that impairment, understood as a disadvantaging deviation from a bodily norm, is one of these morally relevant descriptive properties. So even if a *single* ethical stance or evaluative algorithm could be agreed on, and even if it were found useful in generating conclusions about some situations in which disability plays a role, it would be a bad mistake to expect the conclusions to be ethically appropriate for all disabled people, or even for people with a common disability – hearing impairment, for example – in all circumstances.[8]

Second, if moral understandings cannot in truth be universalized, only generalized, then not only do we have to detail the moral lives of the group in question; we also have to make a decision (and possibly revise it as we go along) about who constitutes the group and who can represent it. In the Duchesneau-McCullough case, for example, whose opinions should have been the focus of bioethical attention – the "disabled community" (in which country?) or the "Deaf community" (ditto)? All hearing-impaired people? All hearing-impaired people in the eastern United States? All hearing-impaired lesbians wanting a child? Adult hearing children from deaf families? Or just Duchesneau and McCullough themselves? If we think that neither universalist nor extreme case-by-case approaches are informative, then we need to be disciplined about avoiding glib over-simplifications like "D/deaf people" and able to state clearly whose articulations are being given ethical priority, and why.

---

[8] Although, as I noted earlier, it is often appropriate for disabled people to act as a single *political* community.

Third, saying that attention to moral experience from within disability will correct a distortion in bioethical thinking is not the same as suggesting that experiential accounts are the only source material for theorizing disability. Experiential accounts are only part of the knowledge of the body that, along with the body of medical discourse and the body representations of popular culture, contribute to local understandings of impairment and disability. How being physically deviant affects a person's moral understandings will depend on how it affects her life, and that in turn will depend on the cultural meaning and values that impairment carries; but it will also be related to the ways these meanings and values are modified by biological, material, and symbolic interactions between the individual and society, *and* on how each individual makes sense of these interactions for herself, *and* on what happens as these microlevel hermeneutics, eventually, feed back into collective understandings.

Among these collective understandings are those of the bioethics community itself. The suggestion that shared features of embodiment predispose a group or culture to find certain moral values and priorities obviously right is one that must be applied democratically, and not just to choices that we find anomalous. I depict the Deaf habitus, for example, as constituting a set of moral dispositions that are manifested in the choices made by members of the Deaf community. But the same holds for the hearing world and (a point that is usually forgotten) for the "social field" of professional bioethics. Bioethicists enjoy their own versions of habitus – it is what enables them, in Bourdieu's terms, to play the bioethical game. A bioethicist's habitus results in part from the social backgrounds that underpin the identities of academics the world over (affluent enough to be educated, disproportionately male, mostly white, mostly not disabled) and in part from the semi- or unconsciously absorbed rules of *how to be a bioethicist*: rules about when to use one word and when to prefer its euphemism, which values can be expressed and which should be hidden, the rules on how to conduct an argument, or how to hold a meeting, an instinct for who should be invited to a consultation, or for standards of dress, or for knowing who are the good guys in the professional narrative, and so on.

Bourdieu wanted to highlight that the structuring of habitus is inscribed very early on, and so its manifestations seem self-evident.

Things out of alignment with it appear obviously absurd or illogical or barbaric. This is a significantly different idea from the one that says frameworks and tacit understandings of morality *can* be clarified using intellectual tools but that people mostly lack either the skill or the will to do so (thus allowing moral philosophers to earn an honest living).

The habitus of professional bioethicists serves to naturalize their imported moral, epistemological, and other assumptions, so that they fade from sight as needing justification: they *just are so*. It escapes notice that these assumptions are tailored to the demands of a particular social and professional world. For bioethicists, it is salutary to remember how Bourdieu (1993, 76) put it: "When people only have to let their habitus follow its natural bent in order to comply with the immanent necessity of the field and satisfy the demands contained within it ... they are not at all aware of fulfilling a duty, still less of seeking to maximize their (specific) profit. So they enjoy the additional profit of seeing themselves and being seen as totally disinterested."

Bourdieu himself was fairly pessimistic about the possibility of changing the habitus, which he saw as owing its potency and persistence to the fact that it operates outside the reach of conscious control. Nevertheless, paying attention to local knowledge as a naturalized epistemology prescribes does two helpful things. It accumulates details about local moral perceptions and understandings, the facts that show where and how they differ. In doing so, however, it demonstrates in a more general way the reality of epistemic constraints that are inherent to lives lived in specific cultural and historical locations. It automatically disrupts the naturalization of the bioethicists' own mental and physical habitus, even if it cannot do a great deal to the habitus itself. Bioethicists who recognize that they are epistemically limited, who know that they are not "totally disinterested" as Bourdieu put it, bring a different kind of expertise to situations of moral difficulty that are never entirely knowable.

Fourth, the standard criticism leveled at this approach is that it is all very well to do the empirical and narrative work of filling in the details of a moral agent's personal, social, or institutional landscape, but once all that information is available, how does it help make a moral choice, or evaluate someone else's? For anyone except the most radical of relativists, it is inadequate to try to justify an act *solely* on the grounds that it fits comfortably within one person's moral framework. We might now have a better grasp of *why* it seemed obviously right to Duchesneau and McCullough to act on their preference for a deaf child, but as bioethicists we surely need to be able to give some more general (even if not universal) kind of assessment.

One response here would be that a naturalized bioethics continues to examine critically the moral authority of local knowledge claims, such as those based on the experience of impairment. While better knowledge of contexts and experiences may prompt morally significant shifts in how behavior is judged, there must be a structure of morality that is retained and against which such judgments can still be made. It is beyond the scope of this chapter to evaluate the numerous attempts that philosophers have made to delineate a universal or general ethics; all I want to say here is that conceding a level of epistemic authority to others is not an argument for moral relativism of the sort that takes different groups as having incommensurable moral codes that cannot be judged against a common standard of some kind. It is more of a particularism whereby, in different cases, similar acts have different consequences and meanings. The incompatibility between the culturally Deaf who see no disadvantage in having a child with a hearing impairment and those who argue that parents have something like a duty to have the best possible child (see Savulescu 2001; 2007) is generated in their different local moral knowledges. Both culturally Deaf and hearing nevertheless operate within a common social-moral framework that gives high value to the welfare of the child, to the vitality of the community in which it lives, to parental liberty to make decisions on behalf of their children, and to individuals' autonomy to run their lives as they see fit. They differ in recognizing the local manifestations of these values: what constitutes damage to welfare, or how might individual autonomy be fostered by a community? For the hearing world, knowing more about the Deaf world's structure, history, and future might turn a preference for a hearing-impaired child into a morally permissible stance rather than an objectionable one. It might also be the case, of course, that Deaf people would shift their positions with better knowledge of hearing bioethicists' arguments.

A naturalized bioethics is not about bioethicists facilitating the moral accommodations of any group of people, whether they are patients, the Deaf community, clinicians, or even (especially) other bioethicists. As an ethical practice, it remains critical and self-critical. A fuller answer to the question of how a naturalized bioethics operates normatively in situations where people's experiences are very divergent – as is often the case with impairment – would outstrip the ambitions of this chapter. And, in a sense, the answer cannot be given in advance. That is, a project of naturalized bioethics involves teasing out the best responses to issues of methodology and normativity as they arise within particular cases, as bioethicists do their work.

2

Choosing Surgical Birth

Desire and the Nature of Bioethical Advice

Raymond G. De Vries, Lisa Kane Low, and
Elizabeth (Libby) Bogdan-Lovis

> All is clouded by desire: as fire by smoke, as a mirror by dust....
> Wisdom is clouded by desire, the ever present enemy of the wise.
> – Krishna to Arjuna, *Bhagavadgita*, book 3

Most of us, academics or laypersons, accept the straightforward and
simple syllogism: scientific discovery → change or improvement in
medical practices → new ethical problems → bioethical advice or
solutions. While there are some cynics among us,[1] the progression
from science to practice to ethical adjustment seems logical, if not
natural. But the real world, alas, is not a clean and logical place. Our
tidy idea of a natural progression conceals a messy process where
competing information, demands, pressures, values, and emotions
interact to produce scientific discovery, new medical practices, and
bioethical advice. We may prefer to see bioethics as part of a well-
organized division of labor, but it is, in fact, one part of the complex
world of science, medicine, and health care.

Called upon to provide reasoned and defensible advice on the
ethical quandaries that emerge from this jumble, bioethicists must
find a way to collect information, strip away confounding factors, and

---

[1] Stevens (2000), for example, posits that bioethical solutions *preceded*, and indeed
made possible, the development of new medical practices. She describes how the
work of bioethicists helped to change the definition of death in a way that allowed
physicians to move ahead with organ transplantation.

A grant from the National Institutes of Health (U.S.) National Library of Medicine
(1G13LM008781–01) supported De Vries's work on this chapter.

zero in on the essential dilemma. Clearing away the clutter provides clarity for bioethics, but it also obscures the social origins of the facts that are brought to bear in bioethical deliberation. When consultant bioethicists consider ethical problems associated with genetic therapy, for example, they ask about risks and benefits of the procedure, scrutinize the informed-consent process, question the effects of altered genes on the population, and consider who will and will not have access to new treatments. They do *not* ask about the more foundational issues: How did this medical practice and the science that supports it come to be (i.e., what are the social and cultural forces that produced genetic therapies as opposed to other approaches to disease)? What influences the desires and demands for these therapies by patients and their families? How does this approach to disease reflect the desires and anxieties of caregivers? And last but decidedly not least: How does the social location of bioethics – in the worlds of medicine, science, and in the larger culture – influence bioethical judgment? In distilling the "facts of the case" of genetic therapy – about risk and benefit, personal autonomy, and justice – consultant bioethicists ignore the way these facts are produced by cultural ideas, social structures, organizational constraints, group norms, and social relationships.

Academic bioethicists may protest that the principlism implicit in our description of the bioethical approach to genetic therapy is passé. They will point to far more nuanced and elegant approaches to ethical quandaries, including casuistry, narrative ethics, and care ethics. Yet nearly all bioethical deliberations that occur in hospital ethics committees, in committees that advise professional bodies, and in research ethics committees invoke the four principles of autonomy, beneficence, nonmaleficence, and justice. This is no surprise. Principlism provides an easily understood and easy-to-apply template for recognizing and resolving ethical dilemmas. Such routinization of bioethical deliberation makes organizational sense. After all, do we really want bioethical advice at the end of life to include reflection on the science that brought us life-prolonging technologies, the culture that shapes the wishes of family members and the anxieties of caregivers, and the place of bioethics in hospital organizations? Well, yes and no. We social scientists are convinced that these issues *should* be part of the conversation, but we also recognize the social conditions that make this kind of broader conversation impractical and thus unlikely. Our goal here is to show what is lost when bioethicists fail to attend to these larger questions. We are convinced that inattention to the social facts of bioethical quandaries diminishes the possibility of achieving the goals of bioethics, whether those goals are described modestly (helping those in the life sciences to see the moral implications of their actions) or immodestly (assuring that medicine and medical science are done ethically).

We make our case by taking a close look at the issue of cesarean delivery on maternal request (CDMR).[2] Unlike areas of medical practice where the presence of bioethicists has become routine and almost taken for granted, this relatively new and still controversial procedure gives us the opportunity to see how social and cultural forces shape bioethical advice. Providers of maternity care have reported a recent – and, by their reckoning, dramatic – increase in women with uncomplicated pregnancies asking to have their babies delivered surgically. The central question engendered by these requests – should elective surgery be used to intervene in what is essentially a natural and healthy process? – has led to lively discussions among professionals and the public. Pregnant women want to know about the risks and benefits to their babies, themselves, their partners, and their families. Physicians want to see the evidence and understand how CDMR affects the health of their patients, the use of their skills, and the management of their practices. Bioethicists want to understand the moral dimensions of choosing more and less technological approaches to care at birth.

Because we are at a remove from the clinic, the questions we ask of CDMR have a more "meta" feel. We start by asking: Why now? How did CDMR become a medical and bioethical issue? What roles have been played by professions, professionals, clients, medical institutions, and third-party payers in the emergence of this issue? How has the evidence brought to bear on CDMR been created and used? How – from what materials and toward what ends – are bioethical arguments about CDMR fashioned? These questions situate medical

---

[2] CDMR is among the most popular of the many terms used to describe the phenomenon of healthy women submitting to a surgical birth in the absence of a medical indication for the intervention.

and bioethical practice in personal, social, and political space, offering a naturalistic account of the way bioethics (and in particular the principle of autonomy) is engaged in the everyday work of medicine. Rather than extracting the moral questions from the environment in which they arise (as is common in bioethics), we examine this bioethical issue as it is found in the social and cultural situation of health care.

SURGICAL BIRTH ON DEMAND

In the late 1990s studies investigating a possible link between vaginal delivery and pelvic floor damage began to populate the medical literature, expanding along with the rise of urogynecology, a medical specialty that focuses on the integrity and function of a woman's pelvic floor. Case studies suggesting a correlation between vaginal delivery and pelvic floor damage were cited as a rationale for introducing informed consent for elective cesarean delivery. This consideration in turn raised a related question of whether informed consent should be provided for vaginal delivery. Obstetric and urogynecological specialists cautiously surmised that harm to the pelvic floor might be averted with surgical delivery. It followed (in a self-fulfilling fashion) that "preserving the pelvic floor" could then be a medically indicated rationale for choosing a surgical instead of a vaginal birth (O'Boyle et al. 2002; Sultan and Stanton 1996; Handa et al. 1996; Devine et al. 1999; DeLancey 2000).

The United States is experiencing a rapid rise in surgical births – in 2005, 30.2 percent of U.S. births were accomplished surgically (Hamilton et al. 2007) – but it is difficult to distinguish between elective and medically indicated caesarean births, and there are no credible data on the extent of CDMR. In spite of this, the program of a 2006 National Institutes of Health (NIH) "State of the Science" conference on the procedure asserted that CDMRs make up 2.5 percent of all surgical births.[3] To support this assertion, those convinced of an attention-worthy rise in the CDMR rate used a statistical sleight of hand: they introduced graphics that showed the number of primary (first-time) cesarean sections rising, even though

[3] See http://consensus.nih.gov/2006/2006CcsareanSOS027main.htm.

maternal risk profiles remained unchanged. Their conclusion? The "unexplained" rise in the rate of primary cesarean deliveries must be the result of maternal request. Disregard for other sources of the rise in surgical births, including, for example, changed professional practice patterns, allowed conference organizers to frame the question in terms of women's choices. The evidence brought to bear focused on balancing respect for women's autonomy with the benefits and risks of surgical birth. By posing CDMR as an ethical dilemma, the NIH conference created space to consider CDMR in terms of women's desires.[4]

The autonomy principle figured prominently in conference discussions. In the absence of direct and convincing evidence of increased risk, how could a physician deny the desire of a woman giving birth? Following the conference, NIH conveners issued a press release with the headline, "Panel Finds Insufficient Evidence to Recommend for or against Maternal Request Caesarean Delivery." A tagline recommended that those women requesting a cesarean delivery should be thoroughly counseled on potential risks and benefits. Neither the press release nor subsequent media coverage mentioned that the evidence supporting the claim that vaginal birth damages the pelvic floor was very weak; this oversight is interesting because concern with pelvic floor damage is a primary rationale for choosing elective surgery. Thus, the practical result of the conference was to conclude that there can be *no* ethical objection when the desire of an "informed" woman for a surgical birth meets the desire of a physician to apply the "best" of medical technology to the natural process of birth.

DESIRE AND SURGICAL BIRTH

How did we get to this point? A lot of time, energy, and money are being spent on a situation that, in statistical terms, is vanishingly small. In a recent nationally representative survey of mothers in the United States, "just one mother among the 252 survey participants

---

[4] The significance of the "problem" of CDMR was repeatedly challenged by skeptical members of the audience during the program. The proceedings of the conference can be watched in the NIH videocast Web site (http://videocast.nih.gov/).

with an initial (primary) cesarean reported having had a planned cesarean at her own request with no medical reason" (Declercq et al. 2006). That is 0.4 percent of the women with a primary cesarean and 0.2 percent of first time mothers. What is at stake here? In order to understand what seems to be disproportionate attention being paid to CDMR, we must look at the way desire influences medicine and bioethics.

We use the term "desire" to replace the more often invoked "interests." It is commonplace for social scientists to describe how interests shape knowledge and practice. Although it is clear that interests *do* shape the generation of knowledge, patterns of practice, and the development of technologies, the connotations of interest often are limited to *material* interests. Desire expands and more accurately describes the interests that inform decision making in health care.

In the case of surgical birth, for example, it often is claimed that obstetricians prefer surgical birth because it is in their (material) interest. In some places, so the argument goes, the remuneration is higher for surgical birth, and even if it is not, the time demands of surgery are comparatively less because an elective procedure can be scheduled, and surgery is more "efficient" than waiting for labor. These arguments may be true, but there are at least two problems with this analysis of the link between interest and practice. First, more than material interests are involved in a preference for surgical birth. It is a rare obstetrician that would choose surgery simply for his or her convenience and pecuniary gain; it is far more likely that a physician, after years of education and the socialization experience of residency, sees surgery as the *best* way to promote the health of a mother and her child. The second problem follows from the first: physicians do not recognize themselves in descriptions of the interest-practice link and thus see little reason to reflect on the non-medical influences on their practice.

Replacing *interests* with *desire* broadens our understanding of professional knowledge and practice. Desire stresses the depth and strength of feeling and implies strong intention or aim. Desire begins with the assumption that medical professionals want to do their best for their clients, but it allows analytic room to explore the genesis of desires, how they represent a mix of material, psychological, social, political, and cultural motivations. Desire has the added advantage of bringing in other actors whose interests are less easily described as "material." In our case, it allows us to explore how CDMR is produced by the desires of women, medical institutions, *and* bioethicists.

Our first glimpse of the role of desire comes in the name used to describe the use of surgery to assist in a birth absent a medical indication. While it may seem simply descriptive, the term CDMR imports professional attitudes and desires. Notice that the active agent is defined as the mother: it is she who is setting the surgical wheels in motion and she whose wishes must be honored. Notice, too, how "cesarean delivery" masks the fact that this procedure involves major surgery.[5] Many women whose babies are delivered surgically are subsequently surprised by the attendant postoperative pain and lengthy period of recovery.[6]

In an effort to be more neutral, to remove assumptions about agency, and to make clear that "cesarean birth" is indeed a *surgical* procedure, from here on we refer to this phenomenon as "non-medically indicated surgical birth" (NMISB).

PROFESSIONAL DESIRE

Professional desires, acquired in the long process of becoming a doctor, influence the creation and use of medical science, define professional fears, and influence the organization of health care delivery. When we look at NMISB through the lens of professional desire, we gain a clearer picture of the forces at work in medical decisions, a necessary but often ignored first step in bioethical deliberation.

Desire Diminishes Science

No one knows what the best cesarean delivery rate should be – or even what is a good range. Obstetricians are obliged to recommend

---

[5] The term "cesarean section" had this same masking effect: most women are unaware that "section" implies "cutting or separating by cutting." Replacing "section" with "delivery" further obscures the fact this procedure is major abdominal surgery.

[6] Compared to women who give birth vaginally, women who have their babies surgically are far more likely to report pain that interferes with their daily activities in the first two months after birth (Declercq et al. 2006, 91).

cesarean delivery in any given case based on the best available evidence of the balance of risks and benefits for mother and child. If the mother agrees, a cesarean is performed. *The statistics shouldn't matter*. (W. B. Harer Jr., past president of the American College of Obstetricians and Gynecologists, 2000, 13, emphasis added)

What role does science play in the decision of an obstetrician to intervene in birth? Harer's statement is revealing: he acknowledges that a doctor's judgment should be informed by the "best available evidence," but in the end he stakes his claim for physician autonomy, asserting that "statistics shouldn't matter." He recognizes that the credibility of medicine rests on science, but he preserves a place for the "art" of medicine, that is, the freedom of doctors to practice as they see best. Science becomes secondary to the wisdom of the physician.

This same attitude is found in the work of Mary Hannah, a physician-researcher widely known for her study that concluded surgery was safer than vaginal birth for babies in the breech position at term (Hannah et al. 2000).[7] Writing about "planned elective cesarean section" with no medical indication, Hannah (2004) concludes that it is a reasonable choice for some women. But she makes her case in a rather odd way. She first describes the *known* risks of cesarean delivery, which include higher maternal mortality, longer recovery time, major bleeding, subsequent placenta previa, neonatal respiratory distress, and unexplained stillbirth in a second pregnancy. She then shifts to a more tentative voice to list the benefits that *may* be associated with surgical birth, including reducing the risk of urinary incontinence, fecal incontinence, unexplained or unexpected stillbirth, and certain complications of labor. Hannah (2004, 814) uses this inconclusive and disputed evidence to advise her fellow obstetricians:

If a woman without an accepted medical indication requests delivery by elective cesarean section and, after a thorough discussion about the risks and benefits, continues to perceive that the benefits to her and her child of a planned elective cesarean outweigh the risks, then most likely the overall health and welfare of the woman will be promoted by supporting her request.

[7] Several more recent studies have challenged Hannah's findings. See http://www.lamaze.org/Research/WhenResearchisFlawed/VaginalBreechBirth/tabid/167/Default.aspx.

Although she qualifies her position ("most likely"), Hannah, like Harer, defends professional autonomy in the face of evidence. Verified and unverified facts have equal weight; statistics do not matter.

There is another interesting commonality in the reasoning used by Hannah and Harer. In both we see how their desire to help women is limited by what they know about birth. Because vaginal birth is already beset by so much intervention, the surgical option seems appropriate to Hannah (2004, 813): "Labour and vaginal birth, complete with hospital stay, continuous electronic fetal heart rate monitoring, induction or augmentation of labor, epidural anesthesia, forceps delivery, episiotomy, and multiple caregivers, may also not be considered 'natural' or 'normal.'" For Harer (2000, 13), surgical birth is a *remedy* for (poorly managed) vaginal births: he points out that incontinence is associated with "episiotomy and sphincter damage" and "use of forceps" and that "cesarean delivery [is] protective against these risks." Both seem unaware of the possibility that birth can be attended in less invasive and disruptive ways and that well-managed vaginal births with minimal interventions are the more appropriate comparison group for studies of surgical birth.

Desire Determines Science

Not only does professional desire give preference to professional autonomy over science; it also *determines* science by dictating research questions and the interpretation of results. This becomes clear when looking at cross-societal variation in medical science: the design, results, and use of scientific studies are products of professional desires forged by cultural ideas and the organization of health care systems and medical research.

The universalizing nature of science obscures this variation. In spite of Payer's (1988) now twenty-year-old observations about culture and medicine, it can be difficult to find differences between, for example, British and Finnish nephrology. A kidney is a kidney, after all. Interestingly, one place where we *do* find variation in medical science is in maternity care, an area of medicine where cultural ideas about women, family, the body, pain, and the efficacy of medical intervention shape both science and policy (De Vries et al. 2001).

Most striking in this regard is maternity care policy and obstetric science in the Netherlands, where nearly one-third of the births take place at home. In no other country with a modern health system do more than 3 percent of births occur at home. Midwives are primary attendants at 71 percent of Dutch home births (general practitioners attend the other 29 percent); midwives are the primary caregiver at 48 percent of all of that nation's births. It is a system that works quite well in terms of cost-efficiency and quality: the high rate of midwife-attended home birth is coupled with the world's lowest rates of surgical intervention in birth and very low rates of infant mortality.

The peculiarity of birth in the Netherlands creates a special problem for Dutch gynecologists and obstetrical researchers. In light of the uniformity of obstetrics outside the Netherlands, and in light of the need to scientifically support health care practices, how do the Dutch defend what seems an old-fashioned way of birth?[8] In fact, some researchers in the Netherlands are committed to the Dutch view of birth, whereas others, whose allegiance lies with the larger world of obstetric medicine, are skeptical of (and slightly embarrassed by) Dutch birth practices. Not surprisingly, those in the first camp do scientific research that supports the maternity policy of the Netherlands, whereas the skeptics do scientific research that exposes the Dutch way of birth as dangerous.

All those who would do research on the mode and place of birth face the same inherent difficulties. First, it is impossible to do randomized clinical trials on this topic. Assigning a woman to give birth in a setting she would not ordinarily choose not only would be unethical but also would create a confounding variable: the emotional state of a woman birthing in an environment she finds unfriendly would influence the outcome of birth. Second, extremely large samples are required to find significant differences in the outcomes of healthy women having their babies at home or in the hospital. Given this reality, researchers have three choices: they can use existing statistics, do "prospective studies" that analyze outcomes based on an "intention to treat" design,[9] or

---

[8] This review of the scientific debate over Dutch maternity care is based on several years of research in the Netherlands by De Vries (2005).

[9] This design, where analyses are based on *planned*, rather than the *actual*, place of birth, is necessary because of the simple fact that most complicated births end up in

devise new measures capable of discovering small differences in outcomes. Dutch researchers have used all three methods, but the best illustration of the way desire shapes obstetric science comes from research using new types of measurement.

The desire to find a better, more scientific way of comparing the outcomes of home and hospital birth led several researchers to develop a research design based on objective measures of umbilical cord blood pH and neonatal behavior. The researchers surmised – not unreasonably – that, in spite of favorable outcomes shown in prospective studies, midwife-assisted birth at home was unsafe. Women who give birth at home in the Netherlands must be healthy, as defined by a set of guidelines published by the Ministry of Health, and thus will have excellent outcomes, regardless of where they give birth. In order to get around this problem, the team devised a research strategy that would allow comparisons to be made even when there was no *overt* morbidity and mortality. Researchers would look for small but significant differences in the pH of blood taken from the umbilical cord. Lower pH values are suggestive of oxygen deprivation (acidosis), which is associated with growth retardation and damage to the central nervous system, and hence less than optimal outcomes for the neonatal brain. In conjunction with measures of cord blood pH, researchers also assessed outcomes using a scale that measured the neurological condition of the newborn.

In a series of articles and papers these researchers proposed, tested, and defended their use of measures of umbilical cord blood pH and neurological scores as a fitting way to examine more closely the outcomes of home and hospital births (see Stolte et al. 1979; Van den Berg-Helder 1980). Throughout the 1980s, several studies were done using these outcome measures, the most prominent of which, published in *American Journal of Obstetrics and Gynecology*, showed care in hospitals to be superior to birth at home with midwives: on average, babies born at home or under midwife care were more acidotic and had poorer neurological scores (Lievaart and De Jong 1982).

This widely read study presented a clear challenge to the Dutch way of birth. Pieter Treffers (a champion of home birth and then

the hospital; to simply compare home and hospital births builds in a negative bias toward the hospital and a positive bias toward home birth.

chair of obstetrics at the University of Amsterdam) and his colleagues replicated the research, paying careful attention to the collection and storage of cord blood. When researchers took pains to assure that cord blood samples from the clients of midwives and gynecologists were treated in an identical manner, the results were opposite to those reported by Lievaart and De Jong: women attended by midwives had significantly *higher* cord blood pH values. The researchers concluded that there was no cause for concern about the use of midwives.

Eager to get these results to the readers of *American Journal of Obstetrics and Gynecology*, Treffers and his colleagues submitted this research to the journal in two studies, but neither study was accepted for publication. Instead, the first was published in the *Journal of Perinatal Medicine* (Pel and Treffers, 1983), an English-language journal published in Germany, and the second was accepted by the *Nederlands Tijdschrift voor Geneeskunde* (Dutch Journal of Medicine) (Knuist et al. 1987).

This case study from the Netherlands reveals that accepted definitions of what is "normal" in pregnancy determine what is accepted by journal editors as good science.[10] Editors of the *American Journal of Obstetrics and Gynecology*, most of whom do *not* share the cultural assumptions of the Dutch, accepted the work of Lievaart and De Jong and rejected the work of Treffers because of what they "know" to be true about birth. They are unwilling to let research evidence influence their belief that "birth is normal only in retrospect."[11]

The "Dutch difference" illustrated here also shows up in the science that directs the use of surgery to birth babies in the breech position at the onset of labor. The often-cited "term breech trial"

---

[10] Two researchers whose work challenged the status quo in obstetrics – Tew, whose epidemiological work in Britain suggested home birth was safe, and Klein, whose research suggested that routine episiotomies were unnecessary – faced great difficulties in getting their research published in British and American journals. See Tew 1995 and Klein 1995.

[11] One interviewee reported that the *American Journal of Obstetrics and Gynecology* refused to publish an article by Berghs and Spanjaards based on their research that showed extremely low interobserver agreement about the interpretation of electronic fetal monitoring recordings taken during the second stage of labor (see Berghs and Spanjaards 1988, 129–40). The letter of refusal stated that it would be "immoral" to publish these results (De Vries, 2005, 207).

done by Hannah (a Canadian) and her colleagues (2000, 1375) concluded: "Planned caesarean section is better than planned vaginal birth for the term fetus in the breech presentation; serious maternal complications are similar between the groups." But in their analysis, Leeuw and Verhoeven (2006), two physicians whose desires are shaped in the Dutch maternity care system, conclude that the data from the term breech trial are "very controversial" and, looking at data from the Netherlands, argue for an increase in *vaginal* delivery of breech babies.

Here we see how ideology about the "best" way to give birth affects both the generation and interpretation of the scientific facts about birth. Desires, shaped by training and practice, influence science. The assumed relation between science and practice is turned on its head: practice is not based on science; rather, science is based on practice.

Desire Varies by Professional Specialty

The desires of medical professionals vary by specialty. While the first years of medical school are quite similar for all physicians-in-training, the later years and the years of residency expose students to different experiences, different regimes of socialization, and different bodies of knowledge. Specialties also differ in typical demands of energy and time, types of clients and complaints, types and rates of remuneration, and nature and amount of interaction with clients.

Urogynecology is a relatively new profession: the United States specialty group, the American Urogynecologic Society, was founded in 1979, and the first issue of the professional journal of this specialty, the *International Urogynecology Journal*, was published in 1989. The specialty grew in response to a particular set of clinical problems, as the society explains on its Web site:

A Urogynecologist is an Obstetrician/Gynecologist who has specialized in the care of women with Pelvic Floor Dysfunction. The Pelvic Floor is the muscles, ligaments, connective tissue, and nerves that help support and control the rectum, uterus, vagina, and bladder. The pelvic floor can be damaged by childbirth, repeated heavy lifting, chronic disease or surgery. http://www.augs. org/i4a/pages/index.cfm?pageid=210, last accessed October 5, 2007)

The Web site goes on to list "some problems due to Pelvic Floor Dysfunction," the first of which is "Incontinence: Loss of bladder or bowel control, leakage of urine or feces."

Not all physicians deal with pelvic floor dysfunction on a daily basis, and this difference in ailments seen and treated leads to a different set of desires. Doctors in family practice, for example, have a view of women that is less specialized and that encompasses many more aspects of their lives. Writing in their specialty journal, *Annals of Family Medicine*, Leeman and Plante (2006, 265) respond to the move toward NMISB:

Patient-choice cesarean delivery may become widely disseminated before the potential risks to women and their children have been well analyzed. The growing pressure for cesarean delivery in the absence of a medical indication may ultimately result in a decrease of women's childbirth options. Advocacy of patient-choice requires preserving vaginal birth options as well as cesarean delivery.

Because they are not driven by daily encounters with the heartbreak of incontinence, family practice physicians emphasize the need to preserve choice in mode of childbirth, even in cases where women desire a vaginal birth for a breech presentation or after a previous surgical birth.

Fear Replaces Confidence

Desire often operates as a pull factor – a yearning to possess a wished-for goal or object. But the pull toward a goal or object can include a desire to avoid other outcomes. In the case of birth and surgical birth, fear is an important source of action. It is worth noting that *all* published studies of fear of childbirth are studies of birthing women: it is simply assumed that "fear of childbirth" means a *women's* fear of childbirth. No consideration is given to the caregivers' fears and how these fears may influence the way babies get born.[12] Before we discuss the fears of women, we mention two ways that fear shapes the desires of physicians: fear of natural processes and fear of legal action.

[12] In their innovative work with labor and delivery nurses, Regan and Liaschenko (2007) have identified a range of attitudes toward birth (from normal, to lurking risk, to risky), and they are at work studying how these influence the course of labor. So far, there is no similar work with physicians.

Technology, broadly defined, has always been present at birth. In premodern times, midwives did not often use instruments to assist at birth, but they had a variety of techniques, including positioning, movement, and hands-on maneuvers, to help a women give birth to her child. During the twentieth century, the technologies of birth became more mechanical and more automated, moving from a simple fetoscope to the electronic fetal monitor, from forceps to vacuum extraction, from simple blood and urine tests to amniocentesis and chorionic villus sampling. While advances in technology offer much, they also move the caregiver away from the natural process of birth and low-technology solutions to the problems of labor. Technology replaces traditional knowledge. With the rise in popularity of the "doptone" (a device that uses sonar to locate and amplify the heart tones of the fetus), caregivers have forgotten how to use a fetoscope. This may seem a small loss, but the fetoscope is capable of giving a wealth of important information about mother and baby. The doptone can pick up a heart tone from nearly anywhere on the mother's belly; the fetoscope requires careful placement and registers the strength of the heartbeat. The latter procedure allows the caregiver to assess the position of the baby and puts the caregiver close to mother, where touch and smell provide measures of wellness. Similarly, the resort to surgery for all babies in the breech position has all but eliminated the knowledge of how to manage a breech birth vaginally. Doctors no longer trust themselves to guide a natural process without technology.

There is also the very real fear of being sued. This fear drives beliefs, actions, and advice to mothers. Stories abound about obstetricians leaving their practices because of fear of lawsuits and the high costs of malpractice insurance (Xu et al. 2007). Silverman (2004, 1) reports that "one in seven fellows with the American College of Obstetricians and Gynecologists has stopped practicing obstetrics because of the risk of medical liability claims." In their study of "cesarean on request" in eight European countries, Habiba et al. (2006, 651) discovered "a consistent, statistically significant trend emerged between obstetricians' self-reported feeling that their clinical practice was influenced, occasionally or often, by fear of litigation and the willingness to perform a caesarean delivery at the patient's request."

The Influence of Physician Desire

With the rise of for-profit hospitals and the push for greater efficiency in the nonprofit sector,[13] a business model is replacing a care model. Cost recovery is increasingly important. Speaking about the cost of cancer treatments, Dr. Robert Geller, an oncologist who worked in private practice from 1996 to 2005 before leaving to join a biotechnology company, points out that cancer doctors know that certain drug regimens are more profitable than others: "It's clear that physicians stopped making decisions based on what made scientific or clinical sense in lieu of what made better business sense" (quoted in Berenson, 2007). The same is true for hospitals and surgical birth. While physicians are often paid the same for vaginal and surgical births, hospitals can bill for far more services for surgical births. In 2003 the average cost of surgical birth was $12,468, compared to $6,240 for a vaginal birth (Baicker et al. 2006).

The desires of nurses also are shaped by physician desire and organizational needs. In their innovative research, Regan and Liaschenko (2007) discovered three discrete orientations toward birth among labor and delivery nurses. Shown a drawing of a woman in labor and asked to describe what was occurring, the nurses went on to characterize birth as a "natural process," a "lurking risk," or a "risky process." These attitudes were correlated with the environments in which the nurses worked: nurses working in a unit that employed midwives (whose desires are less oriented toward medical intervention) were less likely to see birth as a lurking risk or a risky process. According to Regan and Liaschenko (2007, 623), "Nurses' beliefs about the risks of childbirth focus nursing care along a specified trajectory of nursing action whereby the use of childbirth technologies and their associated physiological response might influence the use of CS [cesarean section]."

WOMEN'S DESIRES

How does professional desire shape what women want? The desires of women are heavily influenced by their perception of birth, the

---

[13] With the rise of diagnosis-related groups (DRGs) and managed care, nonprofit hospitals have been forced to find ways to be efficient.

importance of choice, concerns about sexuality, and the demands of work and career. We examine the first three of these influences through the lens of a discussion that occurred on the Web site of a popular media outlet. In September 2006, MSNBC put the issue of elective surgical birth to the public in an e-discussion, inviting readers to respond to the following query in its online health section: "A study shows that the infant death rate for babies born via C-section is three times higher than those born vaginally. Some C-sections are medically necessary, but others are not. What are your views on elective C-sections?"

The subsequent interactive e-discussion generated a rich and telling discourse, touching on the themes most commonly mentioned in NMISB debates. We use selected responses (posted between September 14 and September 20, 2006) to explore what these themes reveal about women's desires.[14] As with professional desires, individual desires do not emerge spontaneously: the desires of childbearing women are threads within a complex tapestry of cultural and social forces.

While a few e-respondents described childbirth as an inherently healthy process, a majority of discussants accepted the prevailing medical perception of birth as fraught with risk. "Caring Mom"[15] claimed: "If C-sections weren't here most of us women couldn't have kids." And "cuddliemamma" pondered: "How many infant/mother fatalities have resulted from c-sections being avoided or delayed?" "SamsMom" tells others that she received *authoritative* reassurance from her doctors that, "when performed in a sterile OR, the risks from a C-section are the same as risks of a vaginal birth." In this pathological view, surgical delivery is a welcome antidote to the "predictable dangers" of birth, supporting the conventional wisdom that birth simply will not work in the absence of medical intervention.

Another prominent theme in the e-discussion was *choice*, calling on a presumed liberal entitlement *to* choose. Notice how the notion of autonomous choice, so important in reproductive health advocacy efforts, is (mis)appropriated here. "Animalover" had an elective cesarean: "I was glad that I had the choice to decide what was best for

[14] Unfortunately, the Web site with these comments has been taken down.
[15] All e-discussion names have been changed.

me and my child. I wish every woman would become more aware of her options." "Haveaniceday" is "VERY pro-c section! And I believe it is up to the mom to decide what she wants, and for what reason." "ProfessorMD" suggests: "The mother must have total and unlimited choice."

The long-term negative effects of childbirth in terms of incontinence and sexuality were on the mind of several e-discussants. "Lonnie" says:

Celebrities get c-sections because it preserves the elasticity of their vagina. My obgyn said that no amount of kegel exercises can bring it back to what it was before a natural delivery.... The new term according to my obgyn for having an elective c-section is "perineum preservation." Would you rather have stitches on your abdomen or on your vagina if you tear?

"SamsMom," who chose a cesarean delivery, notes that during vaginal birth "severe tearing can occur on the mother." She goes on to defend her choice with doctor-supplied "facts" such as "the incontinence rate in Argentina. Women [there] ... have one of the lowest incontinence rates in the world [and] one of the highest C-section [rates]."

The notion that bypassing the vagina for birth is desirable to preserve future perineal, urinary, and anal sphincter function (see Nygaard and Cruikshank 2003) is a curious perversion of the precautionary principle, where wisdom dictates that one should take action proactively to forestall imminent disaster. In this case, the risks and harms of the intervention – major abdominal surgery – are ignored. Many comments by participants repeat the same suspect information (about pelvic floor damage) that influences providers, exemplifying a "medical false consciousness." In turn, this false consciousness presses providers of obstetrical care to support women's autonomous choice of NMISB.

Bioethics' patient-choice literature presumes a rational actor capable of evaluating available options and considering their consequences to ultimately achieve ends that will increase the individual's overall happiness (Jaeger et al. 2001, 246). Critics of mandatory informed consent point to weaknesses in the rational-actor paradigm, noting the many systematic errors of reasoning that occur in estimating probabilities. These critics tell us that overestimates of injury are especially likely for events prone to excessive vividness (Schneider 2006, 57).

The e-discussants offer a case in point: they frame NMISB as an action that selects among expected "risk" options of uncertain labor and birth trajectories. The "childbirth is always risky" frame amplifies the likelihood of bad outcomes (Jaeger et al. 2001), and, seen in that light, the responses to MSNBC's question are both reasonable and rational.

Surgical birth also can be regarded as a rational choice when seen in the context of women's work. One's location in the world of employment is an important influence on one's desires in choices about birth. The number of births to women aged thirty and older has increased markedly in the past thirty years (Hamilton et al. 2007). These women are more likely to be established in their careers and thus must organize their childbearing around the demands of work. A scheduled birth fits more easily with the needs of employers and has the added advantage of allowing family members who live at a distance to organize their travel efficiently and economically.

BUT IS IT ETHICAL? MORALIZING OBSTETRIC DESIRE

There was a time when professional desire was sufficient justification for treatment decisions. In the "golden age of doctoring" (McKinley and Marceau, 2002), the considered decision of a medical professional about proper treatment went largely unchallenged by patients, hospitals, and third-party payers. We now live in a society where professional desire is constrained by insurance companies, risk managers, drug formularies, and yes, bioethicists. Although there is some dispute as to the power of bioethics committees and bioethicists, it is commonplace for professional associations and hospitals to have ethics committees at the ready to review controversial clinical decisions and medical practices.

NMISB is a procedure that begs for ethical advice. The use of an expensive, highly technological, and risky procedure to assist at a birth that everyone agrees could occur without intervention pushes all the buttons of contemporary clinical ethics. As we noted, the opinion of academic ethicists about principlism – that it is simplistic and passé – has little influence on clinical ethics, where autonomy, beneficence, nonmaleficence, and justice continue to be used to make decisions and generate advice. In deciding if NMISB can be justified ethically, ethicists and ethics committees must strike a balance between autonomy (the right of a woman to determine her own care), beneficence (promoting the welfare of the woman and her baby), nonmaleficence (avoiding unnecessary harm to the woman and her baby), and justice (seeking the proper and fair use of health care resources).

One reason the principlist approach has remained popular is that abstract principles can float above, and yet account for, the peculiarities of culture. Regardless of our cultural differences, we can all agree that nonmaleficence is a good thing; but we must hasten to add that what you and I *call* harm may vary. The same can be said of autonomy: in the United States autonomy is conceived in a radically individualist manner, but in other cultures we can adjust the idea to incorporate more familial and communal ideas of autonomy. In the atomistic United States, a free and independent individual should (must?) determine her care, whereas in more communal societies autonomous decisions occur in consultation with, or by decision of, recognized authorities. Pushed too far in this direction, of course, the principles become meaningless. Can we really speak of autonomy if a treatment decision for an adult woman is made by others?

Bioethical advice about NMISB reflects the variation in desires we described previously. This is clearly seen in looking at the responses to NMISB offered by two professional associations of obstetricians, one based in the United States and the other being an international organization: the American College of Obstetricians and Gynecologists (ACOG), and the International Federation of Gynecologists and Obstetricians (FIGO). Interestingly, both organizations base their advice on the principles, but different desires result in different advice.

In 1998 FIGO's Committee for the Ethical Aspects of Reproduction and Women's Health published its position on NMISB in a document titled *Ethical Aspects of Caesarean Delivery for Non-Medical Reasons*. Its opinion, reaffirmed in 2003, was based on the principles of nonmaleficence and justice. The committee starts with two observations: "Cesarean section is a surgical intervention with potential hazards for both mother and child"; and "[Cesarean section] uses more resources than normal vaginal delivery." Given that FIGO members "have a professional duty to do nothing that may harm their patients" and "an ethical duty to society to allocate health care resources wisely," the committee concludes: "At present, because hard evidence of net benefit does not exist, performing cesarean section for non-medical reasons is not justified" (http://www.figo.org/docs/Ethics%20Guidelines.pdf).

ACOG's position on NMISB is found in an opinion from its Committee on Ethics, "Surgery and Patient Choice," dated 2007 (www.acog.org/from_home/publications/ethics/co395.pdf). The ACOG committee considers how each of the four principles of bioethics may be applied to the request of healthy woman for a surgical birth. The principle of autonomy lends support for the "permissibility of elective cesarean delivery in a normal pregnancy (after adequate informed consent)." The principle of justice "regarding the allocation of medical resources must be considered" in the debate over NMISB, but (unlike FIGO), the committee adds, "It is not clear whether widespread implementation of elective cesarean birth would increase or decrease the resources required to provide delivery services." With regard to the other principles, the committee notes that "the application of the principles of beneficence and nonmaleficence . . . is made problematic by the limitations of the scientific data. Different interpretations of the risks and benefits are the basis for reasonable differences among obstetricians regarding this challenging issue." The committee then concludes: "If the physician believes that cesarean delivery promotes the overall health and welfare of the woman and her fetus more than vaginal birth, he or she is ethically justified in performing a cesarean delivery."

AUTONOMY AND DESIRE

The story of NMISB demonstrates how medical science, medical practice, and bioethics are shaped by the desires of professionals, organizations, and patients. Our analysis offers four lessons for bioethicists.

First, like medicine, bioethics is shaped by desire. This occurs in at least two ways: the need to survive professionally and the desire to frame an issue in ways that are familiar. With regard to survival: unlike other professions in medicine, clinical bioethics has no visible means of support. Clinicians fund themselves by seeing patients, and those who teach in medical schools are funded by tuition dollars, but who will fund bioethics consultations? Bioethical advice has no billing code and no RVU (relative value unit).[16] Given this situation, bioethicists must be keenly attentive to the needs of their colleagues in the clinic. Saying no too often will not help secure bioethicists a place. Thus, bioethics is likely to go along with the reigning clinical mentality.

Second, bioethical advice must cast a wider net when looking for facts relevant to the dilemma in question. Because of its roots in philosophy and the humanities, bioethics tends to ignore social context. In a recent listserv discussion that offers an apt illustration, bioethicists weighed in on a case of a woman who refused an "emergency" cesarean section. The facts of the case are these: after twelve hours of labor and more than two hours of pushing, an obstetrician informed his patient that it was time for either a vacuum extraction or a cesarean section. The woman agreed to the vacuum but would not sign a consent that also allowed a cesarean. While the obstetrician was out of the room, deciding how to handle the refusal (what if surgery became necessary during the extraction procedure?), the woman spontaneously delivered a healthy child. The listserv discussion ignored the healthy, spontaneous birth and instead centered on the fine points of law, ethics, autonomy, paternalism, and the duty to rescue. Uninteresting to the bioethicists was the fact that the professional judgment of the physician was wrong. The desires of bioethicists, shaped in the crucible of philosophical debate, center on intellectual puzzles and elegant arguments.

When bioethicists are called on for advice, it is their habit to wade through a sea of facts to find the key issue(s) in question. This important and useful skill serves the needs of clinicians well. In the midst of a heated and emotionally charged family debate about what to do with a laboring woman or a dying parent, bioethical parsimony is useful. But the clean cut of Occam's razor excises facts that are

---

[16] Schneiderman and his colleagues (2003, 1166) have suggested a creative solution: they studied the effect of bioethics consultations on the "use of life-sustaining treatments delivered to [intensive care] patients who ultimately did not survive to hospital discharge." Using a randomized controlled trial where patients were randomly assigned to consultation or standard care (i.e., no consultation), they discovered that ethics consultation significantly reduced the use of life-sustaining treatments *and* was regarded as helpful by a majority of nurses, patients or surrogates, and physicians. In other words, bioethicists are paying for themselves by reducing futile care at the end of life.

essential to good bioethical advice. The "stuff" of bioethical advice – the data from which one assembles a judgment – must include all the social and cultural forces at play in the dilemma in question. In the case of NMISB, to ignore the many ways that desire shapes and constrains the choices of women and caregivers is to concede the power to define the situation to one institution: medicine. When bioethical advice fails to account for the social and cultural contexts of bioethical dilemmas, it is all too easy for critics to label bioethicists as apologists for medicine and science (Elliott 2001).

Third, NMISB and the ethical advice it generates call into question the way autonomy gets used by bioethics in the United States. ACOG's opinion, that there is no ethical reason to deny the request of an informed, healthy woman for a surgical birth, rests on a socially and culturally limited idea of "informed consent." Missing in the information given to a woman choosing surgical birth is discussion of the way in which professional desires shape medical science and medical practice and thus bias the information she receives. Absent also is comment on the way a woman's desires are produced by culture. Like Odysseus – who, in his cautious approach to the songs of the Sirens, recognized that desires could be bent and misdirected in ways that caused harm – bioethicists must be aware that unreflective obeisance to autonomy is dangerous.

The fourth and final lesson of NMISB is that the distinction between autonomy and paternalism can no longer be maintained. We see here (and it is true elsewhere) that informed consent imports paternalism. Concealed in the information given to a woman to obtain her consent is the paternalism of medical science and clinical practice that generate facts in line with professional desire. It is time to rethink paternalism. "False" paternalism – the self-interested assertion of one's will upon another – is clearly objectionable. But "true" paternalism, defined as the selfless love of a parent for a child, recognizes the corrupting influence of professional desire and looks for ways to respect persons – to serve the interests of patients – that go beyond the formula of informed consent.

3

Holding on to Edmund

The Relational Work of Identity

Hilde Lindemann

It was Tosca's apartment, really. The living room was uncarpeted for greater ease of sliding and chasing, should she care to bat her catnip mice under the sofa. Two large cardboard boxes also lay on the hardwood floor, should she care to lurk inside. A pole with perches set at different heights stood before the picture window, should she care to survey the passing scene. And while two scratching posts were available for her use, the state of the furniture clearly proclaimed that she preferred to sharpen her claws on the upholstery. The only concession to her besotted keeper's own taste and convenience was an elaborate sound system flanked by rows of vinyl recordings of baroque and nineteenth-century music, heavy on the Italian composers.

I looked in on Edmund and Tosca about once a week, sometimes bringing a new CD, sometimes just bringing faculty gossip. It had been twenty years since the old gentleman retired, but he liked to keep abreast of departmental politics even though he'd outlived all the professors of his generation, and besides, he enjoyed having me to talk to. The gray tabby would jump onto his lap and demand to be petted, with special attention to the white bib under her chin, and Edmund would tell me all about how clever she was, which operas she liked best, and what the vet had said at her last checkup. He'd tell me about his

Many thanks to Erika Lindemann and James Lindemann Nelson for their help in developing these ideas. Thanks also to Sara Ruddick, Claudia Card, Rebecca Kukla, Joseph J. Fins and his colleagues at New York Hospital-Cornell Medical School, members of the Philosophy Department at the University of Kentucky, the project participants, and other Dutch bioethicists who commented on earlier versions of this chapter.

former students, too, some of whom had kept in touch, and he'd quiz me about my latest research, because, like him, I was a specialist in medieval European history.

When he called me that evening, frightened, to tell me he couldn't breathe for the pressure on his chest, I broke the speed limit getting him to the hospital and stayed with him while they diagnosed a heart attack in progress. The cardiologist on call told us Edmund needed a cardiac catheterization so that she could see exactly which arteries or vessels were blocked. After they prepped him, I did my best to reassure him. "I'll be right here," I promised. "You're going to be okay."

"Who'll look after Tosca?"

"It's all taken care of. I phoned your neighbor."

"If I'm dying, don't let me die here. Let me die at home, with Tosca."

"You're not dying."

"Do they know that you're my decision maker if anything goes wrong?" he asked.

"Yes, it's in your chart. Nothing's going to go wrong, though. They're going to fix you up."

"I want to die at home."

"I know."

In the middle of the catheterization Edmund sustained a second, massive heart attack. He underwent an emergency double-bypass surgery, and when it was over, they took him to the cardiac intensive care unit. They let me see him the next morning, an ashen-faced eighty-five-year-old man on a heart monitor with an IV drip and God knows how many other tubes running from his body to wherever it was that they were supposed to go.

Over the next two weeks I couldn't see much improvement, though his cardiologist, Dr. Stoddard, remained consistently upbeat. At first, Edmund recognized me but wasn't strong enough to talk much, so I downloaded quantities of his favorite music – Mozart, Verdi, Boccherini, Puccini – onto my iPod and he listened to it for hours at a time. His heart was so badly damaged that it couldn't pump adequately, which put stress on his kidneys to the point where they too began to fail. He was too sick to eat, so they fed him with a nasogastric tube. Then, in his third week in the intensive care unit, just as his kidneys were starting to respond to treatment, he developed pneumonia. When I came to see him the next day, there was a breathing tube down his throat and he was on a ventilator.

"What happened?" I asked his nurse.

"He had trouble breathing."

"But you know he doesn't want this – "

"It's only temporary, just for seventy-two hours, to give the antibiotics a chance to clear up the pneumonia."

I didn't like where things were headed, but I agreed that the tube could stay in, on the strict understanding that this was to be only temporary. I'd already gone over with Dr. Stoddard the standardized form Edmund had signed five years ago, which was titled "Declaration of a Desire for a Natural Death" and which stipulated that "if my condition is determined to be terminal and incurable, my physician may withhold or discontinue extraordinary means, artificial nutrition or hydration, or both." It seemed to me that Edmund was sliding further into just the kind of medical morass he didn't want and that I would have to get him out of it.

They kept him sedated so he wouldn't fight the ventilator. When the seventy-two hours were up, they gave him a lung function test, which, in the hospital's unlovely parlance, he failed. Time to call a halt, I thought. Not only has this gone far enough, it's gone too far. I made an appointment with Dr. Stoddard for later that afternoon and asked him to take Edmund off the ventilator so he could die in peace.

"Take him off the ventilator?" he said. "Why, you mustn't even think of it. Professor Randolph isn't dying, you know. His kidneys are doing much better. Much better. In fact, his urine output is back up to normal. And the pneumonia is clearing up too. No, no, we need to be thinking more positively. For one thing, we need to get his weight up. The nasogastric tube seems to be bothering him, so I'd like to implant a PEG tube into his abdomen – just a simple surgical procedure – and I also think his breathing tube would be more comfortable for him if we performed a tracheotomy."

I was appalled. "But you can't!" I protested. "He's been very clear from the beginning that he doesn't want to end up like this. Please don't keep doing things to him. Please. It's time to stop."

Stoddard shook his head. "I sympathize with what you're going through, but you have to understand that patients don't always mean what they say. I've seen it so often, people telling me they don't want to live if it means being on oxygen the rest of their lives, or being bed-bound, or having to go into a nursing home. But then when they find themselves in that situation, they discover it's not as bad as they thought it would be." He gave me a wry little smile. "It's certainly better than being dead."

"How do you know *Edmund* didn't mean what he said? You can't just bulldoze right over his express wishes!"

"But he might have changed his mind. There's still a chance that he'll pull through. Maybe not to where he can go home, but to where he can still get some pleasure out of his life. I can't in good conscience – "

"But he doesn't want – " We spoke simultaneously.

Stoddard blew out a deep breath, as though he were counting to ten. "There's a perfectly simple way to settle this," he said. "Professor Randolph is only temporarily incapacitated, you know. Let's just take him off sedation, and when he wakes up we can ask him whether he wants us to continue treatment."

"No. No, don't do that. I know what he wants. I know *him*. He wants his cat. He wants his music. He wants his old life back. And if he can't have those things, he wants to die quietly. At home, if possible. But if not, at least without all the tubes and machines."

I argued it out with him for another half hour, but I might as well have saved my breath. Stoddard remained adamant: it wasn't time to give up on Edmund. So here we are. I don't have any idea what to do next. My biggest fear is that when they wake him tomorrow he'll say yes and improve just enough to end up in a nursing home, with one complication after another until he finally dies. I've got to stop that, but I can't see how. It's not right. None of this is right. Somehow, I've got to convince them to let him die tonight, before he has a chance to get better.

Many people's preliminary intuitions here will line up on the physician's side of the disagreement: if the patient can speak for himself, he should speak for himself, and the proxy should not try to foreclose the possibility that he might make a decision of which she does not approve. The proxy, while doubtless well intentioned, exceeds her authority by insisting that he not be given the opportunity to change his mind. It's his life, when all is said and done, and if he now finds he can settle for a severely diminished version of it, it's not the proxy's place to stop him. These are widely shared moral understandings, justifiable on the grounds of respect for patient autonomy and the value of human life. I have no wish to unseat them; I endorse them as appropriate and increasingly necessary in an age when professional health care givers wield enormous power over their patients. In this chapter, however, I want to complicate these shared understandings by identifying and describing a feature of close personal relationships that stands in some tension with them but nevertheless seems to be morally valuable: I urge the possibility that Edmund's proxy is holding him in selfhood, maintaining his identity for him under conditions of deep duress.

My aim is not so much to defend the proxy's actions as to demonstrate how standard bioethics' reliance on impartial, impersonal principles of ethical conduct causes it to miss an interpersonal practice, particularly in evidence here, that contributes significantly to the overall moral shape of many instances of medical decision making A naturalized bioethics that pays attention to how people actually interact can motivate the thought that what the proxy is doing for Edmund deserves respect, even if competing considerations also weigh in the balance.

BACKGROUND

Before I begin, a little stage setting is in order. In wealthy nations where health care delivery is driven by continuous advances in biomedical technology, it is not uncommon for people to fear what Philippe Ariès called a "wild" death. In *The Troubled Dream of Life*, Daniel Callahan (1993, 26) explains that by a wild death Ariès meant the death of technological medicine, "marked by undue fear and uncertainty, by the presence of medical powers not quite within our mastery, by a course of decline that may leave us isolated and degraded." A tame death, by contrast, is "tolerable and familiar, affirmative of the bonds of community and social solidarity, expected with certainty and accepted without crippling fear." Callahan notes that in societies where wild deaths predominate, doctors are pushed by an imperative to take life-sustaining technology all the way up to the point where the technology becomes harmful, and only then to withdraw or withhold it. But because of medicine's continuing failure to achieve the precision necessary for this kind of brinkmanship, Callahan (1993, 41) argues, more and more people experience the violence of "death by technological attenuation."

Callahan somewhat injudiciously writes as if a death accompanied by technology were by definition violent, but that is surely wrong. Many people welcome whatever technological assistance they can get at the end of life and are not at all degraded by it. Where such a death is *violent* is when the technology is used to *violate* the person, contemptuously disregarding the person's bodily integrity, injuring or shattering the person's sense of self. In this respect, technology becomes violent in the same way that sexual intercourse becomes violent: when it is no longer welcome.

According to Callahan, the wildness of death has also prompted a shift in what counts as dying: patients in the United States are often not defined as dying until their doctors judge that no further technological interventions will improve their condition. If he is right, it's no wonder that Dr. Stoddard isn't ready to stop treating Edmund – or, for that matter, that he's not yet willing to acknowledge the authority of Edmund's advance directive. The medical practice that surrounds the culture of wild death is governed by a particularly powerful norm: it is worse to err on the side of letting a patient die prematurely than to err by overtreating the patient.

One reason why the norm in favor of treating is particularly power-ful is that, as Robert Veatch (1997, 396; also 1973) has argued many times, physicians have a role-related bias in favor of treatment:

Members of special social and professional groups hold special, atypical values. This is true of all professionals, not just physicians. Something led them to choose their profession; they believe in its goals and believe it can do good things. They should favor the use of society's resources for their profession. This is not necessarily because they will earn more if more of society's resources are devoted to their sphere; it is more because they have an unusual view about the value of the services in the field to which they have given their lives.

Imagine if professors of philosophy were asked to decide the number of required courses in philosophy in a college curriculum. They would plausibly make the wrong choice, not only because they would have an economic interest in remaining employed, but importantly, because they have an unusual view about the value of studying philosophy. Likewise, clinicians should be expected to make value tradeoffs atypically.

If Veatch is right and their unusual view about the value of treatment causes most physicians to believe that technological support and treatment should be given until they no longer work, then, from their point of view, the burden of proof is on the patient to show that refusing further life-sustaining treatment is reasonable. Ideally, the principle of respect for patient autonomy swings the burden back in the opposite direction, but there is a catch: in the physicians' epistemic environment, refusal of treatment can be seen as a sign that the patient is not mentally competent and therefore not capable of exercising her autonomy. So, often, the bias in favor of treatment remains in place.

HOLDING ON TO SOMEONE'S IDENTITY

Against this background, I offer a way of thinking about what Edmund's proxy might be doing as she urges that he be allowed to die before he wakes. A number of rather pedestrian considerations might be motivating her, so I will just mention some of them to get them out of the way before I begin to develop the one that interests me in particular.

First, she might be thinking that if Edmund were awakened and asked if he wanted treatment to continue, he might assent out of fear of dying, rather than because he has given the matter careful thought. Or she might be worried that because he's in such unfamiliar surroundings, he might be particularly susceptible to decisional pressures: there is a body of research that constitutes powerful evidence that people are highly suggestible to figures in authority, even when told to do things they ordinarily wouldn't do. As John Doris (2002, 2) has recently concluded, "The experimental record suggests that situational factors are often better predictors of behavior than personal factors, and this impression is reinforced by careful examination of behavior outside the confines of the laboratory." So the proxy could be afraid that because the authority figures in Edmund's environment (in white coats and carrying stethoscopes) are biased in favor of treatment, Edmund will assent to treatment against his own better judgment. Finally, the proxy might think that the mere ability to understand what he is asked and to say yes in reply is no indication that he is competent to determine his course of care. Given the bludgeoning that Edmund's body has sustained in the last three weeks, including two heart attacks, one cardiac catheterization, one double-bypass surgery, kidney failure, pneumonia, and lung failure, she might be doubting Edmund's ability to think clearly, even if it turns out that he can respond when spoken to.

These considerations call Edmund's autonomy into question. Important as they are, though, there is something equally important at work here that might explain the proxy's attitude and that seems to be consistently overlooked in the bioethics literature. It may or may not explicitly enter her thinking, but it is certainly a favoring consideration that contributes to the moral shape of the situation (Dancy 2004). It is the role she plays in maintaining Edmund's identity.

In the sense that I intend, an identity is a representation of a self: it is a narrative understanding of who someone is. Generated from both an internal and an external perspective, an identity consists of the tissue of stories and story fragments that are woven around the acts, experiences, personal characteristics, roles, relationships, and commitments that matter most about a person – either to her or to others around her. Because people change over time, the stories that portray them either grow to accommodate a specific shift or fall by the wayside and are replaced with new stories. Because people can be self-deceived or mistaken about themselves, third-person stories are sometimes more accurate than first-person ones. And because identities set up expectations for how people are supposed to act and how they may be treated, it is a matter of great moral importance that the stories constituting our sense of someone show the person in either a just or, in some cases, a moderately charitable light (H. Nelson 2001).

Even as none of us can *form* a personal identity without the help of many others, so none of us can *maintain* our identities all by ourselves. Many self-constituting social roles, for example, require others to take up reciprocal roles with respect to them: I can't be a mother if I don't have a child. To be *held* in my identity as a mother, my family and my friends and co-workers need to interact with me as someone who occupies that role.

Identity maintenance takes many forms. Under ordinary conditions, mentally and morally competent adults can do the lion's share, if necessary, of maintaining their own sense of themselves. I am, we shall say, an eighty-five-year-old retired college professor, opera buff, and cat owner, and it's out of that sense of who I am that I go about my daily business. In addition to my own identity-maintaining activity, though, the familiarity of my surroundings and my day-to-day relationships help me maintain my self-conception. My cat Tosca, simply by jumping into my lap and purring, or demanding that I feed her, helps me to be myself: by her interactions with me, she reminds me who I am. Sleeping in my own bed, listening to recordings from my own music library, and cooking my supper on my own stove also contribute to my understanding myself as me.

Narrative recognition on the part of other people is another major source of identity maintenance. My neighbor, acting on the basis of narratives she contributes to my identity, greets me with a friendly, "How's Tosca?" The clerk at the record store, acting on the basis of his own narrative understanding of me, saves the new Riccardo Muti recording of the *Verdi Requiem* for me. My dear friend who visits me every week *listens* to my stories and in that way also affirms my sense of myself as me.

Serious injury or illness, rape, assault, the death or divorce of a spouse, and other traumas can and frequently do play havoc with one's identity. To be critically ill for more than a few days is to lose control over one's physical and mental processes. It puts a stop to one's professional and social activities and interferes with one's memories, hopes, plans for the future, and ongoing projects. It usually involves hospitalization, which means that one is uprooted from one's customary surroundings; denied access to cherished people, pets, and objects; and thrust into a milieu governed by insider understandings to which one isn't privy. All of this contributes to a disintegration of one's self. The physician Eric Cassell (1982) conceptualizes the sense of this disintegration as *suffering:* to suffer is to feel oneself coming undone. Suffering persists until the threat to the identity has passed or until the integrity of the identity can be reestablished in some manner.

It is when we suffer in Cassell's sense of the word that we most need the help of others to hold us in our identities. Torn out of the contexts and conditions in which we can maintain our own sense of ourselves, we run the risk of losing sight of who we are – at least temporarily – unless someone else can lend a hand. Edmund's proxy, whether or not she conceives of it in this way and whatever else she might also be doing, is involved in maintaining Edmund's identity for him.

The Edmund she knows is Tosca's owner, the elderly opera lover who lived contented in his oddly furnished little apartment and claimed her as his friend. The stories by which she constitutes his identity are woven around her interactions with him, and they include the stories he has told her about his life and times. Dr. Stoddard, on the other hand, doesn't know Edmund as well as the proxy does, so the stories that constitute his understanding of Edmund are much more likely to be drawn from the store of widely circulating, medically shared master narratives that doctors use to depict patients as a group. He has never seen this particular patient before this illness, and since his hospitalization, Edmund's been so very ill that the doctor has had little chance to get to know him.

So while the proxy is caring for someone we might call Tosca-Edmund, the doctor sees mainly Patient-Edmund: the Edmund that Tosca-Edmund has become as a result of serious illness. These are not really two distinct people, of course: there is bodily continuity, his memories and personal history have not altered, and his Social Security number remains the same. If what we wanted to know was, Is he the person who was admitted to the hospital three weeks ago? (Marya Schechtman [1996] calls this the Reidentification Question), the answer is yes. But if what we want to know is, Does the tissue of stories that used to constitute his identity still represent him accurately? (this is what Schechtman calls the Characterization Question), the answer may be no.

On an identity view of the moral situation, then, the quarrel between doctor and proxy might easily never have been about respect for Edmund's autonomy – they both might well agree that Edmund should determine for himself the kind of treatment he will receive. What they, on my hypothesis, disagree about is *which* self should do the determining. The proxy thinks it should be Tosca-Edmund, who exercised his autonomy by drawing up an advance directive. The doctor thinks it should be Patient-Edmund, who, if competent, might override Tosca-Edmund's wishes.

Although we have moved the locus of the disagreement, the correct strategy for resolving it might still be the one Dr. Stoddard originally proposed: if you want to know which self should determine Edmund's future, why not wake him up and ask him? The difficulty with moving the old strategy to the new locus, though, is that the outcome is rigged: the current self will naturally choose in its own favor, so when you ask the question, you already have a pretty good idea of what the answer will be. If there is a Patient-Edmund distinct from Tosca-Edmund and he is mentally capacitated when he wakes, he will say that he and not Tosca-Edmund is now in charge.

But, it might be objected, the outcome is always rigged. It was just as rigged when Tosca-Edmund signed the advance directive. In fact, what he was doing when he signed it was trying to insure that Patient-Edmund would never get the upper hand. Why, then, isn't it equally valid, now that so much has changed, for Patient-Edmund to return the favor?

EXPERIENTIAL INTERESTS VERSUS CRITICAL INTERESTS

To get help with this question, we might look to Ronald Dworkin, who, in *Life's Dominion: An Argument about Abortion, Euthanasia, and Individual Freedom*, suggests that if we want to understand why we care about how we die, we must first understand why we care about how we live. Dworkin (1993, 201) distinguishes between two kinds of interests that give our lives their value and meaning. *Experiential* interests are those that have to do with pleasures or satisfactions:

We all do things because we like the experience of doing them; playing softball, perhaps, or cooking and eating well, or watching football, or seeing *Casablanca* for the twelfth time, or walking in the woods in October, or listening to *The Marriage of Figaro*, or sailing fast just off the wind, or just working hard at something. Pleasures like these are essential to a good life – a life with nothing that is marvelous only because of how it feels would be not pure but preposterous.

Critical interests, on the other hand, are those that give life its deeper and more lasting meaning and lend it coherence. We establish close friendships, build a career, raise children, pursue artistic or political goals not only because we want the pleasurable experiences these projects offer but because we believe our lives as a whole will be the better for taking them up. "Even people whose lives feel unplanned are nevertheless often guided by a sense of the general style of life they think appropriate, of what choices strike them as not only good at the moment but in character for them" (Ronald Dworkin 1993, 202). This tendency to want to stay in character, as it were, helps to explain why many of us care not only about how our lives go on but about how our lives end. As we approach death, we don't want merely to avoid pain for ourselves and unpleasant burdens for our families; we also want to avoid dying in ways that are not consistent with how we have lived. Most people "want their deaths, if possible, to express and in that way vividly to confirm the values they believe most important to their lives" (Ronald Dworkin 1993, 211).

Because Dworkin assigns greater moral significance to an individual's critical interests than to her experiential interests, he endorses what he calls the "integrity" view of autonomy: the view that people should be free to act in ways that clearly conflict with their best interests, if that is what they see as preserving their sense of who they are. And this, he thinks, holds for exercises of "precedent autonomy" as well – which is to say that Edmund's interest in living his life in character includes an interest in determining what will happen to him later, under circumstances of serious illness that he has never encountered, even if he misjudges what that experience will be like. His advance directive, stipulating that he wants a "natural" death and appointing a friend who knows him to be his proxy decision maker, is a mechanism for seeing to it that his critical interests, and not just his experiential ones, will be honored. Dworkin, then, has a lot to say in support of Tosca-Edmund's claims to be in charge.

Rebecca Dresser, by contrast, has argued that experiential interests must take precedence when patients are too ill to say what they want. For one thing, people do not seem to value exercises of precedent autonomy: "Surveys show that a relatively small percentage of the U.S. population engages in end-of-life planning, and that many in that group simply designate a trusted relative or friend to make future treatment decisions, choosing not to issue specific instructions on future care" (Dresser 1995, 34). She worries too that in drawing up an advance directive, competent patients might not be very well informed about the physical states they may one day find themselves in, and that they may not understand the meaning or implications of their decisions. Most important for our purposes, Dresser (1995, 35) worries that "the rigid adherence to advance planning Dworkin endorses leaves no room for the changes of heart that can lead us to deviate from our earlier choices. All of us are familiar with decisions we have later come to recognize as ill suited to our subsequent situations." So it is probably not fair to say that Dresser favors the sovereignty of Patient-Edmund – it is more that she would remind us, and rightly, that Tosca-Edmund is a moving target who changes in sometimes dramatic respects over the course of his lifetime. He *is* Patient-Edmund, with the long history, like a comet's tail, of Tosca-Edmund behind him. And he might have changed his mind about the importance of things that mattered to him before he became seriously ill: dying at home, dying naturally, dying without "extraordinary means."

THE ROLES OF THE PROXY

So, should Edmund be waked? I honestly can't say. My own intuition is that it would be cruel to subject him to the fear and other forms of suffering that would surely accompany his arousal, but that may be because I know how this story ended: when the man I call Edmund was awakened, he was too ill to communicate his wishes and died a few hours later. That, however, is no argument; it's an anecdote, and while I hope I have motivated the thought that the proxy is trying, at Edmund's explicit request, to look after his critical interests, I have not made the case that she should do so even though he might be competent to repudiate those interests and espouse new ones instead. So, instead of recommending an action item, let me conclude with some thoughts about one task among others that a patient might have appointed a proxy to perform.

That task, on my analysis, is to hold on to the patient as the person the proxy has known and cared about, making decisions reflecting *that* understanding of who the patient is. Presumably, it has mattered to the patient that his prehospitalization identity be maintained. Why else would he have appointed a proxy in the first place? It can't be because he wants his experiential interests to be safeguarded, as those are the responsibility of the professional health care staff. And while prudence dictates having a family member or friend on hand to make sure the professionals discharge their responsibility adequately, that is not the proxy's primary duty. She is charged with making decisions, and even if the patient does not articulate it in so many words, he may have chosen her to do it or trust her to do it because she is one of the people – perhaps the most important person – who has been *holding the patient in his identity all along*.

Holding, then, does not kick in just in case the patient is permanently incapable of exercising his own autonomy, which is when, under the law, the proxy is empowered to make decisions for the patient. Holding has usually been going on for years, and it can be a matter of great moral importance to patient and proxy alike that the proxy makes sure it continues to go on to the very end of the patient's life. It might not be of the highest importance, of course. There are times when it is more important that a particular patient be treated kindly, or that an unresponsive medical bureaucracy be prodded into action, or, especially if the patient is poor or powerless, that his rights be vigilantly protected, all of which a proxy might also be appointed to do.

Nor is all holding morally positive. Parents sometimes hold on too tightly to their children's earlier identities and in that way infantilize them. Friends sometimes fail to recognize that a person is no longer committed to a project or cause that was once of central importance to her, and so identify her via stories that are outdated. Family members sometimes refuse to see that a person is now in the early stages of a progressive dementia, and then the stories they use to constitute the person's identity no longer represent her properly. Terry Schiavo's parents held on to their sense of who she was long after she ceased to have any of the upper-brain function that is required for a personality or for even the most minimal ability to sustain an interpersonal relationship.

But patient-designated proxies have some reason to think that the holding they do is wanted and welcome. If I am right about how holding works, the proxy designation could simply formalize an arrangement that has been a source of satisfaction to the patient for quite some time. The designation then expresses the patient's view that *this* person knows how to hold him properly, and he would like her to keep on doing it.

Whether anything like this is what people actually intend when they name a proxy decision maker is an open question. My guess is that they do not, because the practice of holding patients in their identities is not one that gets talked about in the way I am doing here. I think, though, that the practice is instantly recognizable, and that if patients were asked why they chose the proxies they did, their answers would reflect something of what I am describing.

I observed earlier that maintaining another's identity is morally valuable work. At the same time, though, it can confer on those who engage in it a tremendous amount of power over the other, whether at the bedside, in a boardroom, or on the phone with a friend. That we have this power over others and they over us shouldn't frighten us, I think, despite the fact that, badly wielded, it turns into tyranny. It is merely a humbling reminder that, in both the short and the long run, we are all at each others' mercy.

4

Caring, Minimal Autonomy, and the Limits of Liberalism

Agnieszka Jaworska

Dr. Atul Gawande reports this history of a patient with extensive and untreatable cancer:

Lazaroff was only in his early sixties, a longtime city administrator ... [with] the hardened manner of a man who had lost his wife ... and learned to live alone. His condition deteriorated rapidly. In a matter of months, he lost more than fifty pounds. As the tumors in his abdomen grew, his belly, scrotum, and legs filled up with fluid. The pain and debility eventually made it impossible for him to keep working. His ... son moved in to care for him. Lazaroff went on around-the-clock morphine to control his pain. His doctors told him that he might have only weeks to live. Lazaroff wasn't ready to hear it, though. He still talked about the day he'd go back to work.

Then he took several bad falls. ... A metastasis was compressing his thoracic spinal cord. ... His lower body was becoming paralyzed.

He had two options left. He could undergo spinal surgery. It wouldn't cure him – surgery or not, he had at the most a few months left – but it offered a last-ditch chance of halting the progression of spinal-cord damage and possibly restoring some strength to his legs and sphincters. The risks, however, were severe. [Surgeons would] have to go in through his chest and

Thanks to the editors of this volume and to all participants in the 2005 Naturalized Moral Psychology Working Group meeting at Groningen University for very helpful comments on earlier drafts. Special thanks to Jodi Halpern and Julie Tannenbaum for numerous insightful conversations; and to Dan Halliday, Caleb Perl, and Cole Leahy for research assistance. I presented an early, shorter version of this chapter at the APA Central Division meeting, Chicago, 2005. The proceedings of that session were published online in the *APA Newsletter on Philosophy and Medicine* 5 (1) (2005): 19–23.

collapse his lung just to get at his spine. He'd face a long, difficult, and painful recovery. And given his frail condition, ... his chances of surviving the procedure and getting back home were slim.

The alternative was to do nothing. He'd go home and continue with hospice care, which would keep him comfortable and help him maintain a measure of control over his life. The immobility and incontinence would certainly worsen. But it was his best chance of dying peacefully, in his own bed, and being able to say good-bye to his loved ones. ...

Lazaroff wanted surgery. The neurosurgeon ... warned [him] at length about how terrible the risks were. ... But Lazaroff wasn't to be dissuaded.

[Preparing for the surgery, Dr. Gawande reviewed the risks again.] "The operation could fail or leave you paralyzed. ... You could have a stroke or a heart attack or could even die." ...

"No one ever said I could die from this," [Lazaroff] said, tremulously. "It's my last hope. Are you saying I'm going to die?"

[Just then, Lazaroff's son David arrived.] "Don't you give up on me," Lazaroff now rasped at his son. "You give me every chance I've got."

Outside the room, David [expressed his reservations]. His mother had spent a long time in intensive care on a ventilator before dying of emphysema, and since then his father had often said that he did not want anything like that to happen to him. But now he was adamant about doing "everything." David did not dare argue. ...

[Although] the operation was a technical success, [Lazaroff soon developed many severe complications and his condition quickly worsened.] [He died] exactly the way [he] hadn't wanted to die – strapped down and sedated, tubes in every natural orifice and in several new ones, and on a ventilator. (Gawande 2002: 208–10, 212–15)

According to Gawande, Lazaroff "chose badly." Gawande suggests that physicians may be permitted to intervene in choices of this kind. What makes the temptation to intervene paternalistically in this and similar cases especially strong is that the patient's choice contradicts his professed values. Paternalism appears less problematic in such cases because, in contradicting his values, the patient seems to sidestep his own autonomy. This chapter addresses the dangers of overextending this interpretation. I argue that it is not so easy to judge when a person is not genuinely exercising autonomy, and that choosing contrary to one's own values does not necessarily amount to sidestepping one's autonomy. The key insight is to recognize the importance of the attitude of caring as an integral part of some expressions of autonomy. This will allow us to develop an alternative picture of minimal autonomy, according to which it is possible to choose against one's values while genuinely exercising autonomy. For practical purposes, in medicine and elsewhere, this means that, in cases like Lazaroff's, those tempted toward paternalism must exercise particular caution before they deem a choice to be disengaged from autonomy: even if a choice contradicts the person's own values, it might be rooted in caring, and then, despite initial appearances to the contrary, it may still command the highest level of protection against paternalism.

TEMPTATIONS TOWARD PATERNALISM

In a wide gamut of contexts, patients ask physicians for assistance with choices and procedures that appear deeply misguided. Think of requests for cosmetic surgery designed to make the patient look more Caucasian, or requests for extra rounds of in vitro fertilization likely to jeopardize the patient's overall health, or a Viagra prescription for someone like the Kinsey fan who takes pride in being able to masturbate to ejaculation in ten seconds flat. Ordinary physicians find many such choices morally unsettling and grapple for reasons why it would be appropriate to refuse.[1]

In one category of cases, it is relatively easy to see what would justify the physician's refusal. In these cases, although the choice is beneficial to the patient himself and perhaps even allays genuine suffering, detrimental effects on third parties render the choice problematic.[2] Not even the staunchest liberals face inherent

---

[1] On some views, each physician always has a right to be "a conscientious objector" and refuse procedures and treatments simply because they offend her moral beliefs. My target here is a deeper justification for refusal, aiming to show why a physician's moral conviction that she ought to refuse certain requests is in fact correct.

[2] There is a spectrum of possibilities here, differing by whether identifiable parties are likely to be directly affected. The request of an AIDS patient not to inform his partner about his condition lies at one end of this spectrum. At the other end are choices that merely contribute to diffuse socially pernicious effects. For instance, choosing to alter one's appearance to remove (seemingly undesirable) racial features reinforces the climate of racial stigmatization and invites the physician's complicity in propagating suspect social norms; yet, it may not, by itself, cause well-circumscribed damage or injustice. (For a nuanced discussion of latter cases, see Little 1998.)

difficulties in justifying why choices that harm third parties or contribute to the weakening of social justice need not be straightforwardly respected. John Stuart Mill (1978, 9) famously recognized this in his very formulation of the principle of liberty.

Problematic requests that do not harm third parties raise more-intricate moral puzzles. In paradigmatic cases of this sort — exemplified by requests to continue in vitro fertilization rounds beyond safe limits – the patients' choices appear detrimental to their own well-being with no adverse effects on others. There are variations here, depending on whether the detrimental effects on the patient are fairly immediate or merely statistically predicted and projected over the long term – as in refusal of prophylactic tests. In a related, yet distinct category of cases, illustrated by the record-setting use of Viagra, the patient's choice appears to be motivated by shallow values but does not undermine either the interests of others or even the patient's own interests, subjectively understood. (In a subset of cases in both categories, a compounding problem dominates the picture: not only does the patient undermine his well-being or pursue small-minded values, but his choice is so ill-advised as to compromise his very dignity and constitute lack of self-respect.)[3]

According to the liberal doctrine of respect for autonomy, choices that are problematic merely because they reflect shallow values, or harm only the chooser's own interests or dignity, need to be respected. On the standard liberal approach, each individual's *capacity* for autonomy is the ground of value and the most fundamental locus of respect. It is up to the individual how she chooses to exercise her capacity for autonomy and whether she does so at all. We need to respect the capacity for autonomy in all its manifestations, however imperfect they may be on a given occasion.[4] In other words,

---

[3] In real-life cases, reasons why medical professionals are tempted not to comply with patients' requests are often mixed. Michael Jackson's request for plastic surgery propagated socially abhorrent norms of appearance and, in this sense, had pernicious third-party effects. It was motivated by vanity – a less than admirable value. It was also not in Jackson's own interest to change his appearance in a way that won him more loathing than admiration. And the results compromised Jackson's dignity, as the details of his appearance and the flaws of the surgery became objects of public scrutiny and ridicule.

[4] Even in very liberal societies, there are regional variations in how this requirement is interpreted. For example, are we required to *ensure* that the patient has a chance

we need to respect the capacity for autonomy even if it is exercised in service of shallow values or against the agent's own acknowledged or unacknowledged interests. Of course, we are allowed to attempt to aid the patient noninvasively in making a better decision – to try persuasion or to improve the background conditions of decision making insofar as they are within our control – but if the agent is unmoved by these measures, we must respect his imperfect decision.[5]

When detrimental effects on third parties are not at issue, ill-advised or imprudent choices may cease to be protected by liberalism only when it can be legitimately determined that the chooser lacks the capacity for autonomy or faces specific impediments to adequate exercise of autonomy that are beyond his control – such as, for example, incorrigible lack of access to relevant information. That is, self-regarding choices can be genuinely problematic, in the sense of lacking the claim to straightforward respect, only when a specific problem with the agent's capacity for autonomy, or the adequate conditions of its exercise, is identified. We may call this approach "strict liberalism": in brief, it requires respect for *all choices of autonomous agents*.

Yet, despite this well-articulated position, when competent patients choose badly for themselves, even physicians very sympathetic to liberalism can be deeply morally unsettled and tempted by the thought that they ought to intervene. Importantly, however, the temptation is not the same with respect to all imprudent decisions of competent patients. The appeal of paternalism is strongest in cases in which the patient's decision seems to go against his deepest interests and values as the patient understands them himself. Consider Gawande's (2002, 215–16) diagnosis of why Lazaroff made a grave mistake:

Lazaroff, I thought, chose badly. Not, however, because he died so violently and appallingly. Good decisions can have bad results. ... Lazaroff chose

to make an autonomous choice concerning his affairs? Waking up a sedated dying patient to ask him how exactly to respect his wishes could seem advisable in the American context, while it is unlikely to happen in Holland. Yet, despite these variations in detail, the idea that every self-regarding choice of a competent patient deserves respect is at the core of the liberal approach.

5 Liberalism does not require an individual to aid others in activities the individual does not approve of, and this limitation may sometimes also apply to physicians. But again, I am concerned here with the possibility of a deeper justification for the physician's response, focused on whether the physician in fact ought to refuse certain requests.

badly because his choice ran against his deepest interests – interests not as I or anyone else conceived them, but as he conceived them. Above all, it was clear that he wanted to live. He would take any risk – even death – to live. But, as we explained to him, life was not what we had to offer. We could offer only a chance of preserving minimal lower-body function for his brief remaining time – at a cost of severe violence to him and against extreme odds of a miserable death. But he did not hear us: in staving off paralysis, he seemed to believe that he might stave off death. There are people who will look clear-eyed at such odds and take their chances with surgery. But, knowing how much Lazaroff had dreaded dying the way his wife had, I do not believe he was one of them.

As Gawande (2002, 216) sees it, "a good physician cannot simply stand aside when patients make ... self-defeating decisions – decisions that go against their deepest goals." Yet why, precisely, does the assessment that a decision contradicts the patient's own deepest goals or values make paternalism particularly appealing? Presumably it is because such a decision appears not to genuinely express the person's autonomy and is "self-defeating" in this sense. We see implicitly invoked here a morally relevant difference between choices made with the capacity for autonomy available in the background, which thereby count as outcomes of the chooser's capacity for autonomy in this weak sense, and choices that are in fact autonomous and thus truly the agent's own. It is relatively uncontroversial that choices that are in fact autonomous should be treated with full deference. By contrast, even those with strong liberal leanings may be tempted to intervene when a person's decision does not seem to truly reflect the person's autonomous will – that is, when, despite having the *capacity* for autonomous decision making, the person makes a decision that does not seem to be a product of a proper *exercise* of autonomy. We can call this approach "liberal perfectionism": it focuses on respect for *choices that are in fact autonomous*.

I do not take a stand in this chapter on whether this general approach to correcting the excesses of strict liberalism is correct. Rather, I am interested in some usually overlooked limits of liberal perfectionism, even when it is accepted on its own terms. I suggest that liberal perfectionism may invite intervention in a larger number of cases than its own commitments permit, because it is often improperly assumed that the agent does not in fact act autonomously. (Related moral uses of the distinction between respecting someone's capacity for autonomy and respecting actual exercises of autonomy are in analogous danger of overextension. Consider that even strict liberals, who oppose all paternalistic intervention in choices of autonomous adults, would still likely judge the moral violation to be much less grave when the person's choice does not really engage or stem from his capacity for autonomy. This view also needs to be cautioned against a paradigm that too readily invites the assumption that a decision is not really autonomous.)

Of course, much depends on our background understanding of what kinds of choices count, at least minimally, as really stemming from the person's autonomy. It is relatively uncontroversial that, to qualify here, a choice does not have to be ideally and perfectly autonomous; for instance, the choice need not fully engage the person's capacity for critical reflection and may still be open to considerable rational criticism. Take the case in which the patient's decision reflects shallow values. Even though the patient may be making a considerable (evaluative) mistake, if the choice adequately reflects the patient's currently professed values, it does seem to be the patient's "own" to a very considerable extent. Several key aspects of the patient's capacity for autonomy have been involved in this choice: he formulated an evaluative perspective, made a specific choice in light of this perspective, and was able to carry that choice into action without external or internal impediments. Intervention with such a choice appears to be a clearly impermissible and severe form of paternalism.

By contrast, when a competent person chooses against his professed values, we are prone to assume that his capacity for autonomy is largely disengaged. Several plausible interpretations support this assumption. One possibility is that the person has chosen against his deepest values because he has succumbed to weakness of the will: he was fully aware of what was best to do, but a particularly strong desire or emotion made a different course of action irresistible. One could interpret Lazaroff's choice in this way: Lazaroff is committed to a good death, and yet, when he is faced with the prospect of dying, his fear of death overwhelms him and leads him to request additional procedures at any cost, against his deepest convictions.

A related possibility is that a person chooses against his deepest values due to a kind of miscalculation. The person is fully aware of what outcome would be best, and yet, in trying to bring about this outcome in his concrete and complex circumstances, he reasons poorly and arrives at a decision that fails to reflect his commitments. There might be different explanations for his poor reasoning: for example, he did not give the matter the requisite attention, he is generally not very adept at means-ends or probabilistic reasoning, or his emotional state skewed his judgment. Again, Lazaroff's decision can be interpreted in this vein: he is committed to a good death, and yet, when faced with the prospect of dying, his fear of death skews his thinking and leads him to believe that the additional surgery will give him the best chance to live or die in accordance with what most deeply matters to him. In saying that Lazaroff "did not hear" the facts presented by his doctors, Gawande strongly suggests this interpretation.

On either interpretation, the choice does not reflect the proper starting point of autonomous decision making – namely, what most deeply matters to the person. If the choice is based on a miscalculation, it is a failed attempt to express one's authentic self in one's actions. If the choice is weak-willed, it reflects the conflicting wayward desire or emotion instead. Either way, the choice is not really autonomous: if the capacity for autonomy were properly engaged, it would not result in this choice.

These familiar interpretations, however, do not exhaust the space of possibilities. There is, as I hope to establish, another common and important way in which a person's choice can go against what may be thought to matter to him most deeply, but in this case the capacity for autonomy is not similarly disengaged. Specifically, when the person *cares* about something that conflicts with his values, he may choose in accordance with his caring, and thus against his values, and yet choose autonomously.

This result carries bad news for sympathizers of liberalism who nonetheless seek a justification for expanding the range of cases in which people can be legitimately prevented from making bad decisions, in the medical context or elsewhere: the requirements of what makes a choice in fact autonomous are less demanding than traditionally assumed, and, consequently, advocates of liberal perfectionism have less room, within the confines of their own doctrine, for deeming a choice fundamentally flawed. Once we rethink what is, at minimum, required for autonomy, it will turn out that an individual may go against his own acknowledged values and against his own preferences as to which of his motivations to act on and still give a genuine expression of his autonomy. This result reduces the impact of liberal perfectionism's project of limiting the permissiveness of strict liberalism by attending to flaws in people's actual implementation of autonomy: some choices that initially may look problematic deserve not only basic respect as pro forma expressions of the chooser's capacity for autonomy but also full deference as choices that are indeed the agent's own.

AN ALTERNATIVE CASE OF MINIMAL AUTONOMY

I proceed by developing three minimal conditions of an autonomously made decision: (1) the attitude that guides the decision must properly represent the agent's self; (2) the agent governs himself by way of seeing reason to pursue what this attitude prescribes; (3) the agent is capable of reflection that leaves him open to a fresh perception of reasons. I will show that actions grounded in caring can meet these conditions even when they contradict the agent's values and even if the agent would prefer to be motivated differently.

1. Attitudes Representing the Agent

On the approach I favor, the appropriate starting point of an account of autonomy is a story about what makes an attitude really one's own, and thus a suitable basis for *self*-governance. Broadly speaking, an attitude is truly the agent's own if the agent cannot properly distance himself from the attitude and see it as a mere happening in his psychology, with respect to which the agent is a "mere passive bystander" (Frankfurt 1988a, 59). This sense of ownership is often called, following Harry Frankfurt's terminology, the attitude's internality. The idea is that for an action to be autonomous (i.e., self-governed), it must stem from attitudes that properly express the self, rather than attitudes that are best interpreted as external happenings.

Philosophical conceptions of internality have been dominated by two models. On the first model, advanced, for instance, by Gary Watson (2004), value judgments or evaluations are paradigmatic internal attitudes. The second model, associated with Frankfurt himself (1988b), links internality to self-reflection, that is, to the ability to step back from one's ordinary first-order motivations and assess them in some way. On this model, however, the self-assessment is not necessarily evaluative. Rather, it can be an assessment by further motives or desires, such as a second-order desire that a particular first-order desire be effective in moving one to act. More generally, to be internal, a given first-order motive must be embedded in the right motivational structure – in the right hierarchy of motives assessing the original motive and thereby conferring an endorsement.

In these ways, internality – and, consequently, the capacity for autonomy – have been understood to require either the ability to make evaluative judgments or the ability to reflect on one's own mental states, or sometimes both. In opposition to this picture, I argued extensively elsewhere that neither evaluation nor motivational hierarchy is needed to account for the phenomenon of internality. The attitude of caring about someone or something is, I have argued, a *nonhierarchical, nonevaluative internal* attitude. Let me briefly recap the contours of this argument.[6]

The account I favor, caring about *P* – about a person, an animal, an ideal – is a complex emotional attitude that comprises various less complex emotions, emotional predispositions, and desires directed at *P*: joys at *P*'s successful flourishing, frustrations at *P*'s failures or setbacks, fearful anticipations of possible dangers for *P*, relief when *P* escapes such dangers, disposition to grieve at the loss of *P*, and so on. Most of these constitutive components of caring are emotions, themselves composed of interrelated simpler components – emotional episodes – such as, in the case of grief at the loss of *P*, for instance: the tendency to dwell in one's thoughts on memories of *P* and of the circumstances in which *P* was lost, having one's attention directed at objects and details associated in some way with *P* and with the events leading to the loss of *P*, the tendency to ruminate in one's thoughts on how those circumstances could have gone differently, and so forth. Caring about *P* is, in the first instance, a matter of emotional vulnerability to *P*, which requires a great deal of emotional integration and sophistication. The component emotions all construe

---

[6] For details, see Jaworska unpublished and Jaworska 2007. My discussion in the next five paragraphs is borrowed, sometimes verbatim, from these articles.

P as a source of importance commanding emotional vulnerability. Or, to put it differently, by virtue of his steady emotional attunement to the ebb and flow of the fortunes of *P*, the caring subject imbues *P* with importance. Further, caring is not a mere concatenation of various emotions that an outside observer would see as related. To genuinely care about *P* from the first-person point of view, the caring subject must *comprehend*, at least implicitly, *P*'s importance: otherwise, importance would simply be imbued in *P* unbeknownst to the subject, rather than the subject's actively imbuing it through his attitude. Note that this requirement of comprehension brings with it considerable cognitive sophistication and complexity. A caring subject must be cognitively sophisticated enough to grasp, at least implicitly, the concept of importance. And the comprehension of the importance of *P* would normally inspire further cognitive activity, for example, further inquisitiveness about the object, or, in a suitably endowed subject, the formation of stable intentions, plans, and policies concerning the object.[7]

As it turns out, children as young as two and three are capable of caring of this sort, usually about their parents or other family members. They exhibit sustained patterns of emotional response like those I have just described (Zahn-Waxler et al. 1992), and their burgeoning general facility with language and concepts suggests that they can grasp the concept of importance. (They grasp seemingly equally difficult concepts, for example, the concept of misbehaving – the difference between accidentally spilling milk and deliberately pouring it on the table.) If I am right that young children are capable of caring, this helps establish that caring is both nonhierarchical and nonevaluative. For first, at this age, children are barely beginning to discover that they have attitudes toward the world, such as wanting, so they are unlikely to direct their wanting or other practical attitudes

---

[7] Note that caring does not have to involve a positive affirmation; caring also has negative equivalents: hate and similar complex emotions. Hating may be interpreted in terms of standard components of caring – caring about the demise and/or suffering of an object: joys at the successful demise of the object, frustrations at the object's failure to suffer, etc. On this picture, hate is still an internal attitude and a functionally suitable basis of autonomous governance. (In this respect, a caring-based view of autonomy parallels an evaluation-based view: when evaluation is seen as a suitable basis of autonomous governance, negative evaluations fill the bill just as well as positive ones.)

at the newly discovered wanting itself. That is, they are unlikely to form motivational hierarchies. And, second, as has been amply documented in developmental psychology literature, these children do not understand the concept of belief as a representational attitude that can be correct or incorrect (Gopnik 1993), so, more specifically, they cannot conceive of the idea that their evaluations are correct and that the lack of recognition of them would be a mistake – which is necessary for the proper grasp of any evaluative concept. Therefore, they cannot form evaluative judgments. Because these children are nonetheless capable of caring, we can conclude that caring presupposes neither motivational hierarchy nor evaluation.[8]

Further, caring attitudes invariably appear to be internal to the agent. Unlike in the case of mere desires, or individual emotional responses such as anger or fear, it seems very hard and even paradoxical to fully distance oneself from one's caring attitudes, to view them as alien or foreign, to feel oneself merely taken over by them.[9] It is common enough to experience a strong desire that one has to fight off like a foreign intrusion, or to have an outburst of anger with respect to which one is a "mere passive bystander," but being a "passive bystander to one's caring attitude" is an oxymoron. This is not to say that it is so hard to *evaluatively* distance oneself from these attitudes. We do, not so mysteriously or infrequently, consider our own caring attitudes bad for us, mistaken, or misplaced, but, even in those cases, we do not normally view them as alien forces or as attitudes that we simply "find occurring within us."[10] (Indeed, it is precisely the internality of the caring – the deep hold that the caring has in the person's psychology – that a person attempting to overcome a caring, for example, a lover of an abusive partner, would likely judge to be bad.)[11] Thus, if our

---

[8] The way I see it, the ability to form preferences about one's own desires and the ability to understand the concept of belief require insights into the workings of a mind, so they are much more sophisticated (and enter later in psychological development) than the ability to grasp the concept of importance.

[9] Of course, it is not so unusual to feel oneself overcome, overwhelmed, or swept away by a caring, in the sense of lacking control over it and feeling helpless vis-à-vis its power. But even such a powerful caring is not normally experienced as an external force.

[10] Phrase borrowed from Frankfurt 1988a, 59.

[11] I thank Gary Watson for this point.

ordinary intuitions about internality are to be trusted, we cannot but be identified with our cares.[12]

(I have relied here on our patterns of associating ourselves with some attitudes and dissociating ourselves from others as sources of intuitions about internality, but it is important to keep in mind that internality is not a matter of how the agent feels about aspects of his psychology and how his attitudes appear to him. For an attitude to be internal, the agent does not need to explicitly and self-reflectively recognize the attitude as his own. The claim that carings are invariably internal is not to be taken as a prediction that all agents will acknowledge their carings as internal; it simply identifies a class of attitudes that always represent one's point of view as an agent. As such, it can apply even to agents incapable of recognizing attitudes as their own or alien, and, more generally, to agents incapable of taking their attitudes as objects of reflection.)

My earlier account of caring can help elucidate why carings are the sort of attitudes that are invariably internal. By combining various individual emotions into a complex structure, carings synthesize and organize disparate elements of one's psychic life, allowing for convergence of several psychological elements into a coherent cluster. In this sense, they support the agent's identity and cohesion over time. Further, by being steadfastly emotionally attuned to the ups and downs of the fortunes of the object of care, the caring subject imbues the object with importance. And once the subject cognitively grasps the object's importance, this can inspire further psychological alignments: most importantly, the formation of stable intentions and plans concerning the object, which keep the subject on track, and thus weave the web of unified agency. Because they connect various aspects of our psychology together, and support our psychological unity and continuity over time, carings are tied to our sense of self more closely than other attitudes – they are more strongly our own.[13]

Pulling my various claims about caring together yields the result that caring attitudes are internal but neither necessarily evaluative

[12] Note that this is compatible with the possibility of giving up on one's caring – with deciding to cease to care and following through. What is ruled out is caring and being dissociated from one's caring attitude at the same time. I thank Michael Bratman for prompting this clarification.
[13] For a fuller exposition of this point, see Jaworska 2007.

nor necessarily constituted by motivational hierarchies. And this means that internality requires neither motivational hierarchy nor evaluation.

Suppose I am right about this. We have now made room in moral psychology for a class of attitudes cognitively simple enough so as not to require reflexive understanding of one's own mental states – be it one's own motivations or the correctness of one's own beliefs – and yet sufficiently complex emotionally to carve out a distinct self from among the chaos of mere psychological happenings. On my picture, caring is indeed such an attitude. Because caring attitudes do not presuppose understanding of one's own mental states, they make less of a demand on a subject's psychological sophistication than do either second-order desires or evaluative judgments. Yet, because these attitudes are nonetheless internal, they are plausible building blocks of (the "self" aspect of) autonomous self-governance.

2. Governance by the Self

Internal attitudes (of which carings are but one subcategory) are appropriate starting points of autonomy, but additional elements are needed for a genuine instance of autonomy. Autonomy involves self-*governance*, so it is not enough for the self to causally bring about action; the self must truly *govern*. One may think that either motivational hierarchy or evaluative judgment would have to be introduced at this stage. On closer examination, however, this turns out to be unnecessary.

True enough, self-governance is normally rightly interpreted as *normative* self-governance, or governance mediated by reasons. The agent must normatively govern herself by way of her internal attitudes exercising normative guidance. One may think that this automatically introduces an element of evaluation. As David Velleman (2000, esp. 120–22) has insisted, however, there is a difference between perceiving a course of action under the guise of the good (under the guise of value) and acting for a reason. A teenager who sees creating mischief and havoc as a reason to engage in a prank does not necessarily judge mischief and havoc to be good. His aim may be to be bad for a change, and he may treat the badness of mischief and havoc as his reasons to act. Similarly, a young child may take his mother's pain to be a reason to offer comfort, without the further understanding, or the further thought, that it is good to alleviate the pain. And, important for us, one likely possibility here is that the internal attitude of caring for his mother leads the child to take his mother's pain as a reason to help. To treat a consideration as a reason to act is to view it as recommending or counting in favor of the action (Velleman 2000, 100). Crucially, though, when a consideration makes sense to the agent in this way, the agent need not regard being guided by this consideration as correct (and not being so guided as a mistake). Thus, young children who cannot yet apply the notion of correctness to their beliefs are able to treat considerations as reasons. In this way, treating something as a reason can be independent from judging it to be good.

Self-governance must involve normative governance by attitudes that are truly one's own, but this may well consist in internal attitudes being sources of what one treats as reasons, which does not necessarily require judging the objects of internal attitudes to be good. The self-governing agent I have in mind would take herself to have a reason to pursue what she cares about. On this picture, the ability to act for reasons is sufficient for the governance aspect of autonomy, and evaluating or judging good need not be involved.

Evaluation is thus unnecessary to this sort of governance, but is *motivational hierarchy* also unnecessary? One may think that some sort of motivational hierarchy is introduced when we require a self-governing agent to take herself to have a reason to pursue what she cares about. Isn't this agent – the objector would say – treating her own caring as a reason? And isn't this a kind of second-order attitude, which takes caring, a first-order attitude, as its object? However, the fact that a person treats (some aspect of) what she cares about as a reason does not imply that she must recognize (or be capable of recognizing) her caring attitude itself as the source of the reason. Indeed, she does not even need to understand that she has this caring attitude. Her caring about P leads her to treat advancement or flourishing of P as a reason, or, better put, her caring about P partly consists in treating advancement or flourishing of P as a reason. No second-order attitude needs to be formed in this process. Moreover, the agent's claim to self-government is not affected by this lack of self-awareness. The agent's internal attitudes can exercise normative guidance through their content without the agent being consciously aware of having these attitudes.[14]

Admittedly, treating considerations as reasons for action does require a kind of awareness of oneself that could be thought of as self-reflection – namely, attention to one's own actions. The agent expresses her attitude about how she does and does not want to act. But this type of self-reflection is, of course, much less demanding than motivational hierarchy.

On my analysis, although governance is a conceptually distinct element of autonomy, its satisfaction is built into ordinary caring, so that a caring agent meets my first two requirements of minimal autonomy in one sweep, simply by virtue of his caring. Caring, as we have seen, is an internal attitude. And treating advancement or flourishing of P as a reason is part and parcel of construing P as a source of importance of the sort that lends one emotionally vulnerable to P. In other words, a caring agent has an appropriate sense of self and is capable of governing his actions accordingly; he is a very promising prototype for minimal autonomy.

3. Mental Freedom

According to the portrait of a minimally autonomous agent I have assembled so far, this agent cares about certain things and guides her actions in light of seeing reasons to pursue those things. Acting on reasons of this sort, however, can still sometimes come short of genuine self-governance. Our theory must stave off the possibility that seeing a reason would simply amount to being in the grip of the reason. This concern is particularly pressing when an emotional attitude is a source of reasons, because being in the grip of an emotion and an emotion-influenced picture of reasons is a common phenomenon. Even ordinary emotions strongly influence a person's

---

[14] The very "treating of a consideration as a reason" may sound like a second-order attitude, where a consideration simply being my reason is somehow taken to be the corresponding first-order attitude. But, according to the way I use these locutions, there is no difference between a consideration being my reason and my treating that consideration as reason. That is, one does not need to have an explicit conception of a consideration as a reason to treat it as a reason. Analogously, one may treat someone as a sex object without even having the concept of a sex object, or treat someone as a queen without ever thinking of her in those terms.

outlook on the world and her assessment of options. More troub-
lingly, as Jodi Halpern (2001) has emphasized in a somewhat different context, emotions such as fear, jealousy, and despair, by
"hijacking" a person's perception of pertinent facts and her expectations for the future, can, in certain circumstances, render her
unable to shake off the emotionally charged view of her predicament.
In this rigid or (as Halpern puts it) "concretized" emotional state, the
emotional view dominates the person's thought processes and is cut
off from ordinary internal sources of possible, even momentary,
correction: the person is no longer subject to the ordinary ebb and
flow of diverse, potentially conflicting emotions, and her emotional
view is also isolated from ordinary cognitive processes of gathering
and assessing pertinent evidence. She is mentally "stuck" in an
inflexible emotional view. A similar rigid adherence to an emotional
view is, I imagine, possible in the case of caring, and it could presumably extend beyond the assessment of facts (whether mom's pain
will get better) to also affect the agent's assessment of reasons
(whether mom's pain is a reason to stop playing and offer comfort).
Just as a person in the grip of fear and the fear-dictated perception of
facts – as Halpern rightly argues – would not be exercising autonomy,
we should say the same of a person in the grip of caring and the
caring-dictated perception of reasons. We thus need to specify what
conditions our candidate autonomous agent must meet to escape
being merely in the grip of reasons.

Again, one may think that appeal to motivational hierarchy or to
evaluative judgment becomes necessary at this juncture. Is it not the
case that, in order to avoid being in the grip of a perceived reason,
the agent must reflect on why she treats this particular consideration
as a reason or, alternatively, must regard her perception of a reason
as correct, thereby making an evaluative judgment? Yet, just as we
saw with the first two aspects, the minimum requirements for this
aspect of autonomy turn out to be somewhat less demanding. What
really is required to avoid being in the grip of a perceived reason
is some openness to the possibility of seeing things otherwise. To
put this in more familiar terms, the agent must see a specific consideration as a reason against the background of the possibility of
reflection – provided we interpret what constitutes reflection very
broadly and do not confuse reflection with assessment of one's

motivational states. Gary Watson's (2004, 30) understanding of practical reflection helps guide us on this last point. Watson reminds us that reflection can be a first-order phenomenon – reflection need not take the agent's own motivations as its object. On this conception, reflection is a process of considering the substance of the various courses of action and their consequences in one's particular circumstances. Further, if reflection of this sort is to help prevent the agent from being in the grip of a perceived reason, the agent must be so constituted as to be open to the possibility that a fresh perception of reasons will result from this process. Of course, to fit the account developed so far, what is needed is a possibility of treating something different as a reason instead, not a possibility of a fresh evaluative judgment. Reflection is typically an imaginative exercise, but even the engagement of the imagination is unnecessary. What we are after here is room for insight that prevents an emotional view from becoming rigid, but nothing near the full deployment of reflective powers. For example, so long as spontaneous shifts of emotional frame are possible (by analogy to a suggestion in Halpern unpublished) – so that one is not relentlessly subject to the caring emotions – the openness to a fresh perception of reasons may be already in place.[15] (And, reversely, even if the caring *is* relentless, the agent is not in the grip of the corresponding reasons, so long as he is capable of imaginatively entertaining alternatives.)

To avoid the charge of being in the grip of a reason, one's perception of a reason need not even be a direct result of the process of reflection. Rather, as I expressed it earlier, one needs to see something as a reason *against the background of the possibility of reflection*. This simply means that the agent must be *capable* of some reflection – but he may have accepted the reason in question in light of whatever reflection (if any) he happens to have actually engaged in thus far.

---

[15] It is, in principle, possible to be in the grip of two conflicting caring emotions, say, one focused on a love affair, the other on one's mother, and simply to vacillate between the two, without one emotion providing a critical perspective to ease the grip of the other. All the same, for the conditions I am describing here to be met, the agent does not have to experience the conflicting emotions concurrently; it is sufficient if insights from one emotional state can penetrate into the other.

Of course, an agent may find himself in circumstances that do not allow for a realistic alternative perspective. For example, when one's life is threatened and one sees reason to flee, it is likely that no amount of reflection would yield an alternative perspective and reflection indeed may be pointless. Even here, though, one avoids being in the grip of the reason if one perceives the reason against the background of the possibility of reflection: what matters is that the person capable of reflection is prepared to question, and potentially modify, his current view of reasons so long as the circumstances allow for an alternative perspective.

The young child from my previous examples is unlikely to meet this requirement. On my view, young children, by virtue of being capable of caring, have internal attitudes and are able to govern themselves internally when they see reason to pursue what they care about and act accordingly. Young children are typically in the grip of such reasons, however, because they are not *capable* of engaging in sufficient reflection to gain any sort of critical vantage point or alternative perspective on the reasons that make sense to them at any given moment.[16] So despite having remarkably well-developed starting points of autonomy, young children are incapable of minimal autonomy – an intuitively welcome result.

In brief, what seems sufficient to avoid being in the grip of a reason is that one takes a consideration as a reason in the context of the possibility of first-order reflection, no matter how much actual reflection one happens to have engaged in thus far.

Altogether, our minimal case of autonomous decision making comprises the following core elements. First, the agent cares about a particular object *P*; this ensures that the attitude that guides the decision making is internal – and thus ensures that it is the *self* to whom the government can be attributable. Second, the agent acts in light of seeing reason to pursue what he cares about; this introduces

---

[16] Interestingly, we can even posit an explanation of why two- and three-year-olds are incapable of reflection of this sort: they don't have the concept of belief, but one needs the understanding of one's beliefs as potentially being mistaken in order to be able to hold in one's head an alternative perspective – to be able to entertain the possibility that things could be different from what makes sense to one now.

the element of *governance* itself.[17] And, third, the selection of this reason for action takes place against the backdrop of the possibility of first-order reflection.[18] This ensures that the agent is not merely in the grip of treating caring-based considerations as reasons. At no point in this picture does the need arise to appeal to evaluative judgments or to a hierarchy of attitudes about attitudes.

IMPLICATIONS FOR THE LIMITS OF LIBERALISM

How, then, does this alternative view of minimal autonomy affect the requirements of liberalism, and the range of cases in which they may plausibly appear excessive?

On the account I have outlined, it is a lot easier to achieve a genuine exercise of one's autonomy than has been traditionally understood, because the high-level cognitive abilities requisite for motivational hierarchy or evaluative judgment formation turn out to be unnecessary. And this means that the capacity to genuinely exercise some form of autonomy is, in principle, easier to come by than has been standardly assumed. One would expect such easing of the requirements for the fundamental underpinnings of autonomy to immediately affect when, in practice, people can be presumed to possess the capacity for autonomy to a sufficient degree so that their decisions merit noninterference under the tenets of strict liberalism. Yet, in fact, this practical effect is likely to be masked. The reason is that, in order to express a capacity for autonomy in particular choices, an agent must possess not only the fundamental underpinnings of autonomy that I have been discussing so far but also vital supplemental powers. These include the ability to engage in means-ends reasoning (so as to be able to advance what one cares about in the concrete circumstances in which one is acting) and the psychological ability to convert one's decisions into actions (i.e., freedom

---

[17] Recall that a caring agent meets the first two requirements of minimal autonomy in one sweep, simply by virtue of his caring.

[18] This means that for a specific decision to count as an *exercise* of minimal autonomy, only the *capacity* for critical reflection needs to be in place. But because an *exercise* of minimal autonomy involves additional elements, it can still be distinguished from the *capacity* for autonomy. This is particularly important to keep straight, given that the distinction between capacity for autonomy and its exercise is at issue in this chapter.

from disorders of the will, such as addiction or extreme impulsiveness). If these supplemental powers require a higher degree of cognitive sophistication than that required by the basic elements of minimal autonomy, the modified understanding of autonomy that I have defended here may not lead, for example, to any changes in our estimates of when, in the course of their development, human beings become capable of making specific choices that merit noninterference, or when they may lose this ability due to mental illness or neurological impairment.

What is more consequential for practical purposes, however, is that the account I have outlined changes the requirements for what it takes to count as genuinely *exercising* one's autonomy. As a result, many more choices than we may have hitherto understood qualify as indeed autonomous. If a normal adult, presumed to have all the prerequisites of autonomy, makes a decision based on his caring attitude, so long as he is not *in the grip of* caring, his choice may be a nondefective expression of autonomy not only when it goes against his well-being, his dignity, or reasonable ideals of conduct, but even when it contradicts his own higher-order desires or long-standing values.

Let us return to Mr. Lazaroff. As we saw earlier, because Lazaroff's choice contradicts his long-standing values, it is easy to interpret him as miscalculating or being weak-willed in the face of an overwhelming emotional crisis – and thus to assume that Lazaroff's capacity for autonomy is disengaged from the choice. I do not mean to deny that this may be what in fact occurred, but, crucially, my analysis makes room for another possibility. It could also be that, although Lazaroff values a good death very highly, he now finds himself deeply caring about simply staying alive. Were all three elements of minimal autonomy present, his choice would count as a true exercise of autonomy. So, let us investigate this possibility.

First, it would be unsurprising if, in this time of acute awareness of his own mortality, Lazaroff's emotional responses – his hopes, fears, angers, disappointments, and other reactions – did now powerfully focus on the goal of forestalling death, whatever the cost. His anger at his son for "giving up" on him is partial evidence that this indeed happened. So it is quite plausible that Lazaroff now finds himself deeply caring about simply staying alive. Second, Lazaroff's caring perception of forestalling death as of paramount importance could reasonably lead him to see any chance, no matter how minuscule, of halting the progression of his disease and prolonging his life as a reason to undergo the surgery. (While mere fear of death could result in a similar perception of reasons, it is also possible, as I am envisioning, that a full gamut of a Lazaroff's emotions has crystallized around the goal of staying alive. In this version, Lazaroff's attitude is much more profoundly his own than a mere fearful reaction, which could be simply weak-willed.) Third, does Lazaroff have the mental freedom to look at his situation and his reasons any other way? Although Gawande's description does not settle this question, it is at least possible for a patient in Lazaroff's shoes not to be rigidly stuck in his perception of every chance of staying alive as a reason to act.[19] For instance, the patient could well be aware that his current feelings go against his considered belief that he ought to assure a good death. He would then likely be able to think through this opposing point of view, and thereby subject his caring-based perception of reasons to critical reflection – while still making a choice in line with his caring.

In short, it is possible for a decision to undergo surgery in Lazaroff's circumstances to be an expression of the patient's caring about staying alive, without the patient's being in the grip of this caring. If this is indeed the case, his decision does count as a genuine exercise of autonomy, even though it contradicts his values. As such,

[19] I concede that it is likely that Lazaroff himself was subject to a rigid emotional view. In fact, he might even have been subject to a rigid emotion of the type described by Halpern, which manifests itself in rigid convictions about pertinent facts, convictions unresponsive to evidence. Lazaroff's might be a case of concretized hope, generating a rigid conviction that the surgery has a good chance of saving him, so that he "doesn't hear" contrary evidence presented by doctors. On this reading, Lazaroff is unable to bring pertinent facts to bear on his choice, and thus his choice cannot express his capacity for autonomy (he has a serious deficit in the first of the two "supplementary powers" I mentioned earlier in this section); accordingly, his choice need not be respected under the liberal doctrine of respect for autonomy. (I follow Halpern's insights here.) Additionally, one may reasonably expect that an emotion that leads to a rigid perception of *facts* is also likely to lead to a rigid perception of *reasons*. If so, Lazaroff's perception of reasons would not be open to critical reflection and his decisions based on caring would not qualify as minimally autonomous on the view I posited. While either sort of rigidity is likely for Gawande's Lazaroff, my point is that this outcome is not inevitable for someone in Lazaroff's position, who, in the face of a very real threat of impending death, ends up caring deeply about staying alive at all cost, against his long-standing value of a good death. And this leaves room for a minimally autonomous version of Lazaroff.

his decision cannot be so easily dismissed by those aiming to curb the excesses of strict liberalism.

Analogous interpretations apply to other choices that may initially look disengaged from autonomy. Imagine a woman faced with two options for treatment of breast cancer: a lumpectomy, somewhat more risky to her health and life, yet designed to largely preserve the shape of her breast, versus a radical mastectomy, at the time considered much safer, but also certain to leave her disfigured. Her choice, if it is based on her long-standing considered values, is clear: she disapproves giving weight to appearance, so she should go for the safer option, the breast removal. But suppose that when actually faced with the choice, the woman finds herself truly caring about her appearance much more than she realized and, on this basis, opts for lumpectomy. Because she chooses against her better judgment, her choice seems to fail to express her autonomy. However, on my analysis, if her choice reflects her caring-based perception of damage to appearance as a reason to reject an option, so long as this perception is open to critical reflection, her choice does qualify as genuinely expressing autonomy.

It is very tempting to interpret patients as failing to engage their autonomy when they pick options that appear unreasonable according to their own judgments. My analysis has made it much harder to indulge this temptation and to use it to rationalize our paternalistic impulses.

In some cases, a caring may not only conflict with the agent's own considered judgment but may be downright pernicious in light of that judgment. Think of a woman recovering from injuries resulting from spousal abuse, who, against her better judgment, decides to go back to her husband and "try again." Emotionally, she cannot tear herself away from the man she loves, even though she fully recognizes that this response is inappropriate and would very much want to change it. Some may see her as having emotionally internalized a culturally pervasive, gender-based, morally perverted ideal of spousal fidelity, and she may even fully accept this assessment. Yet, her choice derives from her caring, and, given her contrary evaluative judgment, it is clear that she is able to reflect on the matter critically. Thus, on my analysis, her choice does embody minimal autonomy. This assessment may seem implausible at first. However, we must not forget that a choice, such as this one, that meets the most minimal standards of autonomy, may still be a far cry from an ideal expression of autonomy: there is plenty of room for criticism here – for permissible persuasion, assistance, and the like. It is nonetheless crucial to recognize that this person is in fact exercising autonomy and that her choice has a very strong claim to noninterference and basic respect. Because the choice expresses a stance on the matter deeply rooted in the woman's psychic makeup, a stance she must acknowledge as her own, it deserves an especially high level of protection against paternalistic intervention.

Some will be inclined to read my analysis as a *reductio* argument that undermines the liberal approach, even in its more palatable, liberal perfectionist version, by showing how minimal and insubstantial autonomy can be. On this reading, given the possibility of minimal autonomy, there is much less to the liberal doctrine of respect for autonomy than is usually thought. However, I do not offer my analysis in this spirit. Even for critics of liberalism, it is hard to deny that respect for autonomy matters to at least some degree, and that it matters especially when the person does in fact exercise autonomy. If one accepts this much, the cases of minimal autonomy cannot be ignored: interference with minimally autonomous decisions does appear to be a very serious moral breach. Of course, this is not to deny that it would be better for agents to improve beyond the minimal level and come closer to the ideal of fuller autonomy. Still, I am urging that the value of minimal autonomy needs to be recognized and that disrespect for minimally autonomous choices is a pernicious form of paternalism.

This is especially relevant in medicine, because, in the high-stakes decisions concerning health, the temptation toward paternalism when the patient ignores his values is particularly great. It is important to realize that the degree of paternalistic violation would not be the same in all such cases and therefore to be attentive to more pernicious forms of paternalism. The sentiment articulated by Gawande, that "a good physician cannot simply stand aside when patients make ... self-defeating decisions," needs refinement. As they contemplate stepping in, physicians should be aware of a possibility they may otherwise miss: even if the patient contradicts his professed values, and is self-defeating in this sense, the patient may still be exercising (minimal) autonomy and so might not be altogether self-undermining. In such cases, the physician's own rationale for stepping in may, in fact, not apply.

Curiously, the concept of minimal autonomy also matters in a very different way to those contemplating the refusal of patients' requests: it affects what could legitimately count as a conscientious objection. It is controversial whether health professionals can make conscientious objections, but suppose we established that they are, in principle, allowable. Those who allow them normally assume, I think appropriately, that to qualify as a conscientious objection, it is not enough that a choice be made with capacity for autonomy in the background; the choice must genuinely embody the person's autonomy. If the medical treatment at issue goes against the physician's evaluative convictions, there is, on this view, prima facie ground for conscientious objection, and, circumstances permitting, it would be reasonable for the physician to recuse herself. For example, it is often accepted that doctors do not have to perform abortions against their moral beliefs. Yet, if a doctor, fully capable of autonomy, succumbs to weakness of the will, and on this basis refuses to treat her patient according to standard medical practice, this patently does not count as a conscientious objection, and opting out is surely impermissible; a doctor who is simply squeamish about performing an abortion cannot recuse herself. Now consider a doctor who believes that it is best to forgo heroic measures on a terminally ill patient but who nonetheless begins to truly care about that patient and therefore wants to keep the patient alive, against her better judgment. Might she have a basis for a conscientious objection to participating in the process of letting this patient die?

On standard assumptions, there are only two options for interpreting this scenario: either the doctor is making the evaluation that it is better to keep the patient alive, which is implausible given her judgment to the contrary; or the doctor is weak-willed, and thus clearly lacking a basis for a conscientious objection. My analysis suggests a third option, in which the doctor's claim of conscientious objection looks reasonable. If her choice is based on a caring, even though it contradicts her better judgment, it qualifies as minimally autonomous. And because the choice is a genuine expression of the doctor's autonomy, it can reasonably ground a conscientious objection. (Recall that the standards for what counts as a caring are rather demanding, so I am not suggesting here an overly easy route to qualifying as a conscientious objector.)

It is well known in bioethics that the principle of respecting patient autonomy may come into conflict with promoting the best interests of the patient, whether understood in terms of well-being, or dignity, or reasonable standards of conduct. What I have tried to establish here is the possibility of deeper and more troubling conflicts. A patient may implement all the elements of autonomous self-governance and yet make choices that are deeply troubling even by her own lights. A patient may request extra rounds of in vitro fertilization against her own better judgment, because she cares so much about having a child. Or a patient may request invasive treatment at the end of life against his better judgment, because, when it comes right down to it, he happens to care a great deal about simply continuing to live. These patients may not be exercising autonomy in ideal or perfect ways, but their choices cannot, according to what I have argued, be classified as not, in fact, autonomous. Refusal of their requests would be particularly injurious to respect for autonomy, much more so than a paternalistic refusal directed at a person capable of autonomy who happens to forgo its exercise on a particular occasion due to weakness of the will, thoughtlessness, denial, or lack of attention. From the point of view of liberalism, the range of cases in which patients ought to be seen as adequately exercising their capacity of autonomy, and thus deserving the highest level of protection from paternalistic interference, has greatly expanded.

5

Narrative, Complexity, and Context

Autonomy as an Epistemic Value

Naomi Scheman

> Those masterful images because complete
> Grew in pure mind, but out of what began?
> A mound of refuse or the sweepings of a street,
> Old kettles, old bottles, and a broken can,
> Old iron, old bones, old rags, that raving slut
> Who keeps the till. Now that my ladder's gone,
> I must lie down where all the ladders start
> In the foul rag and bone shop of the heart.
>   – W. B. Yeats, "The Circus Animals' Desertion"

> Human beings are not at the pinnacle of intelligence, smarter than
> other animals, far smarter than plants, farther still from rocks and
> other non-living things. It is, in fact, the other way around: the rocks,
> being oldest, know the most, followed by plants and by animals older
> than we are. As the youngest, the most recent inhabitants of this place,
> we humans are the most ignorant and have the most to learn from our
> elders.
>   – Paraphrased from Paul Schultz, Elder,
> White Earth band of Ojibwe

In addition to those acknowledged in note 5, my thinking in this essay owes a great deal to others in Minnesota: especially my GRASS Routes colleagues, Susan Gust and Cathy Jordan, Nick Jordan, and members of the Bioethics Center. I greatly benefited from discussions with the editors and the other authors in this section at a working meeting in Groningen in the fall of 2006, and from detailed criticism on an earlier draft from Hilde Lindemann and, especially, Michael Root. Hilde's faith and encouragement have been invaluable.

In Margaret Drabble's novel *The Sea Lady* (2006), a man and a woman in late middle age travel toward a small city on the English coast, near where they met as children, to receive honorary doctorates and – as it turns out, not coincidentally – to meet for the first time in thirty years. They had parted after a brief and disastrous marriage following a love affair that, in its intensity of both passion and happiness, shadowed the rest of their lives. The book ends shortly after their reunion, leaving open what will occur between them.

Humphrey is a distinguished marine biologist, renowned as a perceptive observer of the complexity and interdependency of aquatic life. His career and reputation have, however, been overtaken by the disciplinary shift away from the study of animals in the sea toward the study of cells and molecules in the laboratory. Ailsa is a pioneering feminist critic of art, literature, culture, and everyday life. A desultory scholar, she has been an energetic thinker and a charismatic provocateuse, brilliantly bringing together eclectic mixes of theory and subject matter that helped to shape the spirit of a time – radical, restless, and rhyzomatic (rooted not in the stability of depth, but in the network of surface entanglements).

I want to explore a possibility suggested by Humphrey and Ailsa's tentative reconciliation at the end of the novel. Seeing that reconciliation in terms of the coming together of C. P. Snow's "two cultures" – the careful scientist and the allusive aesthete – is thwarted by Humphrey's current status as an outsider to the culture of science. His scientific discipline has, to his dismay and disapproval, embraced the mereology that has characterized modern laboratory science. From a mereological perspective, the properties and behavior of objects are the consequence of the properties and behavior of their parts. Objects of study need to be abstracted from their surroundings in order to discover how they are the (kinds of) things they are in virtue of the constitution of their parts. Humphrey's complexly contextualized knowledge of the sea creatures he studied seems at least as distant from this conception of science as from Ailsa's richly suggestive, but unsystematic, musings. Both he and she see knowledge of the world in terms of relationships – of contiguity as much as of similarity – and knowledge of things as inseparable from the contexts in which those things take shape. Those affinities were camouflaged by the very different positions in which they stood to the authoritative culture of science – Humphrey as an obsolete remnant of an earlier, premodern, age and Ailsa as the seductive siren of avant-garde, postmodern critique. The authoritative culture of serious knowledge not only dismissed them both but did so in terms that disguised their affinities and held apart their potential for collaboration – in fashioning either a personal life together or a way of seeing the world that married his attentiveness to detail to her flashes of analogical insight.

How might the ethical and epistemological norms that underlie modern science – including both biomedical research and a great deal of (especially evidence-based) medical practice – differ if Humphrey and Ailsa were to help to shape them? What, in particular, would research and clinical ethics, specifically as protecting the autonomy of human subjects and patients, look like if knowers and the objects of their knowledge were not abstracted from their relationships with each other and with the worlds in which they live, and if those relationships were themselves conceived of as epistemic resources? Standing as the "before" and "after" to scientific modernity, Humphrey and Ailsa set in relief its distinctive ways of knowing: as different as they are from each other, they share a passionate commitment to what modern science downplays – context, connection, contingency, and particularity.

WHY DOES AUTONOMY MATTER?

Respect for the autonomy of one's (human) subjects is a core concept in the ethics of research, but autonomy is typically characterized individualistically, as something that persons simply have and that others are called upon to respect by not violating. Furthermore, respect for autonomy is conceptualized as arising from considerations extrinsic to the distinctively epistemic aims of science. I want to argue, rather, that scientists need to recognize and act upon a specifically *epistemic* interest in the autonomy of their research subjects (if any) as well as in the autonomy of others who stand to be affected by their research or who are in a position to know and care about the objects of that research. Furthermore, acting appropriately upon this epistemic interest requires a conception of autonomy as relational and contextual, as manifested in particular interpersonal situations, through mutual engagement. Such a conception is also ethically preferable in that it reveals the connections between autonomy and other aspects of human flourishing, making it clearer why it matters, both to the person whose autonomy is in question and to others.

Ethical rules concerning the use of human subjects in research are typically regarded as putting the brakes on the unacceptable behavior in which scientists might engage, were they guided solely by narrowly scientific norms. Such a characterization has its roots in the two emblematic scenarios out of which such rules arose: Nazi experimentation on prisoners in concentration camps and the Tuskegee study of the unchecked progress of syphilis in poor Black men. These two cases, along with less notorious others, merged with the cultural image of the "mad scientist," whose madness constituted, rather than undermined, his [*sic*] scientific genius. As the dark side of the scientific and technological progress of modernity, epistemic lust was regarded as needing to be held in check by something external to the search for truth.

Not all ethical norms for science share this epistemologically extrinsic quality. In particular, those that serve to protect the scientific enterprise itself seem directly related to the search for truth. Thus, prohibitions on falsifying data, or even on stealing the work of others or misusing research funds, are seen as intrinsically, even if not immediately, related to the aims of scientific discovery. The mediating link is the need for scientists to trust each other and to trust the workings of the institutions (from laboratories to universities to journals) that make their work and its dissemination possible. The trust of wider publics is not, however, seen as similarly intrinsic to the enterprise: even when bemoaning public ignorance or irrational credulity, scientists do not usually regard that lamentable situation as affecting the quality of the science they do – except in the indirect way of leading to reductions in public funding or the enactment of restrictive legislation. This distinction – between the scientifically intrinsic nature of trust among scientists and the scientific irrelevance or merely instrumental relevance of public trust – marks a substantive difference in how scientists (are supposed to) think about those toward whom they have ethical responsibilities.

In the case of fellow scientists, respect is rooted in participation in a shared enterprise and the need for each other's intelligence and perspectives: the trust engendered by respect (or endangered by disrespect) is intrinsic to the relationships that constitute a necessarily collective enterprise. In the case of research subjects or of the public more broadly, both respect and the trust it engenders are either epistemically irrelevant or merely instrumental: members of the public, unlike other scientists, are not collaborators in a collective activity, but merely objects (research "subjects"), supporters, victims, or beneficiaries of the activities of scientists. This difference – between treating others respectfully because one recognizes the need for their active engagement in and with one's work and treating them respectfully because to do otherwise would be either morally wrong or instrumentally troublesome – is the difference between having and not having a specifically *epistemic* interest in others' autonomy. I suggest that the picture in terms of which scientists do *not* have such an interest in the autonomy either of their subjects or of others variously related to their objects of research is mistaken. Rather, the requirement of respect for the autonomy of human subjects ought to reflect a broader, epistemic interest in the autonomy of diverse (human and, as my paraphrase from Paul Schultz suggests, nonhuman) others.

Underlying the view of human subjects as needing to be protected from, rather than as collaborating in, scientific research is a conception of knowers and the objects of their knowledge (human or not) as fundamentally and normatively separate. Blurring the boundaries between them is thought to pose not only an ethical but, more fundamentally, an epistemic threat. The disciplining of the researcher and the isolation and abstraction of the object of knowledge are meant to prepare them for an encounter that will not fundamentally change either of them but rather allow them both to be most essentially themselves. The researcher, as generically rational and disciplined, is able to reveal the nature of the object, abstracted from the confounding variables of its life outside the laboratory. Recent work in science studies has argued for a deeply different way of thinking about the encounter between subjects and objects of knowledge, according to which the material-discursive context of that encounter helps to constitute the objects being studied.[1] Much as

---

[1] As I was doing the final revisions of this essay, I received two books that articulate such a conception of the epistemology and ontology of science. One, Karen Barad's *Meeting the Universe Halfway: Quantum Physics and the Entanglement of Matter and Meaning* (2007), develops her theory of *agential realism*, which she draws from Niels Bohr's physics and philosophy; the book is brilliant and, it's to be hoped, germinal in its revolutionary

the normative "view from nowhere" has been criticized as neither possible nor, even as an ideal, conducive to actual objectivity (Haraway 1988), so the laboratory has been argued to be a quite particular place, the site of quite particular relationships, which shape all the participants in the construction of knowledge that occurs there (see, e.g., Latour 1979; Pickering 1995; Rouse 2002; and Traweek 1988).

Because that knowledge is meant to apply to, and to be applicable in, the world outside the laboratory, it is important to ask what the knowledge is knowledge *of*. Real problems arise about the applicability of research findings beyond the research setting, and one way of framing those problems is in terms of whether, and to what extent, the objects of the research are relevantly different from the objects in the wider world they are taken to exemplify. Given the conceptual (and frequently material) abstraction of objects of research, as well as their subsequent reinscription within the specific parameters of the research context, the applicability of research depends on tracing relationships between objects of research and the objects to which the research is meant to apply, whether those objects be people or rocks or the genomes of plants.

I argue for an epistemology and ethics of research that draw attention to the contexts in which objects (and subjects) of knowledge exist both in the laboratory and "in the wild," into which discoveries will eventually move, as drugs are administered to patients, seeds are planted in fields, and public policies are enacted in communities. It can take at least as much material and conceptual labor to successfully integrate scientific knowledge into the world as it took to extract the objects of that knowledge from it. The tools for this labor will not, however, generally reside in scientists' toolboxes. Some of the tools will be found in the engaged praxis and situated knowledge of those

conception of a metaphysics that is relational and – hence, she argues – ethical all the way down. The second, *Pluripotent Circulations: Putting Actor-Network Theory to Work on Stem Cells in the USA, Prior to 2001* (2006), is a doctoral dissertation by Morten Sager in History of Ideas and Theory of Science at Göteborg University, which develops and applies a version of actor-network theory (ANT), drawing primarily on the work of Bruno Latour and Michel Callon, to argue similarly for the emergence of objects of study – reality – in and through material-discursive practice. Strikingly – and this is not an aspect of their work with which I was familiar – both Barad and Sager (and other ANT theorists) articulate and employ a conception of agency that is not confined to the human or even the animate or organic.

who are enmeshed in the world out of which the objects of knowledge were extracted and refined, and others will need to be collaboratively custom-crafted. A central aim of this chapter is to say something useful about the nature of those tools and about the work to which they need to be put. I want to suggest that Hilde Lindemann (Nelson)'s work on the role of narrative in "holding another in personhood" (H. Nelson 2002 and Lindemann in this volume) can be generalized to account for the ontological continuity between the contexts of research and of application (whether theoretical or practical: my concern is not just with research applications in the usual sense but with the more basic notion of "aboutness" – our being able to say that research actually applies to our lives and to the world around us). I want to extend Lindemann's use of narrative to consider non-humans, as well as humans, as both the objects of narrative and as narrators; and it will be as narrators that research subjects (and other objects of research, as well as other people and things related to those objects) will be normatively autonomous.

NARRATIVE AND ONTOLOGY

> If they are not machines, then what are organisms? A metaphor far more to my liking is this. Imagine a child playing in a woodland stream, poking a stick into an eddy in the flowing current, thereby disrupting it. But the eddy quickly reforms. The child disperses it again. Again it reforms, and the fascinating game goes on. There you have it! Organisms are resilient patterns in a turbulent flow – patterns in an energy flow.
>
> – Carl R. Woese, "A New Biology for a New Century"

In returning to the "rag and bone shop of the heart," Yeats's poet speaks to all those, scientists included, who are tempted by the clarity, cleanliness, and uplift of grand and pure ideas. And the return is for real: he does not just root around for inspiration, or data: he casts his lot with the refuse, the old, the broken, the "foul." Yeats means to draw himself, and us, back to where those grand and pure ideas start, and to where we must return, lest those ideas take on the appearance of a life of their own, a life we are at risk of being seduced into regarding as realer or more important than the messy one we're living.

This (re)turn of attention to the ordinary is a naturalizing move, seeking norms that emerge from the details of practice, rather than originating in some privileged elsewhere. Our attention is also drawn to narrative, to details as meaningfully connected in a particular context. In its most basic manifestation, narrative is simply *space and time made salient*: here and now, then and there, once upon a time, long long ago and far far away. Stories are organized from a point of view; salience is perspectival, a matter of how the world appears from here, to the narrator now, in the light of her, his, or its own particular interests, needs, desires, and capacities. Narrative is also intrinsically connected to autonomy, in particular to "perceptual autonomy": the ability to recognize, articulate, and effectively communicate how the world appears from one's particular location in it. Those in subordinated, marginalized, or closeted social locations typically learn, in order to be taken seriously, the skill of periscopic vision: refracting their line of sight to correspond to the privileged "view from nowhere."[2] Autonomous narration thus requires that the narrator be situationally capable of and credited with a legitimate, nonperiscopic point of view.[3]

Narrative begins in the ways in which aspects of the world are differently salient for and to different things – as geological formations bear the traces of volcanoes and the rise and recession of rivers and glaciers, while perhaps remaining mute about the dry or rainy summers, warmer or colder winters that leave their traces in the rings of trees, or about the presence of flora and fauna that shape each other through the co-evolution of predator and prey. At its most

[2] See Haraway 1988 and P. Williams 1991, especially the latter's account of two parents (she says they must be lawyers, but they could as well be philosophers) trying to persuade their terrified toddler that the "slavering wolfhound" drooling over him is essentially no different from the laughably harmless Pekinese he towers over: dogs are dogs, at least from their perspective, informed not only by height but by Science.

[3] It is, of course, true that we no more have direct, unmediated access to narratives than we do to anything else. Anything we say about the narratives of geological formations or anything else will be our story about its story. Such iterative narrativity complicates matters in practice, but my fundamental point remains: we need to practice the respectfully interactive telling of nonhumans' stories, just as we need to practice the respectfully interactive telling of the stories of persons whose capacity for autonomous narration has been problematically denied. My attributing the role of narrator to nonhumans is part of the shift in conceptions of agency also characteristic of theories and methods such as actor-network theory and agential realism. See note 1.

fundamental, narrative and narrative saliency constitute the ontology of complex objects as more than the sum of their parts. As I have argued elsewhere about the self, any object can be thought of as a *locus of idiosyncrasy* (Scheman 1993b), as fundamentally adverbial, a way of being in the world, a nexus of causes and effects, distinctively salient to its surroundings, as they are distinctively salient to it. What makes something a *thing* (an organism, but even an ordinary-sized physical object, like a rock) is its *integrity*, its propensity to continue in existence as the particular (sort of) thing that it is, along with its entering as an organized whole into relationships of cause and effect. Its integrity (its separateness and distinctness) is thus essentially bound up with its relationships with other things in its environment: it and they reciprocally define each other's boundaries, capabilities, susceptibilities, and identities.

It was reflections such as these that led me to appreciate the inverted "smartness" pyramid I learned from Paul Schultz, which I initially had difficulty understanding with any degree of literalness. Think, for example, about ordinary cases of (human) embodied knowledge, such as knowing how to perform activities that we would clumsily fail at if we tried consciously to enunciate each step of what we were doing. In almost as ordinary a way, we speak of our bodies as remembering previous experiences: think of vaccinations and allergic reactions. Our bodies, as complex entities, bear the traces of earlier experiences and act in the present in ways informed by those experiences.[4] Similarly, as a locus of idiosyncratic saliencies, a cliff-side or a tree or a species bears a story about the times it has lived through and that have made it what it is. Our learning that story requires our respecting the perspectival autonomy of that thing, listening and attending specifically to its integrity, its being what it is, in this place, over time. It is what it is because of what it has witnessed, and the specificities of its witnessing were shaped by its being the sort of thing that it is. We need to attend as well to our own relationships to the things we are learning from, to how we come to be where we are, to what we want of these things and how what we want relates to the histories and the relationships that predate our arrival.

---

[4] The immune system is an especially interesting site for reflection on bodily constitution of identity. See, for example, Haraway 1989.

This sort of attention helps to bridge the gap between the laboratory and the wider world. In her discussions about those who cannot, or can no longer, narrate their own lives, hence hold their own personhood, Lindemann (this volume) describes a special case of what (she also argues) is generally true: we are not the sole narrators of our own lives, the sole arbiters of our ontological structure and boundaries. Nor do the relationships that help to constitute us as the particular beings we are remain within the specific contexts in which they most centrally arise: they accompany us, to greater or lesser extents, more or less tenaciously, as we move from place to place. What is true of us is true quite generally, and tracing the relationships and the narratives that cling to and continue to help to constitute objects of research plays an important role in the applicability of that research. As Lindemann's narrator accompanies her unconscious friend through the decisions about his care, by embodying and voicing the story of who he is, so too do the voices of those who are narratively entwined, in the wider world, with the people or objects in research settings need to be heard in those settings, in order to maintain the ontological continuity needed for the applicability of research.

As the doctors treating Lindemann's unconscious patient risk treating not *him* but the congeries of symptoms that reveal themselves to their diagnostic tools and modes of perception, so similarly researchers risk learning about an object constrained and defined by their tools and methods in ways that are discontinuous with the lives of the objects in the contexts from which they were abstracted. As in Lindemann's story, what we need to aim for is not the irrelevance of the expert's tools and perspective but rather a larger story into which the story they reveal can be inserted; we need accompanying narratives to preserve the "aboutness" of the expert's knowledge. Respecting the autonomy both of the objects of study (including, but not limited to, human subjects) and of those things and persons with which they are enmeshed in "real life" is thus not an ethical demand superimposed on epistemic norms but rather constitutive of those norms. And the autonomy in need of respect is, as feminist theorists have argued, relational, not to be understood in terms of separateness or of the primacy of already bounded individuals (Mackenzie and Stoljar 2000; Keller 1985; and – specifically in the context of medical ethics – Kukla 2005).

Although it is not easy to determine what such respect would actually look like, it is clear that its demands will be frequently in conflict with established scientific practice. Think, for example, of the controversies surrounding archaeology's collection and study of ceremonial objects. There is a tension between the meaning such objects have for descendants of their original users and the means employed by archaeologists to study them – starting with removing them from the sites at which the archaeologists found them. This relocation engenders mistrust on the part of those whose relationships with the objects are the last links in the narrative chain that constitutes the objects' sacredness. The severing of those relationships – or their inaccessibility to researchers – means that however the objects come to be known, they will, in important ways, not be known as the particular sorts of things that they were. Similarly, the scientific study of plants that have ceremonial or healing roles in various traditional societies raises questions about the identity of what is being studied: to what extent do the "purified" samples and isolated "active ingredients" correspond to the plants as they are used indigenously? To what extent can the healing properties of the plants be abstracted from the practices that surround their indigenous use? Taking such questions seriously entails engaging with those whose lives and practices have been entwined with the plants, those entrusted with the stories of the plants' powers; and the possibility for such engagement is undermined when those people, practices, and stories are treated as irrelevant to the search for the presumptive essence of the plants.[5]

CLINICAL EPISTEMOLOGY

A recurring theme in doctors' stories of becoming patients is discovering that, as patients, they are not presumed to know anything about the illness or injury they are currently suffering and for which they are being treated. Being the patient, that is, does not put one in

---

[5] In addition to Paul Schultz, I am especially indebted in thinking about these issues to Maggie Adamek, Jill Doerfler, Craig Hassel, Karl Lorenz, and George Spengler, especially in connection with the conflicts between the University of Minnesota and the White Earth Reservation concerning the university's research on wild rice (*Manoomin*), a grain sacred to the Ojibwe.

a socially recognized position to contribute distinctively to efforts to understand either the problem or the effects of attempted solutions. The fact that it is doctors' own bodies that are ill and injured and their bodies that are experiencing the effects of the treatments, far from especially qualifying them to speak about how things are going, marks them as epistemically compromised.

This epistemic disenfranchisement is similar to that experienced by other social groups – notably children, women, homosexuals, and the disabled – who are taken, by their membership in the group (defined and named by others), to be in no position to have reliable beliefs about their own lives. In the case of children (and people with severe cognitive disabilities), there is a degree of justification for this view: young children, or those with the cognitive abilities of a young child, are typically unable to comprehend the more complex aspects of their own lives and well-being. But even in such cases, as children's rights and, especially, disability rights activists have argued, this dismissal is carried farther than is either necessary or justifiable, as well as being extended to people with disabilities that in no way hinder their understanding of their own lives.

As feminist, queer, and disability theorists have argued, in the case of women, variously queer, and disabled people, the presumption of epistemic incompetence, concerning especially one's own life, is a cornerstone of sexist, heterosexist, and ableist ideology. Being the scrutinized object of the gaze of the epistemically privileged, presumptively unable to return that gaze or, specifically, to regard oneself with any authority, is at the heart of the discursive practices that create homosexuals, transsexuals, the disabled, and perhaps even women as such – as particular sorts of people, rather than people who just happen to have certain sorts of sexual desires and proclivities or to have bodies or minds that differ in certain ways from what is considered "normal."

But it is hardly necessary to "extend" such an account to cover patients (or research subjects). Rather, what in the cases of women, homosexuals, transsexuals, and the disabled requires argument and engenders controversy is, in the case of people being treated for illness or injury, lying incontrovertibly there on the surface. Such people are *patients*, something you cannot be, no matter how gravely ill or grievously injured, unless you are under the care of someone taken to be in a position to diagnose your condition and prescribe and administer remedies for it. Your place in the relationship that constitutes your patienthood (specifically and especially within Western, science-based medicine) defines you as subject to an expert gaze presumed capable – as you are presumed incapable – of naming what is wrong with you and directing the course of your treatment.

One might object that patients are continually being asked how they feel, whether it hurts when the doctor presses there, where their pain is on a scale of one to ten and whether it is worse in the morning or the evening. True enough, but like the things that "native informants" tell anthropologists, the answers to such questions are taken as mere raw material for authorized knowers to interpret in the light of their own observations and using their theoretical tools. As I have argued elsewhere, following Uma Narayan and other postcolonial theorists, indigenous knowledge is treated as though it were a bodily secretion that "natives" give off, that they cannot help but know and deserve no credit (not even a personal footnote) for knowing (Narayan 1997; Scheman 1997). Nor does this knowledge, for example of the healing properties of plants, give them power: rather, taken by the expert outsider and spun into something else, it becomes part of a tool kit for the outsiders to use in subordinating and exploiting the "natives." From the perspective of the outsider expert, the indigenous people don't really know what they're doing, nor do they know what they have. It takes the expert's science to turn folk practices into real knowledge, as it takes that science to turn raw material into standardized pharmaceuticals; and it is the added value of scientific expertise that is taken to be the real – commercial, patentable – value of the healing substances. Similarly, patients' reports of their perceptions and sensations are informative without counting as knowledge. They serve the same function as do measuring instruments (from thermometers to CT scanners), with, however, the drawbacks of vagueness, nonstandardization, and idiosyncratic subjectivity. Doctors' reliance on what patients tell them is thus merely a necessary expedient, the best they can do until the invention of devices that will provide better, objective, and objectively comparable data.

How should we characterize what patients know about themselves and their conditions if they are to count as legitimate contributors to the acquisition of knowledge about their own injuries and illnesses – if they are, that is, to be active participants in their own health care? On the philosophical model of privileged access to what only we can know, and we cannot help but know, patients are set up for the treatment accorded "native informants," whose unimpeachable contributions are treated not as their moves in a conversation but as a harvestable natural resource. The very unimpeachability of what one says – its being raw data, rather than a contestable claim – marks one's dismissability as an epistemic partner (Narayan 1997). Patients need, as do "natives," to contribute something impeachable, subject to critique, to engage with and to be engaged by, in order to participate as subjects in the project of coming to know what's going on with them and what to do about it.

Patients clearly are in a position to make such contributions. They can detect regularities and patterns in how they feel, they can hazard hypotheses about where in their bodies sensations are originating, they can note correlations between how they feel and things that are going on in and around their bodies, and they can note apparent similarities between their experiences and the descriptions of symptoms of various disorders. In all of these cases, they might be wrong: they might misremember, or under- or overestimate the severity of their pains, or they might be succumbing to the hypochondria that has afflicted medical students when they first encounter descriptions of the symptoms of obscure diseases and that now afflicts everyone who turns to the Internet to check out some new twinge, rash, or change in a bodily function. Paradoxically, being thought liable to mistake is a necessary though not, of course, sufficient condition of being taken as participants in the conversation. What matters is that the judgment that the patient is wrong not be taken as an excuse for dismissing her, as one would dispose of a faulty thermometer, or at least send it back for repairs: one wouldn't *argue* with it.

It is precisely that engagement, the giving and taking of critique, that marks the sort of respect for autonomy that has epistemic value. It is when the doctor sees the patient as an active participant in coming to know what the problem is and what to do about it that the doctor is in a position to learn from what the patient knows and believes, not just from what the patient's body shows. In such a relationship the doctor is committed not just to respecting the patient's autonomy, in the sense of not violating bounds of selfhood

the patient is presumed to have independently of the clinical relationship, but rather to valuing the patient's autonomy as interpersonal and emergent, and as valuable *to the doctor* because of the
contextual, relational, and idiosyncratic knowledge the patient
comes to have.

Such knowledge is not only thoughtful and fallible; it is typically
narrative. Its value lies precisely in its being not an unmediated
report of a bare sensation, but rather a contextualized counterweight
to the scientific knowledge that the clinician brings, and hence an aid
to the clinician committed to bridging the gap between generalized
knowledge and the particularities of this patient's situation. Such
considerations can be extended to the setting of biomedical research
and the relationship between researchers and their subjects. If
patients have a difficult time making their voices heard, research
subjects face the same obstacles plus an additional one: unlike
patients, they are not in general presumed to have any direct interest
in what is going on.[6]

The active engagement of research subjects can inform research,
even when the researchers think they know what they are looking for
and active collaboration is not required for them to obtain it. The
frequency of unexpected side effects and, more happily, of seren-
dipitous discoveries argues, however, for fostering relationships
within which subjects can reflect upon and discuss their sensations
and perceptions beyond those they are specifically asked to attend to.
Such discussions with patients and subjects do take place, especially
when research is conducted in a hospital setting, but they involve
nurses, in which case the discrediting may have as much to do with
the messenger as with the original source of the message. As Joan
Liaschenko and Debra DeBruin have argued (2003), the richer and
less structured interactions that nurses typically have with patients
and subjects put them in the middle of the ethically problematic
overlap of what are meant to be distinct narrative frames (treatment
vs. research) with distinctively different casts of characters (patients
vs. subjects). But the complexity of those interactions can also help to

---

[6] The question of subjects' stake in research is, in fact, typically addressed in the
context of clinical trials, when the concern is ensuring that subjects have no
expectation that the experimental treatment will benefit them.

maintain the individual identity of the patients and subjects and foster their perceptual competence and autonomy, leading to the emergence of potentially useful information.

COMMUNITY-BASED PARTICIPATORY RESEARCH

The meanings of our lives and experiences, including of those experiences connected with whatever it is that researchers are seeking to learn about us, are not ours alone, as individuals, but are embedded in the communities to which we belong. We develop a voice and the ability to articulate the world from our own particular perspective. One principal value of community-based participatory research is the ability to tap into communities of meaning, thus increasing the likelihood both that the data obtained will be as complete and accurate as possible and that the integration of research findings into people's lives will go as smoothly as possible.

From the definition of a researchable problem, to the recruitment and retention of subjects, to their compliance with research protocols and the honesty and richness of their responses, to the analysis of findings and translation into interventions, the trusting, active engagement of community members, with the confidence and the power to make a difference, can be invaluable (Jordan et al. 2005). In this sense, any research involving human subjects, and much that does not, can be community based and participatory: all that is required is that others than the designated researchers have relationships with the objects of knowledge, and hence be in positions to know something about those objects and their relationships with other things in the world, and that the relationships among researchers and community members be genuinely reciprocal and respectful.

From such a perspective we can raise questions about communities' standing in relation to the potential promises of benefits and risks of harm from research that do not immediately founder (as such questions now tend to do) on the issue of whether anyone is authorized to sign the informed consent form. Just as the requirement of researchers' respect for the autonomy of their subjects neither starts nor ends with informed consent, so the requirement of respect for concerned communities demands sustained engagement and real relationship, and promises not just ethical acceptability but epistemic advantage. Communities are the repositories of the narratives in terms of which the researchers' findings will, for better or worse, be – or fail to be – integrated into the wild; and the multiplicity and contradictoriness of those narratives are reason for, not against, engaging with them. Unlike the logic of the laboratory, based on abstraction and generalization, community-based knowledge is based on logics of salience and connection, of particularity and idio-syncrasy, on narratives of space and time, on history and hope.

The cultivation of relationships of trust between researchers and the communities within which they work may, as critics of commu-nity-based research charge, pose temptations to tell people what they would like to hear, but it can more seriously provide solid ground on which difficult truths can be articulated, listened to, and heeded. When the process of research itself is empowering to a community, such truths have a context in which to be understood and taken on, rather than just being dropped from on high. Communities can frame more useful, in part because more truthful, stories about themselves, rather than leaving that framing in the hands of researchers or more socially, economically, and politically powerful others.

Scientists need to respect communities for the same, intrinsic reasons they respect other scientists, as active participants in making meaning and as contributors to discovery. Cultivating such respect requires guarding against both scientists' arrogance and communi-ties' diffidence and deference on the one hand and mistrust on the other. It requires cooperative work to create discursive space for "subjugated knowledges," importantly including space for mutually critical engagement, rather than uncritical appropriation. This dis-cursive space needs to be commodious enough to hold diverse per-spectives and ways of making sense, while being sufficiently structured by shared understandings to reveal points of disagree-ment needing resolution.

ACROSS THE DISCIPLINING DEMANDS OF MODERNITY

To return to Humphrey and Ailsa, their affair took place in the romantic realm outside of normal time and space – the "green world" of Shakespearean comedy, a magical retreat from normality, after which the characters return to the everyday world, that is, to marriage (Cavell 1981). For Humphrey and Ailsa, that return was disastrous: there was no way for them to be together in the same version of a real world. What separated them was modernity, and the ways neither of them fit into it. Humphrey's way of being a scientist was distinctively premodern, while Ailsa's cultural *bricolage* was distinctively postmodern. Their shared discomfort with the disciplining of modernity may have initially brought them together, but it failed to provide them with any other (sufficiently real) place to be. I want to connect Humphrey and Alisa's problem to a problematic linking of the pre- and the postmodern that periodically surfaces in feminist and other liberatory theorizing. The linking comes up in discussions about individualism and related aspects of modern ontology that reveal similarities between feminist accounts (e.g., of personhood) and analogous accounts in premodern Europe (often tinged by anachronistic nostalgia) or in various indigenous societies (often romanticized). Feminists can end up defending themselves against charges, on the one hand, of making common cause with reactionaries or, on the other, of appropriative exoticizing. While both worries need, in particular situations, to be taken seriously, it can be instructive to focus instead on what is peculiarly distinctive about modernity, rather than allowing it to be the unquestioned background against which the similarities among premodern Europe, various indigenous societies, and present-day feminist theorizing can seem both striking and problematic.

Those similarities can, rather, throw into relief the peculiarity, in particular, of atomism and individualism, as pictures within which Eurocentric modernity is trapped. The relevant manifestation of individualism in this context concerns not subjectivity and personhood (the usual focus of discussion) but rather the ontology of reality-as-revealed-by-science, in particular the atomistic conviction that the properties and behavior of large objects *must*, at least in theory, be accounted for in terms of the properties and behavior of smaller objects that make them up. Causality, on such a view, is "from the bottom up," that is, from the smaller and simpler to the larger and more complex. Atomism so understood is a hallmark of scientific modernity; and, in this sense, biology became modern through the shift of emphasis – from organisms in their environment to cells and molecules in the laboratory – that Humphrey deplored. Biology came so late to modernity, in fact, that physics, the presumptive authority on the ultimate constituents of reality, had already abandoned the atomistic commitment that had arguably largely accounted for that authority (for a similar observation, see Woese 2004).

Neither Humphrey nor Ailsa is comfortable with the discourse of scientific modernity. While Humphrey seems trapped in the past, though, Ailsa is sailing into a brave new future. The question on which the end of the novel leaves them – and us – hanging is whether they – or we – have the resources to reach across the disciplining demands of modernity to find other ways to live. We will need to draw on a very mixed bag of humanly available resources, while recognizing that "humanly available" is far too abstract. We risk tripping over the cultural divides imposed in large measure by the very different relationships in which the specific manifestations of those resources stand to hegemonic modernity. If it is difficult for Humphrey and Ailsa to help themselves to each other's strengths – Humphrey's disciplined attentiveness to detail, Ailsa's associative imagination – how much harder is it to imagine, for example, postmodern metropolitan feminists helping ourselves to the insights of present-day traditionally grounded indigenous peoples, even – or especially – when we inhabit their ancestral homes.

If we are to imagine such a thing, it will need to be piecemeal, as particular ones of us, in particular relationships, care across various differences about particular problems, specific to those who share a place and a time and enough of a story about what matters there and then. Scientific researchers, even those most comfortable in laboratories, have important roles to play, but they can play those roles well, even by epistemic standards, only insofar as they think of themselves and the knowledge they create as framed by, and responsible to, the relationships in which, whether they recognize it or not, they are enmeshed.

6

Toward a Naturalized Narrative Bioethics

Tod Chambers

> As regards plots I find real life no help at all. Real life seems to have no plots. And as I think a plot desirable and almost necessary, I have this extra grudge against life.
>
> – Ivy Compton-Burnett

For someone trying to find a variety of details about movies, the Internet Movie Database is an exceptional resource. At this Web site one can find a film's certification, full cast and crew, production companies, trivia, external reviews, trailers, photo gallery, and writing credits. One can also find plot summaries. Interestingly some films have more than one plot summary, for the database in a manner typical of the antiauthoritarian leanings of the Internet permits anyone to add a plot summary in a film's listing. Look for example at two summaries for the film *Eternal Sunshine of the Spotless Mind* (http://www. imdb.com/title/tt0338013/plotsummary). One is written by jhailey.

A man awakes disheveled; impulsively, he skips work, heading instead to the shore. On this chilly February day, a woman in orange, hair dyed blue, chats him up: she's Clementine, he's Joel, shy and sad; by day's end, he likes her. The next night she takes him to the frozen Charles River. After, as he drops her off, she asks to sleep at his place, and she runs up to get her toothbrush. Strange things occur: their meeting was not entirely chance, they have a history neither remembers. Our seeing how the lacunae came to be and their discovery of the memory loss take the rest of the film.

Another is provided by austin4577.

This is the story of a guy, Joel (Jim Carrey), who discovers that his long-time girlfriend, Clementine (Kate Winslet), has undergone a psychiatrist's (Tom Wilkinson) experimental procedure in which all of her memory of Joel is removed, after the couple has tried for years to get their relationship working fluidly. Frustrated by the idea of still being in love with a woman who doesn't remember their time together, Joel agrees to undergo the procedure as well, to erase his memories of Clementine. The film, which takes place mostly within Joel's mind, follows his memories of Clementine backwards in time as each recent memory is replaced, and the procedure then goes on to the previous one, which is likewise seen, and then erased. Once the process starts, however, Joel realizes he doesn't really want to forget Clementine, so he starts smuggling her away into parts of his memory where she doesn't belong which alters other things about his memories as well.

These two summaries are quite different. While some overlap exists in characters and the themes of a romantic relationship and memory loss, each of the authors relates the story in a distinct way. Such divergences have been accounted for by narrative theorists as having their origin in the difference between the "basic story material" (Prince 2003, 73), or what the Russian formalists referred to as *fabula*, and the particular presentational mode used within a specific narration or *sjuzet*. So the fabula of the Hamlet story is essentially the same for William Shakespeare's *The Tragedy of Hamlet, Prince of Denmark* and for Tom Stoppard's *Rosencrantz and Guildenstern Are Dead*, but the sjuzets of the two tellings are quite different due to differing focalizations of the texts. For narrative theorists, this distinction is particularly important when analyzing narratives that rely on their rhetorical effect by playing with time sequence (as the film *Eternal Sunshine of the Spotless Mind* does). One could imagine a very different sjuzet in Hamlet in which we watch every scene in Shakespeare's telling but in reverse order. We would watch Hamlet die and then end with the appearance of the ghost. The story would have a profoundly different emotional effect as each scene reveals how we finally arrived at the tragic end. From a traditional narratological perspective, both jhailey's and austin4577's tellings share an essential fabula, and the deviations are simply the result of have differing sjuzets. In fact, this also means that the film itself is simply another sjuzet of some basic story material.

Wallace Martin (1986, 109) notes that, while conceptually such a distinction permits one to talk about the narratological rhetoric of a particular telling, it "is achieved at a certain price: it implies that what the narrator is *really* telling is a chronological story – one that the reader tries to reconstruct in the right temporal order – and that the elements of narration are deviations from a simple tale that existed beforehand." This criticism of narrative theory has been most seriously presented by Barbara Herrnstein Smith. In her oft-cited essay "Narrative Versions, Narrative Theories," Smith (1981, 212) notes that "a lingering strain of naive Platonism" has been an ongoing feature of contemporary narrative theory. Such distinctions between fabula and sjuzet encompass a belief that there is "basic story" or a "deep structure," which is "independent of any of its versions, independent of any surface manifestation or expression in any material form, mode, or medium – and thus presumably also independent of any teller or occasion of telling and therefore of any human purposes, perception, actions, or interactions": in short, there exists somewhere a versionless version. Yet, Smith counters, the attempt by narrative theorists to find the deep structure of fairy tales is itself a fairy tale. She looks, for example, at the supposed unity of the various versions that have been cited for the story Cinderella, which were at one time cataloged to having 345 variants. For Smith, our (i.e., academics') ability to find a basic story in all of these tellings simply represents the assumptions of a particular interpretive community; readers do not have an innate ability to find deep structures but rather have been educated to do so. Smith (1981, 216) notes further that even if two people share the same conventions for telling a narrative, the summaries are often themselves different depending on the performative context for the telling: "Thus, one would present a different plot summary of a given novel if one's motive were to advertise it to potential buyers or to deplore its sexism to a friend and still different if one were summarizing the novel in the course of presenting a new interpretation of it or of writing a critical biography of its author." The "basic story" of the narrative theorists is not so much a master narrative as rather a particular telling that is conditioned by the purpose of relating the narrative. Smith is not saying that there is no association between one story and another, no relation between the movie *Eternal Sunshine of the Spotless Mind* and the stories told by jhailey and austin4577 but rather that there is little evidence to believe that there is some fabula, some basic narrative structure that exists outside of particular tellings.

Arguments like Smith's may be viewed as an attempt to attack the very work of narrative theory, but I think this would be an inaccurate interpretation. Instead, it should be a call to turn away from questing for the Holy Grail of an ur-narrative and instead to turn toward the full context of actual tellings. In this vein, Ross Chambers (1984, 3) opines that narrative theorists should be attending to what in common parlance is referred to as the "point" of a story. Understanding the reason for presenting a story reveals more about the rhetoric of narrative than looking for some acontextual basic story. "Consider, for example, a 'faggot' joke told by gay people among themselves, by straight people among themselves, by a straight person to a gay person, and even, just conceivably, by a gay person to a straight person. In each of these cases, the significance of the story is determined less by its actual content than by the point of its being told, that is, the relationships mediated by the act of narration." In the end, Chambers contends that by not attending to the point of stories we miss how stories are used to do things in social life, how they function within human relationships. Scholars like Smith and Chambers seem to be advocating a move away from story structure and toward storytelling events.

It is my contention that in order to naturalize narrative medical ethics one must also attend not to stories but to storytelling, that is, to understand that stories do not exist to be "found" but are continually engaged in rhetorical work.

THE LIFE STORY FABULA AND MEDICAL ETHICS

As in literary criticism, a similar lingering strain of naive Platonism seems to reside in the use of narrative in ethics. While the strain seems considerably weaker than in the structuralist tendencies within narrative theory, a similar belief in an acontextual narrative impoverishes our understanding of how narrative actually functions in social engagements and moral reflection.

A number of moral philosophers at the end of the twentieth century came to see narrative as being an essential alternative to the seemingly impersonal nature of rule-bound Kantianism and the potential nihilism of a deconstructed and Nietzschean worldview. In *After Virtue*, Alasdair MacIntyre argued that one of the essential qualities of the human animal to function as an agent is the ability to see oneself within a story. Lacking the ability to construct such a narrative is to leave one unable to make sense of one's own actions as well as those around one, so MacIntyre (1984, 213) comes to conclude that the human agent is "not only an actor, but an author." But the most important authoring that we can do is to be able to understand our life as functioning within a narrative whole. It is only with a narrative sense of the self, that is, one that maintains some degree of cohesion over time, that the self can be considered accountable for actions in the world. Margaret Urban Walker (1998, 109–10) points out that "*narrative* understanding of the moral construction (and reconstruction) of lives is central to understanding how responsibilities are kept coherent and sustainable over substantial stretches of lives that, in important – but not imperial – ways, remain people's own." Lacking a life story, one would have what Charles Taylor refers to as the "punctual self," a person who has the capacity for self-consciousness but not anything else. This Lockean notion of the self lacks a narrative sense of being in time and thus oriented to some good. A narrative self for Taylor (1989, 48) permits an orientation within moral space that is analogous to our ability to be oriented in physical space; "we determine what we are by what we have become, by the story of how we got there."

Although she is drawn to the utility of narrative in moral understanding, Walker (1998, 120) finds the notion of a single dominant narrative as simply too all-inclusive to represent accurately our moral lives: "There are ... reasons *not* to assume that such story lines are, can be, or should be global or largely unified or strictly continuous. *Can* one imagine a totally or maximally unified life?" Such a notion Walker (1998, 121) finds to be "either desperately simple or intolerably suffocating." If Walker is concerned with the potential danger of being forced to live in a single unified story, Hilde Lindemann (H. Nelson 2001) attends to another potential danger in a narrative-based understanding of morality: unified narratives, though positive in their ability to create cohesion and meaning, can be tools for both liberation *and* oppression. With this insight, she provides a necessary corrective to MacIntyre's seemingly unreflective advocacy of narrative unity for the sake of unity. In order to provide a more sophisticated narrative-based moral philosophy, Lindemann supplies

criteria for determining if a narrative identity is morally credible or is
merely the expression of an oppressive master narrative. She sees the
construction of *counterstories* as one potential response to such master
narratives; counterstories provide narrative unity that repairs the
damage to the self caused by some prior oppressive narrative. But
Lindemann does not valorize all counterstories, for one person's
counterstories can become an oppressive master narrative to
another. While some of the case studies Lindemann draws upon are
derived from issues within bioethics – as anyone familiar with her
intellectual biography would expect – her conception of narrative
repair should be seen as part of the larger category of moral philosophy rather than being confined to bioethics; she responds primarily to moral philosophers who are generally not considered to be
medical ethicists. I note this only because the shift from narrative
ethics to narrative medical ethics entails not merely a turn to a particular application of narrative within ethics but a shift in the
grammatical form from the first to the third person.

As the use of the personal narrative was translated from moral
philosophy to the applied arena of medical ethics, the particular type
of personal narrative shifted from a concern with the autobiography
to the third-person genre of the biography. For the moral philosopher, the autobiography becomes a genre tool for responding to the
question, What is the good, what narrative am I a part of, and how
should I live my life? For medical ethicists, the biography is brought
forth to answer a different question; for the medical ethicists the
question before them is not inward toward understanding personal
authenticity but rather outward in a more Levinasian manner toward
authentically responding to the needs of another. The moral philosopher asks, What is my story? The medical ethicist asks, What is
this person's story?

To be able to find the patient's story grants the medical ethicist the
ability to use the form of narrative as a tool for guidance in recommending the most plausible next chapter or, in some instances, the
most satisfying ending in a person's life. If one thinks of a human life
as being narratologically structured – and one can make a strong
argument against this idea both morally and empirically (see
Strawson 2004) – then one has implicitly accepted the particular logic
of narrative form. Peter Rabinowitz (1998, 141–69) points out that

narrative discourse relies on a series of "rules" or "conventions," which are shared by both the teller and the audience. Whether one is "finding" the patient's story or "constructing" it, these conventions determine our expectations about how narratives hold together. One of these conventions concerns the expectation of coherence: "once done reading a text, readers usually try to tie it up in some way" (Rabinowitz 1998, 158). Even narratives that seem to lack coherence derive their power from breaking this convention and thus reinforce the importance of the convention (D. Miller 1981). The rule of coherence plays a vital role in narrative ethics, for in knowing a patient's story, one is able to see how it fits within a single narrative.

FINDING VERSUS CONSTRUCTING PATIENT BIOGRAPHIES

In 1990 the journal *Second Opinion* began a new series called Case Stories. Steven Miles and Kathryn Montgomery Hunter (1990a, 54), the editors of this series, begin by noting that because "human understanding is grounded in narrative, ethics has always been in some sense a storytelling enterprise." In a later discussion of these issues, Miles and Hunter (1990b, 62) focus on storytelling as "the substance of communication within families and between friends, lovers, doctors, and patients. Telling, hearing, and interpretively retelling stories is how people come to understand themselves and each other and appreciate their duties to one another." The first case that they select, the one that becomes a demonstration of their approach, concerns a woman who died alone in a hospital. Miles (1990, 55) begins his description by revealing his sources.

This is not a proper biography. I did not know Margaret Hull. I talked to no one who knew her, except for the brief professional contacts on the day of her death. I found her story by abstracting data from the medical record. Her "chart" took up six thick binders, describing 14 hospitalizations, 73 clinic visits, 21 emergency room visits, and innumerable laboratory reports and administrative procedures.... The lengthy collection of notes does not narrate a story. An astute medical student is the only person to record the notable onset of a potentially life-threatening cardiac dysrhythmia seven years after the fact. A nurse notes the patient's fear the night before cancer surgery. These are recorded as data, not as human history. These moments suggest the outline of a coherent story. That Margaret Hull's story was lost at the medicalized end of her life shows how alienated medical conceptions of our duties to others have become.

As Miles himself admits, there are no instances of storytelling from which he gained Hull's narrative: the data for his analysis come from chart notes, which do not "narrate a story." Yet there remains in Miles's account a belief in the existence of a particular story, a particular biography of Margaret Hull that has been lost by medicine. Like the narrative theorists' fabula, Miles envisions that all of these fragments are part of a disembodied story that lies in wait for his discovery. Miles is the teller but also from his perspective the story he tells is simply the story he finds. In the end, we see from Montgomery's final discussion of their "narrative ethics" project that it is not storytelling that interests them or guides moral reflection as much as it is the belief in a patient's "life story." Hunter (1990, 64) argues that our identity is itself the life story. She seems attentive to the way someone's story will be a particular interpretation of the events of their life, and this includes the moral problem that brings them to the attention of an ethicist, yet there lingers within her view a belief that there is a story to be found.

Howard Brody's *Stories of Sickness* also argues for a kind of life-story fabula. Brody is interested in how sickness affects a person life, and he claims that this can best be understood through the notion of a life story. He views his work as being a philosophical extension of an observation by Oliver Sacks: "If we wish to know a man, we ask 'what is his story, his real, inmost story?' for each of us *is* a biography, a story" (as quoted in Brody 1987, xi). Brody criticizes analytical philosophers for believing that they can talk meaningfully about human identity by examining "time-slices" of a person's life. This chopping, for Brody, is an inaccurate representation of our life world and thus provides little assistance in understanding human action. In contrast to this, Brody (1987, 44) proposes that narrative is the "fundamental observable" quality of human life, and thus "a time-slice is an abstraction from the more basic entity of the entire life narrative." Medical ethics can benefit from a life narrative perspective by attending to "the portion of the usual human life history one is considering."

Brody's understanding of the life narrative is indebted to MacIntyre. And narrative for MacIntyre (1984, 211) exists outside of human construction: "Narrative is not the work of poets, dramatists and novelists reflecting upon events which had no narrative order before one was imposed by the singer or the writer; narrative form is neither disguise nor decoration." In her discussion of MacIntyre's approach, Lindemann (H. Nelson 2001, 62) argues that MacIntyre fundamentally misunderstands "what a story is," that is, it is constructed "by selecting incidents and themes from the minutiae of our existence and explaining their importance by how we represent them in narrative form. Autobiography, then, isn't life." And neither is biography. MacIntyre (1984, 212) is aware that there can be opposition to his position, and he quotes Louis O. Mink: "Stories are not lived but told. Life has no beginnings, middles, or ends; there are meetings but the start of an affair belongs to the story we tell ourselves later, and there are partings, but final partings only in the story." MacIntyre responds by noting that the fact that there is death demonstrates that life naturally has a narrative ending. It is difficult, however, to see the event of the end of life as the same thing as being the end of a narrative. MacIntyre (1984, 212–13) has an even more difficult time justifying how life has genres outside of a particular telling and responds by discussing the various versions of the life of Thomas Becket:

In some of the medieval versions, Thomas's career is presented in terms of the canons of medieval hagiography. In the Icelandic *Thomas Saga* he is presented as a saga hero. In Dom David Knowles's modern biography the story is a tragedy, the tragic relationship of Thomas and Henry II.... Now it clearly makes sense to ask who is right? ... The answers appears to be clearly the last. The true genre of the life is neither hagiography nor saga, but tragedy.

And thus ends MacIntyre's argument for the true genre of the Thomas story. It seems to MacIntyre simply self-evident what its true genre is. The genre of Thomas is not a particular cultural convention nor is understanding it as tragedy the result of human construction, and for MacIntyre this "clearly makes sense." In his own analysis of the Becket affair, Victor Turner (1974, 69) found the Icelandic saga as particularly helpful in allowing him to see "the fatalistic quality of Becket's relationship to Henry, its social historical dimension, so to speak, while the other histories dwelt in the main on Becket's freely making the choices which placed him in his final predicament." So what is self-evidently a tragedy to MacIntyre is for Turner self-evidently a saga.

NATURAL VERSUS INSTITUTIONALIZED STORYTELLING

Within conventional storytelling activities, are the genres of biographies and autobiographies natural forms of storytelling? I am using "natural" here not in opposition to unnatural storytelling but rather as the social linguist William Labov and the narratologist Monika Fludernik use it, in opposition to storytelling that is nonspontaneous, highly framed, and stylized. Fludernik (1996, 12) observes, "It is from this angle that some cognitive parameters can be regarded as 'natural' in the sense of 'naturally occurring' or 'constitutive of prototypical human experience.'" While it may seem that the concept of natural narratives encompasses all forms of oral storytelling, Fludernik confines the notion to "spontaneous conversational storytelling," which is distinct from formal oral telling genres such as folktales and oral poetry; these oral genres "constitute a more literary (i.e. institutionalized) form of storytelling" and thus they depend upon "different kinds of competence and performance levels from those sufficient for everyday spontaneous conversation." Fludernik submits a basic typology of storytelling that differentiates the spontaneous form from its institutionalized sibling. She identifies three genres of natural narratives (experiential conversational storytelling, narrative report, and jokes/anecdotes) and three nonspontaneous types (folkloristic oral storytelling, epic poetry, and life story). The fact that she categorizes the life story as an institutionalized form of narrative – and thus one that is not a natural form – should be of particular interest to those who wish to use narrative in the analysis of moral issues.

Fludernik begins her discussion of the life story by noting that it can occur during "spontaneous conversation," but her Norman Rockwell–like parenthetical example, "('Granny, I've always wanted to ask you what happened to you during the war'),' seems to actually demonstrate what an odd concept this is. It is clearly not an example of autobiography but instead a type of memoir. Even in instances in which the life story is given a very distinct institutionalized form, as for instance the common activity in Alcoholics Anonymous of telling one's story, it is the experience of recovery that becomes the fulcrum that gives structure to the storytelling event. Fludernik notes that the most common form of the life-story genre occurs in the very non-spontaneous genre of the ethnographic fieldworker trying to "collect" oral histories. Fludernik (1996, 59–60) admits that "the life story obviously is no complete autobiography. Very rarely indeed is there a situation in which people will be led to narrate their entire life from their birth to the present moment." Instead it is the academic that creates a genre that in some manner pretends to be an example of a spontaneous storytelling genre. Even in instances in which eth-nographers argue for storytelling as an essential part of individual and communal identity, the life story is not ever shown to be part of the life of any particular individuals in the community. In her eth-nography of elderly Jews in California, Barbara Myerhoff (1978, 34) presents transcriptions of personal storytelling events but these events were not spontaneous, for the "Living History" events were the creation of Myerhoff herself as a means to collect stories, which she argues are a spontaneous part of their lives.

Walter Ong argues that the kind of storytelling that promotes the ordinary everyday life story arrives with the transformation from an oral to a literary culture. In a primary oral culture, story characters are normally "heavy characters" or, to use E. M. Forster's (1985, 67, 69) term, "flat characters." Such characters are "constructed round a single idea or quality" and thus "are easily remembered" after the tale is told. The reason for these relatively simplistic characteriza-tions is for Ong (1982, 70) the result of an essential need within oral storytelling to work as a mnemonic, for "colorless personalities cannot survive oral mnemonics." It is with the advent of the tech-nology of writing that the human animal is able to be relieved of the needs of memory to pass on knowledge through stories. Eventually we put aside these heavies and develop narratives that feature "the ordinary human life world," of an Emma, a Mrs. Dalloway, a Lucky Jim, or, Ong's own example, a Rabbit Angstrom. There are simply extraordinarily few social events in which one is asked to tell one's life story. Partly this is because storytelling entails an extended break in a conversation. All communication events involve what sociolinguists refer to as turn constructional units (TCU), that is, we take turns during the conversation. Mary Louis Pratt (1977) observes that storytelling entails being permitted to take a particularly long turn in the conversation and thus is a contractual agreement between the teller and the listener(s) that what is being related is worth the extended TCU. But to respond to the inquiry, Tell me about yourself, by telling one's life story would be a bit like responding to the casual inquiry, How are you? with an actual detailed account of one's state of being rather than simply responding, Hi, how are you? While natural storytelling would entail a break in conversation, the TCU would normally be permitted only for an anecdote, not for the life story. Novels, themselves virtual requests for an extended TCU, often provide an imagined encounter in which there is a fictionalized narratee. For instance, in the first line of *The Catcher in the Rye*, J. D. Salinger plays with both the kind of narratee that the actual reader is expected to take on and the expectations that come with these narrations: "If you really want to hear about it, the first thing you'll probably want to know is where I was born and what my lousy childhood was like, and how my parents were occupied and all before they had me, and all that David Copperfield kind of crap, but I don't feel like going into it, if you want to know the truth."

Even MacIntyre (1999, 75), for all his insistence on the importance of a life story, seems unable to muster much of a narrative when asked in an interview to reveal "What would you emphasize in your own narrative?" While his answer is longer than an introduction given for a person prior to a public lecture, the two pages of text seem to be a relatively thin story. When the interviewer asks, "Have you any plans to write an autobiography?" MacIntyre interestingly responds, "Answering the previous question has already stretched my autobiographical powers to their limit" (77). This seems an odd remark but an utterly true one, for few of us have the skill necessary to do the very act of self-storying that MacIntyre thinks is required in order to live a fulfilled life. MacIntyre finishes his answer by observing, "To write a worthwhile autobiography you need either the wisdom of an Augustine or the shamelessness of a Rousseau or the confidence in one's own self-knowledge of a Collingwood" (77) and he then admits that he lacks all three talents . This final statement is also interesting for the way MacIntyre qualifies his answer. Anyone could probably write an autobiography but to write one *worthwhile* seems to entail special skills. I suspect that what MacIntyre means by worthwhile is that it would be worth someone else's time to read it. In this, MacIntyre acknowledges something that he pays little attention to in his discussion of the importance of the life story; one does not merely tell stories but, like philosophical trees in forests, there always must be an audience for the story to exist. While many may keep journals or diaries, I doubt many people write autobiographies without an intended audience outside the self. In other words, life stories should be viewed as performative events that always involve an act of communication between people.

HUNTING FOR A NATURAL NARRATIVE MEDICAL ETHICS

In *The Wounded Storyteller*, Arthur Frank comes closest to analyzing a natural narrative medical ethics. Frank has been critical of how bioethicists, including those interested in attending to narrative, continually attend primarily to the stories of health care professionals rather than to patients. We have an ethical obligation, according to Frank, to listen to these illness stories. Frank (1995, 53–54) sees illness as itself a "call for stories." He means this in two ways. First, becoming ill demands that one re-create one's self-story, which can be profoundly damaged by the onset of the illness. Second, ill persons are literally asked to engage in storytelling by the people around them. "Stories of the illness have to be told to medical workers, health bureaucrats, employers and work associates, family and friends. Whether ill people want to tell stories or not, illness calls for stories." Frank (1995, 54) recalls how, when he had an abnormal chest X-ray, he had on one day to tell "a version of my illness story eight times." Frank's analysis focuses primarily on the institutionalized storytelling of the memoir and the autobiography, which tend to be sites for narrative self-repair, rather than natural storytelling events. Yet Frank (1995, 158, 159) is keenly attuned to the performative dimensions of storytelling, and this can be seen in his notion of a narrative ethic that focuses on "thinking with stories," which entails "allowing one's own thoughts to adopt the story's immanent logic of causality, its temporality, and its narrative tensions." For Frank, this process "requires attending to how a story is *used* on different occasions of its telling." Stories are not merely told but retold, and in a Heraclitean manner one can never tell the same story twice.

A naturalized narrative ethics attends to the use of stories as a rhetorical tool rather than simply as part of a general life story. In order to reveal the rhetorical features of storytelling within medical ethics, one must attend to Ross Chambers's (1984) question of what is the point of telling the story. One must guard against the desire to create a single unitary narrative out of the storytelling performances and instead keep the storytelling grounded in its rhetorical situation. A good model for this can be seen in a study of storytelling in eastern Texas. Folklorist Richard Bauman (1986, 5–6) came to conclude that not only can narratives be an instrument for knowing but they can also be "an instrument for obscuring, hedging, confusing, exploring, or questioning what went on, that is, for keeping the coherence or comprehensibility of narrated events open to question." The types of storytelling Bauman examined in Texas were not only the type that permits, in Walter Benjamin's (1968, 83) words, "the ability to exchange experiences" but also the type that allows the teller to shape the experience of others, and this shaping could take place as much by concealing reality as revealing it. In his observations on the negotiations for trading hunting hounds, Bauman reveals that the storytelling often does not "fall into clear-cut categories of factual and fictional, truthful and lying, believable and incredible." Instead, both sides are aware that the storytelling functions as a rhetorical tool in the trade, and thus both people involved in the trade remain heedful of the rhetorical power of the storytelling event: "Any man who keeps more'n one hound'll lie to you."

From these studies, Bauman argues for an approach to story-telling that attends not merely to the narrative told but also to the event of narration. He cites the sociologist Erving Goffman's observation that "when individuals attend to any current situation, they face the question: 'What is it that's going on here?'" (Goffman et al. 1997, 153). During a storytelling event, Bauman (1986, 6) argues, a second question becomes layered upon that initial question, one that concerns the narrative told: "What is it that's going on there?" It is this relationship between the two that gives a narrative its rhetorical power. Without attending to the relationship between the two stories, one can find oneself like David in the second book of Samuel, who listens to a story told by the prophet Samuel and is trapped because he does not see that the relationship between the narrated event and the narrative event concern his own misconduct.

Medical ethicists interested in using a narrative approach tend to try to combine all the small, natural narratives into a single master narrative. They tend to see the true narrative as simply "out there" waiting to be found and collected rather than as entangled within social events. Perhaps the most vivid examples of this tendency to construct rhetorically charged master narratives can be found in those highly publicized cases that involved decision making and incompetent patients. In *When Illness Goes Public*, Barron Lerner traces the variety of narrative constructions surrounding the Libby Zion case. Lerner (2006, 201–21) reveals how Zion's life was continually refashioned in different ways to promote a particular view of the events. In a similar way, Terri Schiavo's life became the subject of a number of master narratives "uncovered" by politicians, disability activists, bioethicists, family members, lawyers, and conservative Christians. Each of these expressions of "Terri's story" was a rhetorical move to sway decision making. By contrast, a naturalized narrative ethics reminds us to see these events within social politics, whether the large national politics of Schiavo or the small hospital politics in Miles's Margaret Hull. One can never step outside of a particular storytelling event in order to provide a Platonic version of any of their stories. It is not merely that there is no Nagelian view from nowhere but that there also cannot be a telling without a performative context. Each telling becomes entangled with the social dynamics of the particular place and time. When Miles analyzes the chart notes in Hull's story, for example, he fails to view the chart within its performative context of the clinic. Each note is a micronarrative and the point of each of the tellings can be at times epistemological, legal, declarative, or managerial; in other words, every chart note should be understood as a distinct speech act.

A naturalized narrative ethics must not simply attend to the story but ask questions that concern the relationship between the narrative event and the narrated event, that is, reveal the rhetoric of the telling. Who told the story? When was the story told? Where was it told? What was the conversational frame in which the story was evoked? Is this a counterstory? To whom was it told? What was the teller trying to do with this story? Has this story been told before? Does this story relate to other storytelling events? By answering these questions, we can begin to thwart any attempt at the construction of a single narrative and instead keep the stories embedded in the ongoing social life of the people involved in the medical decision. Doing this forces us not only to notice how stories are naturally evoked in medical ethics decisions but also to attend to the power struggles within that decision making. When medical ethicists construct the patient's story, they are themselves simply another part of this ongoing exchange of stories, for they are also engaging in a rhetorical move that tries through a storytelling performance to alter the shape of the decisions. Only by moving from a concern with stories to an integration of storytelling can we naturalize narrative medical ethics.

II

RESPONSIBLE PRACTICE

7

Motivating Health

Empathy and the Normative Activity of Coping

Jodi Halpern and Margaret Olivia Little

Despite an explosion of research demonstrating the substantial health gains that can be made by shifting certain choices – in what we eat, in how (or whether) we exercise, in whether we smoke or follow through on medication regimes – progress on improving health-affecting behaviors has been less satisfactory than hoped for. In particular, there has been a frustrating gap between raising patients' awareness of the health risks certain behaviors carry and conveying such risks in a way that actually motivates a change in behavior. Too often, even when clinicians and other health educators provide clear, realistic, and repeated information about effective methods of risk reduction, people behave in ways that ignore or worsen those risks. Extensive communication campaigns about the risks of obesity, for instance, have done little to stem the tide of morbid obesity (Morrill and Chinn 2004). People often underreact to daily or cumulative threats, such as those of heart disease (Holtgrave et al. 1995; Hart 2005), even as they overreact to dramatic but less threatening events like the shortage of influenza vaccine (Slovic et al. 1990; Snowbeck 2004). And when a frightening event does occur, such as feeling a worrisome breast lump or chest pain that might signal a heart attack, people can become paralyzed by anxiety rather than seeking care (Schoenberg et al. 2003; Sanders 2003).

Given these challenges, researchers have been hard at work to identify more effective ways of communicating health information and to develop, more broadly, an empirically grounded account of human motivation and agency. One of the most vibrant and influential arenas of such research is the field of risk communication, which aims to identify factors that impede and those that facilitate people's ability to absorb and be motivated by information about risks, including risks to their health (Glik 2007; Leventhal et al. 2008). Researchers have already identified a wealth of factors – psychological, physical, and social – that influence how people understand and respond to information about risks to their health and have proposed frameworks for understanding how people act in response to risk information.

Important as this work has been, we believe that it has also been hindered in a crucial way. Attempting to develop a model of agency based in and reflective of factual data, the field's empirical research is mediated by a theoretical model of agency that, for all its ubiquity in the social sciences and philosophy, is deeply flawed. Reliance on its premises, we believe, can lead clinicians to misdiagnose the bases of recalcitrant health behavior, to shift too readily into a managerial or "design" stance toward those who exhibit such behavior, and, most importantly, to miss potent tools for changing health behaviors. Some of the barriers to helping people change toward healthier behavior can be traced to this impoverished view of agency, one that the field of risk communication itself promulgates.

In this chapter, we articulate what we believe to be a missing piece in even progressive models of risk communication. At the core of human motivation, we believe, is the normative activity of *coping* – of maintaining a sense of self and world as meaningful, stable, and secure. Understood properly, this activity is as deserving of respect and assistance as are the activities of theoretical and practical reason. Shifting to this richer picture of agency, we believe, helps us to understand why empathy is a key, indeed indispensable, tool to motivate behavioral change – and to motivate it in a way that promotes respect for the humanity and individuality of people while refraining from a judgmental approach to improving health (Fitzgerald 1994).

THE LIMITS OF RISK COMMUNICATION

Over the past fifty years, advances in the treatment of infectious diseases have greatly expanded life expectancy in developed countries. Efforts at further improving health in these countries now increasingly focus on changing certain behaviors – dietary indiscretion, lack of exercise, smoking, alcoholism, and other substance dependences – that are major contributors to heart disease, diabetes, and cancers. This shift has been matched by an increasing appreciation of patients as stewards of their own health and agents who deserve information to safeguard that health (Bandura 1998; Ory et al. 2002). Together, these developments have increased emphasis on the importance of informational health campaigns: if only, it seemed, people could be adequately informed about health risks, they would take the steps rationally indicated for improving the selected health outcomes. Clinicians have increasingly been urged to regard their role as one of *health educator*: to see the scope of their job as extending not just to diagnosing illness and dispensing medicine but to engaging actively in conversations with patients about their habits in order to encourage behavioral changes (Haynes et al. 2002; Leventhal et al. 2008).

Motivating people to change unhealthy behaviors is thus one of the current linchpins of efforts at improving health. It is also one of the most challenging. As any physician can attest, getting people to follow through on these recommendations – to exercise, say, or to perform their monthly breast exams – can be enormously difficult. Convincing patients to change their diets is a challenge, even when they understand the ways that diet directly affects their health (Durose et al. 2004). Counseling often fails to influence people to continue taking medications to manage high blood pressure or asthma (Horne 2006; Proulx et al. 2007). When it comes to actually influencing people's daily habits, health education goes only so far.

Of the various barriers to changing health behaviors, the three following examples are noteworthy. First, medical recommendations are sometimes ill matched with the concrete social and material constraints faced by various patients. Urging condom use when it will lead to social rejection is untenable. Educating people about the importance of adding fruits and vegetables to their diets is of little help in neighborhoods that lack grocery stores. The exhortation to leave an abusive relationship offers little to women who cannot afford to raise their children or who cannot escape their abusers in the long run.

Second, classical approaches of "inform and exhort" tended to operate on the assumption that people agree on and value to the same degree the heterogeneous thing we call health. As various groups gained voice in public dialogue, though, disparities became evident – for example, women differ on what matters most to them in reproductive and delivery contexts, and members of the deaf community differ on the prospect of cochlear implants (Lane and Bahan 1998; Hyde and Power 2006). Public agendas are not always private ones; the priorities of medical practice guidelines do not always capture what matters most to individual people in their own lives (Halpern 1995).

Third, dramatic empirical evidence began to challenge the informational model of risk communication. In a variety of well-documented areas, from dietary- and exercise-related behavior to substance use, emergency preparedness, sexual practices, and more, multiple channels of empirical research show that emotional factors are crucial in people's ability to absorb information and then to act on such information (Covello et al. 2001; McComas 2006; Leventhal et al. 2008). Research on risk perception has identified a number of major psychological factors that influence how emotionally threatening a person finds risk information, and how likely a person is to accept the communication as valid in the first place. To give just a few examples, people tend to have an exaggerated perception of threat when they see a risk as unfamiliar, out of their own control, irreversible, inequitable, poorly understood, uncertain, or caused by human actions rather than nature (Covello et al. 2001). People less readily accept risk information as valid when they do not trust the institutions conveying the information, when they are told they are personally and directly in harm's way, when the risk is perceived to be ethically objectionable, and when there are identifiable victims; people are also resistant more generally when the risk communication evokes fear, terror, or anxiety (Covello et al. 2001). Indeed, in conditions of distrust and skepticism, people can be frightened by information even as they seem not to believe or act upon it (Slovic 2000; Elder et al. 2007). Simply *believing* risk information, much less deploying it, is already a highly complex emotional process subject to variegated human motives and vulnerabilities. In short, "add information and stir" does not always work – and can be counterproductive.

As awareness of these limitations has grown, several innovations have been put into practice. Acknowledging the social and material constraints faced by various groups, clinicians are increasingly advised to focus more on providing information that people can actually use in their daily lives. This approach includes emphasizing incremental but realistic interventions, such as taking a walk after dinner, rather than ambitious but unworkable ones, such as joining an expensive gym. Further, clinicians are reminded to attend to patient's individual goals and familial and cultural practices so that the health that is aimed for is in accord with the person's contextualized values.

Even more dramatically, models of risk communication began to move away from simply providing information and toward addressing the emotional conditions necessary for absorbing that information. The health communication literature now contains an increasing appreciation of the need to do qualitative research to identify emotional aspects of communication, such as a communities' "rituals" for confirming whether risk information is believable, and the factors that influence people's sense of control, worry, outrage, dread, and perceived benefits of intervention (Kreps et al. 2005). Additional research urges the need to minimize negative emotional factors, such as fear, and to maximize positive emotional factors, such as perceived benefit or sense of fairness (Covello et al. 2001). Indeed, one of the central-most arenas of risk communication research is now directed toward identifying emotional factors in behavior modification.

As important as each of these steps has been, they have also brought in their wake certain unfortunate tendencies. For one thing, as important as it has been to acknowledge the social and material constraints faced by various populations, doing so has brought with it a tendency on the part of some to construe members of those groups as passive victims. Addiction and burnout, not to mention the material constraints of poverty, are all real phenomena, but construing people as victims can carry a fatalistic and disempowering message. For example, while there are important social findings behind the term "learned helplessness," the term itself is felt by some to be disrespectful and can ultimately reify systemic problems and project them onto disadvantaged social groups.

Further, as important as it has been to acknowledge a diversity of values relevant to health interventions, there has been a tendency by some progressives to an unfortunate form of cultural relativism. In an attempt not to repeat the top-down errors of the classical model, some have urged that the way to avoid threatening people's self-esteem is to avoid judging anyone: all behaviors make sense from each person's perspective, no one acts badly. Such an approach is crude at best. For one thing, there is a limit to the moral tolerance appropriate to others' behaviors: if drug use is overly stigmatized, the cost of severe drug addiction to individuals, families, and communities is all too real. Further, while educators need to genuinely attend to cultural factors, superficial attempts to instill "cultural competency" can lead insensitive clinicians to take predetermined views of patients based on demographic categories that ignore the nuance of individual differences (Tervalon and Murray-Garcia 1998; Hunt and de Voogd 2005).

More deeply, if more abstractly, this form of relativism purchases acceptance at the price of *distance*. It is a form of interaction that highlights – and stops at – our separateness, rather than attempting to uncover common elements of humanity that may be present in another's choices and behaviors. Knee-jerk dismissals of others' unhealthy behaviors as expressing "their" values can end up regarding "them" as very separate human beings from "us." In the end, this form of disidentification can prevent the alliance building and trust necessary for effective communication.

Finally, while it has been crucial to acknowledge the limits of informational models of communication, doing so has brought with it a steep price in respect. Clinicians desperate to save their patients' lives and promote health often find themselves frustrated and uncomprehending when confronted with behaviors that seem to defy these goals (Halpern 2007). People's choices thus become difficult to respect, and risk communication becomes seen as the tricky business of trying to circumvent the disruptions that interfere with rationality, rather than facilitating rationality's efforts. This can shade into a tendency to regard others as objects to be manipulated rather than agents to be respected.

Progress notwithstanding, contemporary models of health risk communication are marked by certain limiting tendencies. When faced with health-compromising behavior that is recalcitrant in the face of information and advice, the options are stark: there is either a victim to be pitied, an unfamiliar value to be deferred to, or a population to be beneficently "managed" rather than normatively engaged. None of them, we would argue, are approaches well placed to empower or to maintain respect for those being served.

RETHINKING THE MODEL OF AGENCY

We believe that these tendencies can be traced to a common source, a particular model of agency and motivation. Underlying most empirical work in motivation is a model of agency so familiar that its influence is hard to overstate. It is a theory common to the social sciences; more than that, it is a picture tacitly assumed by analytic philosophy.[1] Put broadly enough, all will agree that agency is an enterprise of setting and achieving ends. According to the usual model, though, that enterprise is understood in a very specific way: agents are decision makers whose task is to make changes in the world – acting causally to bring about the states of affairs their goals represent – by deploying the twin faculties of *practical* and *theoretical reason*. Each of these faculties is governed by its own set of norms, defined by its relevant "direction of fit": beliefs aim at matching themselves to the world, while desires aim, as it were, to make the world match their content.[2] If all is working well, practical reason picks out appropriate ends, theoretical reason identifies accurate means to their achievement, and motivational energy travels unimpeded toward those means.

Of course, as the model emphasizes, there are a number of ways these two activities can go awry, yielding results the agent herself would acknowledge as poor. Theoretical reason can suffer from framing biases, perceptual illusions, and errors in calculative reasoning. Practical reason can suffer from obtuseness (in which ends endorsed by the agent are not noticed as implicated in a choice) as well as lack of will power. Emotions in particular, the model emphasizes, are a significant source of these various distortions.

---

[1] A few analytic philosophers, especially those in the feminist tradition, have also pressed on the limits of this approach. See, for instance, Mackenzie and Stoljar 2000. For an excellent psychological treatise on the need for others' help in sustaining agency, see Fels 2005.

[2] The locus classicus is Anscombe 1957, 56.

They are a particularly powerful (because particularly primitive) instance of the sort of mental perturbation that gets in the way of sensible action. Emotions cloud perception, distort reasoning, and tempt the will to decide against its own considered values.

When faced with such errors, there are several things we can do, according to the model, to help right matters. When faced with ignorance of the facts, we educate (trans fats are more unhealthy than saturated fats); when faced with calculative mistakes and framing biases, we make explicit the proper inference (the risks of not wearing a seat belt are greater than those of flying); when faced with constricted values, we try to persuade that different ends are worth adopting (having a body weight appropriate to one's body frame rather than to fashion runways); when faced with obtuseness, we remind people of ends they already accept but have not noticed as presently salient (taking your hypertension medicine will help you to be around for your children); when faced with a lack of will power, we look to negative and positive reinforcements.

If none of these methods work, it is time to throw in the normative towel, so to speak. The person is revealed as one for whom normative engagement, at least on the present issue, will not work, and methods of help shift to "managerial" modes in which causal levers of influence are identified and deployed. Until then, though, the job of those who seek to help is to inform, reveal framing biases, correct calculative errors, remind of important ends, cheerlead, scold, and offer incentives.

Yet a deeper picture of the sort of creatures we are suggests that this account of agency is deeply incomplete. For there is *another* normative enterprise at the heart of human agency. Key to being a human self, rather than merely a knower of facts or pursuer of ends, is maintaining a certain subjective reality – a sense of oneself as relatively intact and secure and of one's world as relatively safe and familiar. The self as a self does not come already made; we need to work to achieve it. Being complex, this project involves several core elements: to have a felt sense of self-continuity; to maintain an understanding of oneself as effective and worthwhile; to sustain attachments to others; to have a sense of one's own social world as familiar and understandable (Deigh 1983; Bandura 1998). In order even to be able to set new ends and investigate the world, we must have a sense of wholeness and familiarity, a sense of self as at least minimally continuous, of the world as at least minimally secure, of others as at least minimally connected to us.

This is the *existential enterprise*: of feeling secure and at home in a world with others. Yet this project of maintaining a meaningful and secure sense of self and world is, as it were, always up against something. Mortality, the onslaught of loss, the possibilities and realities of immense suffering – all of these are threats inherent in the lives of creatures like us. If it is a task to achieve a sense of self as whole and world as home, it is also a task to sustain it. A key project of agency, it turns out, is the task of maintaining and sustaining a sense of wholeness and familiarity when confronted with threat.

This is the activity of coping: of finding, maintaining, and recovering a sense of security and meaning in a universe full of loss. Such an activity is foundational to how human beings learn, reason, adjust, grieve, and aspire. It is also normative, fundamentally teleological. If its norms are to be consistent with the facts, they are not aimed at gathering the facts; if its norms are to be consistent with the ability to set and achieve goals, they are not aimed at altering the world. Rather, coping has a normative structure and telos of its own, oriented, ideally, toward meaningful connection and security in oneself.

As with any normative enterprise, one can do well or badly by it. To cope well is to maintain a secure sense of self and world in a manner consistent with realism and psychological growth over the life-span. Thus, just as the enterprises of theoretical and practical reason can go awry, so too can this one. We can do a better or worse job at structuring our subjective reality – we can compose it in a way that is consistent with genuine growth and maturity or we can regress and use old defense mechanisms under stress.

What does it look like when coping goes awry? When the going gets tough, when matters get complex enough relative to a person's developed capacities, distortions and blunders can arise. The system breaks down, and people meet their need for psychological security in ways that are not consistent with the facts or their broader interests. Thus, we can be motivated to maintain a belief that all is well, even if it is not, rather than reducing actual danger. We might practice denial, in which one refuses to countenance a belief in the face of evidence. Indeed, the need for felt security can act as an

informational gatekeeper, affecting whether one can take in information in the first place, much less process and act upon it in an
integrated way. Or, again, we can practice "magical thinking," in
which we project onto reality that which we would like to be the case.
Or we might practice avoidance, in which not just real situations, but
even frightening ideas are kept out of awareness. These are just some
of the ways in which the self sometimes maintains a subjective sense
of security at the expense of its more objective well-being – at the
expense of health, physical safety, genuine intimacy.

Just as with theoretical and practical reason, if things get bad
enough, we can shift from normative engagement to a managerial or
design stance. A point will come when we need to work around the
capacity rather than facilitate its exercise. At other times, these tendencies toward denial and the like can be recognized as the missteps
of a capacity that is fundamentally intact but vulnerable to blunder.
We need a little help. If people exhibit poor choices and are recalcitrant to information, advice, and cheerleading, agency need not be
absent, any more than a mathematical error means that theoretical
reason has broken down. It may mean that they need others' help to
strengthen their ability to cope.[3]

FOSTERING COPING

If this claim is of general importance, it is of crucial relevance to the
task of risk communication. For risk communication by its *nature*
deals with information that is threatening. Such information is
essentially, not incidentally, threatening: the tacit speech act of risk
communication is, "Watch out!" Even if a particular individual does

---

[3] In our view, the philosopher's notion of *akrasia*, or weak will, is revealed as a
heterogeneous phenomenon. As classically defined, akrasia occurs when agents
choose an immediate pleasure (such as that second piece of cake) over goals (such as
weight management) that they themselves would endorse as more important. Weak
will is complicated, but there are two very different etiologies of such a phenomenon
(and hence two very different classes of strategies to counter it): one is a breakdown
in the motivational energy of practical reason, in which energy is too diffused or
low; here cheerleading, or discipline, or the distraction of a different and more
productive immediate pleasure can all help. But sometimes the gap is due to a
positive resistance produced by an (ill-advised) way of maintaining one's sense of self
and security. This can be addressed not by cheerleading or discipline but only by
methods adequate to the fundamental telos and logical structure of coping itself.

not feel scared by the information, the information conveys the possibility of some threat to her person or her home (including cared-for others) in the world; risk information hence has the potential to shake up people's organized adaptive or defensive view of the world. Unless people are helped to tolerate and integrate the information in a way that allows them to maintain, or regain, self-efficacy and a feeling of being at home in the world, efforts at health modifications will not work.

Take, for instance, the task of delivering bad news. We know that when people are severely threatened, they have a very hard time hearing or believing bad news, never mind integrating it or changing their behavior accordingly. Thus, caring clinicians learn to convey bad news, such as a loved one's sudden death, in bite-size chunks: "Your sister was in a car accident. It was a very serious one. She was very badly injured when she came to the hospital. We did everything we could do to help her but she was hurt too badly. I have something very, very sad to tell you. [pause] We could not save her life." The point in doling out the information slowly is not that it is *cognitively* hard to process, like some complex math equation. Rather, the point is to help the person take in the news in a way that allows her psychological edifice to gradually shift rather than be radically displaced. If the proposition "Your sister is dead" is easily stated, its implications for a person's place in the world are enormous. Incremental statements can help the person make a very initial start at a transition from a world in which her sister is alive and well to one in which her sister is dead.

Or consider motivation. We know that trying to motivate people with brute appeals to fear ("If you keep smoking, you will die") is often counterproductive. The psychological need to maintain a sense of self and home is an urgent one. Thus frightening risk communication can precipitate a conflict between the need to soothe oneself by denying, ignoring, or disbelieving the information, on the one hand, and the practical need to take in the information and take action to protect oneself, on the other. Especially when the frightening message is about a danger that is diffuse and distant, or when the fear is presented without help in tolerating it, this can exacerbate unhelpful denial rather than cause people to take useful steps to prevent the harm in question.

The message is clear: to be effective, risk communication needs to be in synchrony with the fundamental task of coping. Only when this is true are people situated in such a way that interventions aimed at giving them more traditional motivational tools – pep talks, incentives, habit reminders, and the like – make sense.

Yet, ironically, the need to maintain a sense of self and home is often undermined by standard attempts at risk communication. Take the example of obesity. Increasing attempts to emphasize the medical risks of morbid obesity have all produced frustrating results. Considered in the light of what we have said about coping, though, such results make eminent sense. Overweight people experience negative messages from others, diminishing their sense of self-worth, and are often socially ostracized, threatening their sense of at-homeness in the world. Given the urgent need for security in oneself and a place in the world as preconditions to self-efficacy and agency, asking such people to take difficult measures to lose weight essentially places them in a catch-22 position, in which they need to feel self-love and acceptance *now* if they're to effect the changes needed to lose weight, but feel they must lose weight *before* they are worthy of love and a meaningful place in society.

In contrast, consider the "Healthy at Every Size" project (Bacon et al. 2005), a radically different approach to health in the face of obesity. It seeks to help obese women feel more secure in being how they are right now as a basis for motivating a healthier life-style. To do this unequivocally, the program avoids any goal of weight loss or of restricting the enjoyment of food, focusing instead on messages of self-care. The results of the program included improved blood pressure, blood lipids, and exercise tolerance – thus the enduring reduction of major cardiac risk factors.

When health communicators convey threats, the information has to interplay with, and ride atop, people's ongoing task of maintaining a sense of self and security in the world. If information arises that confronts that existential edifice, that information and its practical import can be absorbed and again helpfully deployed only if given in ways that allow the subject to incorporate it or productively shift that edifice. We believe, indeed, that this message is at the core of sound health communication: good risk communication must *foster coping*. How? As psychologists have noted, there are several methods for fostering coping in others, including humor and use of narrative. One particular mechanism, however, deserves emphasis. We want to defend the importance of *empathy*, already known but underplayed in the literature, as means to empower agency in the face of threat.

THE POWER OF EMPATHY

As we use the term, empathy is the use of one's *imagination* and *emotional resonance* to try to picture as much as possible what another person is experiencing in order to understand them with greater depth (Halpern 2001). Defined in this way, empathy is hence distinct from caring and sympathy. Although caring and sympathy involve resonating with others emotionally and feeling motivated to help them, they do not necessarily involve a curiosity to learn more about what exactly those others are going through. In contrast, such curiosity is central to empathy. More specifically, it is a curiosity about what the situation looks and feels like from the perspective of someone inside the situation. This is quite distinct from observing or thinking *about* the other person's moods and observing them from the outside, as it were. Indeed, while empathizing, one is not necessarily even thinking about the other person from some third-person point of view. In empathizing with a patient with anorexia, for example, a therapist may momentarily take on the patient's view of food as threatening, imagining what it feels like to avoid eating at all costs, temporarily setting aside her own professional view of the patient as ill and desperately in need of food. We might describe this as a shift from a third-person observer looking at another person to a quasi-first-person perspective looking at the world through the person's eyes.

The power of empathy in clinical health communication is strongly documented. Research in medicine on giving serious cancer diagnoses, for instance, has shown that the caregiver's empathy has a profound impact on the patient's and family's responses upon hearing the diagnosis (Ptacek and Eberhardt 1996; Ptacek and Ptacek 2001). Patients whose physicians empathized with them were able to take steps to seek treatment and support sooner than others and showed better self-efficacy and agency in response to a frightening, uncertain situation. Years later, patients and families remember feeling more hopeful and better able to cope, because they felt truly accompanied by their doctors.

Empathy, it is clear, can help people tolerate, absorb, and respond agentially to threatening news. But more specifically, empathy can help motivate people who are having difficulty taking steps to protect their own health despite having received clear information and been given opportunities to change. When faced with recalcitrant health-compromising behaviors, the salient task involves empathizing, not just with the person but with the *dilemma* that can drive the person's denial.

The idea of empathizing with a dilemma is taken from recent trends in psychotherapy, a field which, like risk communication, tries to help people hear what they would otherwise defend themselves against acknowledging or assimilating. The field of psychotherapy has evolved from an intellectualized view of the therapeutic process to a much more emotionally complex view. Current thinking in diverse psychotherapy professional groups emphasizes the value of empathizing with the patient's most anxiety-provoking emotional dilemma as the way to help the patient take in difficult information and be empowered to move with it. Experienced therapists find that when they empathize with the patient's complex needs for self-protection, this helps the patient's unconscious defenses soften and allows difficult information to become more tolerable. Even if the very same information has already been conveyed and deflected, this approach allows more productive movement around the dilemma.

If empathizing with a *person* involves an imaginative act of seeing through their eyes, empathizing with the *dilemma* is even more specific in its focus. Here there is an attempt to look through another's eyes at the tensions presented by the problematic situation. One is still not merely observing another's behavior from the outside, as it were. Rather, one is trying to see what the other thinks is important, but one is also trying to see what the other person is working hard to deny or avoid, and thus to take in aspects of her perspective that she herself may be only partially aware of. The focus of such empathy is not on *watching* the other's behavior; it is a focus *from* her perspective to try to discern what is most difficult or challenging about her situation from that perspective. "Problematic behavior" is secondary to a person's perception of the challenge she faces; it is her attempt at solving this challenge, however poorly; hence the behavior is not as basic as the person's perception of a dilemma or problem. Rather than wondering, from a third-person perspective, what makes a person with a normal metabolism eat excessively to the point of seriously endangering her health, one might ask what dilemma she might perceive as her most basic one. That is, what is the underlying problem, as she sees it, to which her eating is a kind of response – inadequate, perhaps, but a response nevertheless?

How does empathizing with the dilemma help people to better approach their underlying conflict? First, the person's complex motives – both her strivings toward well-being and her need to cope psychologically with her concerns and fears – become a shared object of deliberation, and hence an aspect of reality that listener and speaker can experience together. Sharing this process opens up possibilities for brainstorming alternative responses and allows a shift in modal awareness from what is to what might be, emphasizing the dilemma as something that can be changed. This generates realistic hope from within the individual's own vision of her life trajectory rather than approaching patients with the kind of generic cheerleading implicit in models to "inform and exhort."

Second, because empathy involves emotionally appreciating its object (here, the conflict leading to health-compromising behavior), empathy has a profound anti-shaming effect. This is especially important regarding private and potentially stigmatized health behaviors, such as those involved in sexual activities and parenting. While people find the emotion of shame itself very threatening, by empathizing with the person's dilemma, communicators can greatly reduce that shame. Empathizing with the dilemma allows us to recover common ground: we can understand the felt conflict that drives the choice, even if we do not endorse the choice itself.

Third, empathic communication conveys that the patient and listener have shared humanity and vulnerability. Empathy is a way of *accompanying* others. When we experience empathy from another, we feel connected to them in a deep way; empathy creates solidarity between listener and speaker. This is crucial, for the simple notion of being accompanied in one's fear helps one to bear it. Feeling connected to others, feeling part of a "we," can itself drastically reduce anxiety and help coping. Indeed, if trust is an important factor in determining a patient's ability to absorb and believe risk information, as recent literature indicates, one of the most effective ways of establishing trust is by showing genuine concern for the patient (Roter et al. 2006). Notably, whether the health care provider indicates such concern and establishes trust is one of the most important predictors of patient adherence to treatment.[4]

Fourth, empathizing with the dilemma provides a more respectful stance for approaching differences among persons, whether in social and material circumstances, in familial or cultural values, or, crucially, in the power differences likely to exist between health care provider and patient. *All* of us, this model says, share a psychological need for coping, including the provider (whose own life will contain conflicts, and efforts, better and worse, at coping). If it is a common predicament, it is also inflected by our differences; we construe this task in particular ways depending on our individual and group identities. Central to empathy is genuine curiosity about how the world looks from the other person's perspective, and in this case, curiosity about the particular contours of the person's health dilemmas. For example, changing a food custom might be experienced as a kind of betrayal of an elder, changing a child-rearing custom might be a threat to family closeness, or asking a partner to use a condom might threaten his inculcated sense of masculinity.

In sum, empathizing with the dilemma helps to foster productive coping by engendering an openness that helps the recipient of such empathy accept information that she was guarding against and consider options that might otherwise be missed. The respect that such empathy conveys also helps another retain (or regain) a sense of self-efficacy and agential options by decreasing shame, by helping people feel accompanied and part of a "we," and by helping support a more egalitarian interest in the contextual and

---

[4] Although it is beyond the scope of this chapter, we have explored elsewhere the important difference between the kinds of concern that foster attentiveness and listening on the caregiver's part – that is, empathic curiosity – and the concern that seeks to overly reassure the patient and winds up leading to less disclosure of information and poorer therapeutic results. See Halpern, 2001.

diverse cultural influences on each of our health conceptions and aspirations.

PUTTING FEAR IN ITS PROPER PLACE

Empathic communication of the form urged here stands in marked contrast to the treatment of emotion in prevailing models of risk communication. As we mentioned, the empirical literature on motivation tends to see emotions as primitive impulses to be worked around. One model, the "mental noise" approach, identifies negative psychological associations – risks associated with fear, a low sense of control, and the like – and urges risk communicators to convey messages in ways that will cause as little "turbulence" as possible by avoiding these negative psychological associations (Fischhoff 1989; Covello et al. 2001). Another recent model, the so-called dominance model, advocates that risk communicators avoid negative emotional associations while emphasizing positive aspects of the message (Covello et al. 2001; Glik 2007).

The adage to simply reduce fear and increase positive thinking is far too inflexible a prescription for empowering people to make crucial and complex health decisions. For one thing, fear is sometimes unavoidable – and reasonable. If you suspect you may be having a heart attack, feeling fear is part of a perfectly natural response. Further, fear can be a potent way of shifting people out of dangerous complacency. Notably, many people describe how they are able to finally improve their dietary and exercise habits only after having a mild heart attack and genuinely grasping their mortality. While grounded optimism is truly beneficial for health and quality of life, a superficial emphasis on reassuring people, on accentuating the positive and avoiding the negative, is unlikely to engender realistic coping. To prevent bad outcomes from otherwise silent problems such as hypertension, people may need *more* conscious anxiety and concern about their health; thus, concrete reminders like regular public service messages, which generate some anxiety and fear, can be highly effective.

The prevailing models misidentify what the goal with respect to fear really is. If brute appeals to fear are a poor choice for risk communication, it is not because fear itself is necessarily a primitively infecting state but because, without adequate support, such appeals can trigger counterproductive means to self soothe. What is critical is not to try to *extinguish* fear but to help people to *tolerate* realistic fear and retain agency in its presence. It is not reducing fear per se that is beneficial; it is reducing *denial*. What those dealing with threats need are elasticity and agency in the face *of* negative emotions, not some formulaic reduction of these feelings.

On the usual models, if health choices seem recalcitrant in the face of information and advice – if someone fails to quit smoking, continues to overeat, or does not evacuate his home during a hurricane, all despite being informed of the risks – the choices are limited. If we do not want to disengage with them as agents, we must see them as powerless; if we do not want to see them as powerless, we must see them as endorsing the choice they make, revealing that they hold idiosyncratic and possibly incomprehensible values. Often, though, what makes best sense of an individual's configuration is not that he is trying to act according to his genuine preferences, but that he is attempting, often unconsciously, to shore up his subjective sense of self and ongoingness in the world.

The project of helping people cope with risk is better served by engaging emotions rather than working around them. More specifically, it is better facilitated by empathizing with the dilemmas that can drive denial. Further, empathic solidarity combined with empathic curiosity helps risk communicators both seek common ground and respect the differences among people, noting that people express their sense of self and home in radically contextual terms. One's moment in history, one's familial, neighborhood, and cultural context, one's gender identity and sexuality, and many other factors will give concrete expression and form to how one copes, and thus to how one responds to health communication.

Instead of picturing the clinician or health care educator and the patient on opposite sides, with the educator seeing things realistically and needing to prod the patient to get past his or her puzzling choices, this approach casts both side by side. Existing approaches have sought to overcome long histories of paternalistic errors by promoting an attitude of neutrality – deference to counterproductive behaviors as idiosyncratic values that we "respect" by disengaging with their content – at the cost of trying to understand what it feels like to be in the patient or public's situation. Such distancing ultimately disrespects the people being served. In contrast, the approach we describe here emphasizes curious engagement with our common human predicament, in all its diverse manifestations, and the ways in which we can help one another navigate it.

8

Economies of Hope in a Period of Transition

*Parents in the Time Leading Up to Their Child's
Liver Transplantation*

Mare Knibbe and Marian Verkerk

"I wonder how many miles I've fallen by this time?" she said aloud. "I
must be getting somewhere near the centre of the earth. Let me see:
that would be four thousand miles down, I think – " (for, you see, Alice
had learnt several things of this sort in her lessons in the school-room,
and though this was not a very good opportunity for showing off her
knowledge, as there was no one to listen to her, still it was good
practice to say it over).

– Lewis Carroll, Alice's Adventures in Wonderland

When infant patients and their parents tumble into the world of liver
transplantation, they are not as lighthearted and curious as Alice – the
hospital is not a Wonderland. However, they do discover, as she does,
that they are leaving the ordinary life they shared behind. The geography lessons that Alice learned in school have become somewhat
pointless; they do not seem to tell her where she is. The same happens
with family habits and self-understandings when a child is threatened by
disease and the need for liver transplantation. In retrospective interviews with parents about their child's liver transplantation, the time
leading up to the transplantation is depicted as a period of transition.
Their child's threatening disease has abruptly interrupted their lives,
and indeed, many parents indicate that somehow their life stopped in
this period: "Your life comes to a halt," as one of our respondents put it.

We thank the participants in the Naturalizing Bioethics workshop that was held in
Groningen, May 2007, for their very useful comments on a first draft of this chapter.

In this period of transition, parents must reconsider their responsibilities, making up their minds about living-donor liver transplantation. How should they care for their child and family? Should they donate or wait for a donor liver? Can they accept their partner's decision to donate? Can they afford to wait? Can the family cope with an extra patient?

In our interviews, as parents testify to different ways of carving a route through this period of transition, hope seems to be a central quality. With Margaret Urban Walker (2006), we understand hoping to be as basic to human life as breathing. Hope is therefore not a state of mind that distinguishes this period of transition from other phases of life. Like breath, however, hope comes most forcefully to one's attention when it is in short supply: when an imagined future vanishes, or when "your life comes to a halt." It is the threat to hope, and the response of protection and nourishment that re-create "hoping space," that makes hope a central theme in this period of transition.

Hope also is closely connected to agency. The connection goes both ways; hope cannot be understood without agency, but agency is not possible without hope, whether big or ordinary.[1] The lives of our respondents came to a halt when the (ordinary) hopes that they used to have for their child and family seemed to be closed off. To start picking up their lives again, they had to find new hoping space. In many ways, parents actively regulated their attitudes and activities to nourish and protect what hopes they had, thereby creating the conditions for agency. In short, hope seems to be necessary for threading or carving a way into the new moral landscape that parents face after their child has fallen ill.

In this chapter, we first outline the period of transition in which hopes were lost and new hopes needed to be found and protected. Then we offer a conceptual analysis of hope, rejecting several models in favor of a dynamic conception that allows us to make sense of what the parents in our study were going through. Finally, we offer suggestions for what can contribute to good hoping in the period leading up to transplantation. Throughout, we use our observations of a liver transplantation team and the semi-structured interviews we conducted over a one-and-a-half-year period with parents who

---

[1] For a more extensive discussion of the connections between hope and agency, see, for example, McGeer 2004.

donated or had considered donating a liver to their child. The observations and interviews are part of an ongoing research project entitled "Living Related Donation: A Qualitative Ethical Study," being carried out at the University Medical Center, Groningen.[2]

PERIOD OF TRANSITION

With something like amazement, many parents recall their ways of thinking and acting in the period leading up to transplantation. "I lived through these two years in a daze," one mother told us. As parents try to reconstruct their experiences in an interview, they make clear that the illness of their child was unsettling but that it resettled them as well. Parents recollect having a different state of mind and functioning in a way that was unlike their usual ways. Although there is a great variety in the stories that parents tell about this period of transition, all parents had to deal in some way with the progression of the disease in their child, the uncertainty of the waiting list for donor livers, and the uncertain prospect of possible donation.

To give an impression of this transitional period, we present a fragment of a conversation observed in the outpatient clinic. Most of the children who need a liver transplant are born with biliary atresia, a condition in which the ducts that carry bile from the liver to the gall bladder are blocked or absent, leading to liver damage and cirrhosis of the liver. David is such a child. At six month of age, he had just been referred to the Groningen transplant center because the doctors at his former hospital thought that he would not be able to live much longer on his old liver. The pediatrician explained to the parents how he saw the stage they were in at that moment, and he looked backward and forward with them at the possible developments:

When biliary atresia is discovered, the liver has already been damaged by the bile that is obstructed. A kasai operation[3] can restore the bile flow;

---

[2] This study included twenty-two parents, two uncles (opting for donation), and one aunt of twelve families in which the possibility of living related liver transplantation was examined and considered. In four of the twelve families, living related liver transplantation was performed. The children in eight families had transplants using a deceased donor liver. In this chapter we focus on the theme of hope in the interviews with parents and leave the topic of living donation aside.

[3] In a kasai operation, a piece of bowel is used as a bile duct.

however, this solution is only temporary. This morning we saw a twenty-year-old boy who lived with the kasai for a long time before he needed a liver transplant. Usually, though, it doesn't last that long. You are here now because the bile flow seems to be hampered in spite of the kasai operation. This can change; we don't know. To prevent more damage, diet is very important. But the changes are difficult to predict. And while we don't know how long things will go well, we do know that at a certain moment, David will need a transplant. To prepare for that moment, we want to screen him now for liver transplantation. Ultimately, we only do liver transplantation when there are no other treatment options, but to be ready when the time comes, David has to be on the waiting list.

In the time leading up to transplantation, the condition of the child and family was constantly viewed as something that could develop in different ways; it might be getting better or it might be getting worse. Generally, the expectation was that in the short term the condition would get worse without transplantation. It was a period in which patients and their parents were constantly betwixt and between. Hope, with its ways of "dealing with temporalities," was a condition of carving a route through this period and meeting its challenges.

The challenges that parents face in this transitional period can be summarized as being of two kinds. First, parents had to adjust and often readjust to the progression of the disease in their child, and to the prospects of transplantation and possible donation. Second, parents had to accustom themselves to a medical practice that was new to them. Within this practice, they had to come to shared understandings of their situation, of the disease, and of the treatment options for their child.

CONCEPTIONS OF HOPE

Hope is discussed in different ways in health care contexts. In a first way, the discussion about hope is connected to the giving of information and to the way patients handle information. Here, hope (A hopes that P) is defined in terms of two components: desire and subjective probability (Day 1970; 1998). A desires P and believes that P is to higher or lower degrees probable but not certain. To hope well in this view means that the beliefs are well informed and realistic. Especially in situations of terminal care, this gives rise to moral dilemmas. Should we inform the patient about the fact that she is dying and thereby take away all hope for survival, or should we give her hope and therefore not inform her about the actual state she is in? (W. Ruddick 1999).

Adopting this belief-and-desire conception of hope in health care has practical implications. The emphasis on beliefs and information in discussions about hope often underpins a certain role division in handling hope. The focus is mostly on *beliefs* of patients or their parents and on the *actions* of professionals who might be able to do something about these beliefs. This focus gives the impression of an active party, influencing hope, and a passive party, the object of influences. This picture cannot do justice to the hope-related activity we found in the stories of parents about the time leading up to liver transplantation of their child. Parents actively regulated their information intake, attention, and thoughts regarding outcomes.

In a second way of proceeding, hope is incorporated as part of the treatment or counseling of patients. On this approach, hope is connected not only to belief and desire but also to well-being and agency. In an example of this second conception, developed by the oncologist Jerome Groopman (2005, xii), hope generates a kind of chain reaction in patients, in which each link of the chain improves the chances of healing: "For all my patients hope, true hope, has proved as important as any medication I might prescribe or any procedure I might perform." Groopman does, however, distinguish real hope and giving real hope from false hope that is based on manipulative information giving. The insight about the importance of hope leads Groopman on a quest to discover how to handle the hopes of patients and family, how to guide or support them in hoping well. Other authors have adopted a similar approach, seeing hope as part of the treatment of patients: "Along with medical treatment, health care professionals have identified hope as a deterrent to illness and death, and a necessary component of healing" (Westburg and Guindon 2004, 1). Hope is also seen as something that can help patients cope with the course of a disease. Furthermore, patients with strong hopes are usually more cooperative about treatment regimens than patients with weaker hopes.

At first sight, this conception of hope seems to be broader than the conception that is based on desire and belief. It connects hope to well-being but also to the agency of patients and health professionals.

Hope is presented as a state of mind that *causes* or *stimulates* certain (more responsible) behavior. Professionals strive to inspire hope, in order to invite patients to act in specific ways. If we look at the practical use of this conception of hope, though, the patient still seems to be the more passive party in interactions regarding hope. In that respect, this conception does not differ from the first. The professional, being the active party, is still in the position of giving hope or taking it away. Because hope is good for fostering patients' involvement in their treatments, and because hope can make patients vulnerable, health professionals have to handle hopes in a careful manner. The second conception seems to suggest a cause-and-effect chain of connections: actions of professionals influence hope, and hope in its turn influences the well-being and agency of patients. It is acknowledged that hope often results in a more active involvement of patients (or parents), but the activity involved in hope itself is still opaque.

In a third conception of hope, the clinical psychologist C. R. Snyder (1995; also Snyder et al. 2002) gives a more explicit account of the connection between hope and agency, defining hope as a process of thinking about one's goals. This process embraces two components: agency (the motivation and energy to move toward the goal) and pathways (the ways to achieve that goal). According to Snyder, hope can be seen as a cognitive appraisal of one's goal-related capabilities. As an example of "agentic thinking," Snyder et al. (2002, 258) cite phrases that people with high hopes tend to say to themselves: "I can do this" and "I am not going to be stopped." Thoughts about pathways are about planning, how to reach a goal, and what to take into account. This definition gives a more clear-cut place to the *activity* involved in hoping; it consists of two kinds of goal-directed thinking: agency thinking and pathway thinking.

The third conception, however, also has its problems when it comes to understanding the hopes of our respondents. The conception is too goal directed to come to an understanding of either the hope-related activity in the stories of our respondents or the significance of hope in the period of transition that is our focus. In Snyder's conception, agency is strongly linked to gaining control and to chosen goals. One can wonder whether having a goal is a necessary condition for hope. Often hope is less ambitious and searches more for desired outcomes than for chosen goals. Parents in our study hoped that their child would come out of the transplantation in the best possible way or that life would be less filled with anxieties. Hoped-for outcomes are not always very articulate. In the transitional period, the outcomes were often reimagined and adjusted; they were not clearly defined from the start. As we argue later, this activity of reimagination itself can be understood as part of what it is to hope.

The three conceptions of hope we discuss here do not help us to come to a satisfactory understanding of the hope-related activity in the stories of parents we interviewed. To enable an understanding of hope in those stories, we need a more dynamic conception of hope, one that allows for less ambition about reaching chosen goals while maintaining a sense of the involvement of agency in hoping.

To develop a more dynamic notion of hope, Margaret Urban Walker (2006, 48) proposes to describe hope as an emotional stance or a patterned syndrome that is "characterized by certain desires and perceptions, but also by certain forms of attention, expression, feeling, and activity." One can recognize hope in oneself or in others not in single mental features but in patterns of these "phenomena of hope."[4] As Walker writes, there is no single "recipe" of specific ingredients in precise proportions that constitute hope, but there are patterns of ingredient perceptions, expressions, feelings, and dispositions to think, feel, and act that are part of the repertory of hopefulness.

In developing this conception of hope, Walker discussed four features of hope that make up hopes of people in different con-stellations and interplay. One feature of hope is its *futurity*: hope is directed at a state of affairs that has not yet come to pass. Hope can be oriented at a near future or a far-away future, but it is always forward looking. Even if I hope that things (in the past) went well, it will be something I will find out in the future. A second feature is the *desirability* of what is hoped for: the state of affairs that is hoped for has to have some value for the hoping agent. One cannot hope for an outcome that one does not value at all. The desirability is a feature that can give hope in a health care setting a specific dynamic. In health care, patients, their parents, or other family members often

---

[4] Walker borrows the notion of "phenomena of hope" from Wittgenstein's *Philosophical Investigations*.

need time to learn to value the best possible outcomes of a treatment. Third, there has to be a "nonzero" *possibility* of what is hoped for. The hoping agent has to believe that the state of affairs she hopes for is at least possible. If one considers a desired future to be impossible, one will lose hope for that future, however desirable it may still be (although hope can still be directed at possible futures with a very low probability). Finally, Walker mentions with special emphasis the *efficacy* of hope: the dynamic tendencies of hope to steer thought, feelings, attention, speech, and actions. We dwell on Walker's explanations of the efficacy of hope in somewhat greater detail to come to an understanding of the agency involved in hoping.

To understand what we are doing when we hope, we should look at the "dynamic tendencies to attend to, or be attuned to what is hoped for in a way that tilts or propels us toward making it so" (M. Walker 2006, 47). The agency involved in hoping consists of several exercises of thought, activity, expression, and attention. Walker (2006, 45) outlines these aspects of hoping as the "efficacy" of hope and states that hope's "nature is to engage our desire and agency, so that in hoping, the world is, in some respect that one cares about, construed as open to the outcome one favors." This characterization fits the diverse reports of our respondents about the ways they managed to live through the time leading up to transplantation. In this formulation, *interpretations* of the world and *acting* in the world are pictured as two locations on a continuum; beliefs about the world are *actively* formed and continuously adjusted interpretations of one's situation and its openness to a certain possible and desirable future. Interpreting one's situation is an activity that is sustained by other activities as well. Activities of our respondents could involve seeking or avoiding contact with other parents of liver transplant patients; asking for second opinions; and surfing the Internet or staying far from it. With regard to regulating information, attention, and contact with others, some of our respondents tried to feed their imagination with hopeful scenarios, whereas others tried mainly to keep their imagination from straying to frightening scenarios. With these diverging activities and interpretations, parents had different ways of construing a health care environment, open to good outcomes for their child.

EVALUATING HOPE

How can we recognize good hoping? And how can professionals form a supportive environment for the good hope of parents? In Walker's account of good or misplaced hope, correct beliefs are less important than the activity, imagination, feeling, expression, or other forms of agency that are engaged in hoping. Walker states that hope can be false or mistaken only if one believes there is a possibility where there is none. One can rarely be certain that there is zero possibility of attaining a desired object, however, so that leaves room for hope. Even if there is only the slightest possibility of realizing what one is hoping for, hope cannot be false. And even if hope were based on a mistaken belief that the impossible can happen, one should be careful about advising against such hope because people have a need not only of what they hope for but also for hope itself. Hope, we repeat, is a condition for agency. Without any hope, ordinary or grand, people are left with only inertness, terror, and despair. One could advise against certain imprudent actions inspired by hope but not against hope itself.

To recognize hope that is good, given the abilities and inabilities of parents in this transitional period, we can evaluate the "economy of hope" – that is, the investment and engagement of energy, thought, attention, feeling, and activity made in hoping.[5] We can try to assess whether the energy engaged in hoping is well spent. We can examine, for example, how the future is imagined and invited in one's actions, attention, and thoughts. We can evaluate its desirability: is the future that one hopes for and invests in really desirable and valuable, or is one investing in something of little value? We can check the assumed possibility of a desirable future or we can evaluate hope's dynamic tendencies – the exercises of thought, attention, and activity made in hoping. Does this hope elicit a good kind of activity and state of mind? Does it not lead to neglect of things that deserve attention? Our respondents invested their energy and attention

---

[5] Victoria McGeer (2004) coined the term "economy of hope" to refer to approaches to hope in which hoping well is understood as "having the right quantity of hope." We use economy of hope to refer to the (quality of) engagement and investment of energy, attention, thought, and activity.

in different ways in their hope for good outcomes. In some cases, one can question the wisdom of the investments of hope they were ready to make.

To outline the kinds of questions that can be posed about the economy of hope, we discuss the investments of hope Jonathan's parents made. Jonathan's parents had three children together, were divorced, and had both found new partners. After Jonathan was put on the waiting list for liver transplantation, his parents developed different views on his illness and on living liver donation. When Jonathan was three, he was diagnosed with biliary stenosis; his bile was slowly poisoning his liver. He coped reasonably with his health problems until he had an esophageal bleeding at the age of eight. He was then put on the waiting list for a liver transplantation to avoid a second bleeding of the esophagus or stomach, because the doctors thought that he might not survive a second time. One pediatrician had pictured the risk of another bleeding as a time bomb; without a liver transplant, it would eventually happen again, but it was hard to tell when it would happen. In the interview, Jonathan's father reported that the heavy metaphor had alarmed him. He had asked for further explanation; how critical was the situation? The pediatricians had reassured him that Jonathan was still doing well and that he had some time to wait for a liver transplantation. The father agreed to wait for a deccased donor liver and to become a liver donor in case of emergency; he thought that not risking his health unless it was really necessary would be better for the sake of his wife and three children. "You keep balancing, but you continue to ask yourself, is it still responsible to wait? That is what you want to know, but they can give you no guarantees, but as long as they gave me the impression that we were not in an emergency situation, we stuck to this scenario [of waiting]."

Jonathan's mother saw her son's situation as more urgent. She thought the situation could rightly be called a time bomb and reported having been on tenterhooks for quite a while. If the doctors had not refused her as a donor, she would have donated instantly. "Since I am forty and I have a dangerously ill child who has his whole life still lying before him, I would be very happy to donate, and if I would die for him, well it might be less simple than it sounds but I don't think I have a problem with that.... The children will manage, they still have a father, and others, they will be okay."

Jonathan's parents invested their attention, energy, actions, and thoughts differently; they had different economies of hope. Jonathan's mother was ready to invest her life in her son to give him the best chance. She was unconditionally committed to her son's well-being and could not be sidetracked by considerations regarding her other children, who were doing well, or by other aspects of family life. She had no second thoughts about liver donation; it would be worthwhile if her son could have a future, with or without her. By contrast, Jonathan's father imagined a future that included the whole family. With every change in their situation, he considered what would be best for Jonathan as well as others involved; he talked with others about donation and relied on the estimates of the pediatricians about Jonathan's condition. After accepting the reassurance of the pediatricians, he felt less pressed by the danger to his son.

Questions about good hope are connected to other values in life; answers depend on the kind of futures we value, on ideas about a good state of mind, and on involvement in situations with specific risks and uncertainties. How should one live with this risk and the uncertainty about its magnitude? Is it better to accept this uncertainty as a new and ongoing part of life, as Jonathan's father did, or is it better to realize that normal life has stopped, and sort out what is most important in the future, as Jonathan's mother did? These are the kinds of questions that have to be discussed by those involved when evaluating economies of hope.

The features of hope that Walker describes can help us think about good hope; however, they cannot be isolated when evaluating hope. When evaluating, we have to connect specific features of hope to a broader view of the economy of hope. A broad view of economies of hope, with variously patterned features, can generate insights that are more useful in practice than general judgments about good and false hopes or "high and low hopes" (Snyder's words). Instead of judging hope to be altogether good or bad in virtue of one characteristic, a focus on the economy of hope can help to identify and respond to good and vulnerable aspects of specific hopes.

TWO FEATURES OF HOPE

To think further about good hoping in the period of transition that is our focus, we discuss different shapes of hope in our interviews and observations with parents of patients requiring liver transplants. We focus on two features of hope and good hope in particular: the futurity of hope and the social character of hoping.[6] These features deserve special attention because they are related to the specific characteristics and challenges that constitute this transitional period. Remember that we sketched this period as the time in which parents had to learn how to live with the progression of the disease in their child and the uncertain prospects of transplantation, and in which parents had to accustom themselves to a medical practice that was new to them.

A focus on the futurity and social character of hoping sheds light on three variations in patterns of hope. First, different temporalities can be involved in hoping. Some parents oriented their actions and attention toward short-term problems of that moment; they tried not to look further than one step ahead. Others tried to vividly imagine good long-term outcomes of transplantation. Second, hopes can be directed at goals but also at vague and indeterminate outcomes. Third, there can be different divisions of hoping labor between patients, parents, professionals, or other caregivers. Our respondents had different ways of involving others in their hopes. We think it is important to properly recognize these differences in patterns of hope before judging specific economies of hope.

Futurity

In which ways can the future of what is hoped for be part of hoping? In many discussion of hope, the futurity of what is hoped for is conceptualized as the desired goal that lies in the future. Snyder, for example, started his research on hope by asking people to tell about their goal-directed thoughts. We think that goal-directed thought and action is only one way of hoping. A hoped-for future is not necessarily clearly outlined to a hoping agent. In our interviews we

[6] Walker does not treat its social character as one of the features of hope; however, she does endorse its social character in her discussion of other features.

can roughly distinguish three ways of attending to the future, each of them part of a different economy of hope. We outline two ways of attending to the future and discuss a third way more extensively.

In a first way of attending to the future, parents tried to imagine vividly what they hoped for. They sought contact with other parents to learn about the recovery of other children after transplantation and about the well-being of other families. They listened to stories and information selectively. As Barbara explained, "No, I had little need for information; I did feel a need to talk to other parents, because you want to hear a lot of stories. But you just want to hear many many positive stories. You only want to see the positive situations."

In this way of attending to the future, parents paid less attention to information about risks of transplantation and donation, or to stories about patients who died. Parents who told about this way of dealing with information reported being aware of the risks, but their attention was grasped by stories, gestures, or expressions that could sustain their imagination of a hoped-for outcome. Some parents explained that it made no sense to think a lot about complications and problems of transplantation and living donation, when that was the only lifesaving treatment option for their child. As there was no choice to make, there was no reason to consider the risks carefully.

In a second way of attending to the future, parents prepared for all possible scenarios to realize the best possible outcome. In this mode, parents tried to gather all the information they could find about the disease and treatment of their child, in order to gain more control. Margaret reported, "You absorb anything that might have something to do with it. In order not to miss anything, to avoid being taken by surprise. So you know what is going wrong, what you can expect, what is the situation at hand, and what can happen."

This general openness to stories and information was emotionally stressful. Parents who thoroughly informed themselves often stumbled upon stories about patients who died and about medical mistakes. However, they developed a thorough understanding of the child's disease and the transplantation options. As they encountered different perspectives and found information about other transplant centers as well, these parents were in a position to compare and evaluate the team's attitudes and policy regarding transplantation and living donation. In this critical position, there was more they could do themselves to realize a hoped-for outcome.

A third way of attending to the future, "living day by day," is exemplified by David's mother Selma: "I did not want; I could not look too far ahead. I was living only day by day, and how David was that day, and more than that I could not, I couldn't use."

Our interpretation of living day by day as a way of attending to the future needs explanation. We interpret the way Selma lived through the time leading up to transplantation at greater length. To understand her way of attending to the future, however, we need to look at others surrounding her as well.

In our discussion of the transitional period leading up to transplantation, we presented the pediatrician's explanation of David's disease and treatment, given in the first conversation that David's parents had in the transplant center. In his explanations, the pediatrician considered different possible future scenarios. He focused on a timeline that in his eyes seemed practical to consider. David's father, however, tried to look further ahead. He asked the pediatrician to offer a picture of the future: "We are also trying to get a picture of the future, like how will things go after transplantation, what can we expect? ... How long can you live with a liver transplant? Or is that still unknown?" The pediatrician expanded his comments, citing a few statistics:

No, we don't know exactly how long someone can live with a liver transplant that he received as a child. Somebody [with a liver transplant] recently turned twenty-five. But it remains uncertain how things will go. Of all the transplanted children, 80 to 85 percent can lead a normal life and go to school. They all have to use medicines against rejection for the rest of their lives, but with that, they can do all the normal things.

At the moment of that first conversation in the transplant center, these uncertain prospects of an 80 to 85 percent chance of a normal school-life with medicines for the rest of their lives could seem both unbearable and hopeful. David's father tried to picture the best possible scenario he could hope for. To David's mother, it seemed impossible to look at this uncertain future. In her questions, Selma focused on a smaller time frame; she tried not to look further than one step ahead. Her questions to the pediatrician were mainly about diet, where to ask questions when problems would arise, and about the pain her son had to bear that day. Living day by day was the only way Selma could get through the time of waiting for her son's transplantation.

Can we say that Selma had hope for good outcomes, if she did not try to picture them? The timeline that she had in mind was not that in which an ultimate outcome of her hope (if she had hope) would be realized. Using Snyder's conception of hope, one could conclude that she did not really have hope, or that she only had small goals. We will not endorse these conclusions. With her care and practical questions, she invited outcomes that she knew would be better than the outcomes invited by neglect or mistakes. She knew this, even though she could not bear imagining what these uncertain outcomes would look like. With her small timeline, practical questions, and involvement, it seems that for Selma hope started with *acting* toward an uncertain but preferable future of all possible futures, not with setting a goal or imagining the outlines of a future. In this she was supported by the pediatrician, who did imagine the possible out-comes and could advise her on ways to invite a future life for her son. Her hope thus rested on her trust in the pediatrician and the team he represented.

We stated that for Selma hope started with acting toward a favored outcome, imagined by others, not with imagining it herself. One can ask, however, whether it is possible to hope and continue hoping without somehow imagining a hoped-for outcome. If we accept that hoping involves inviting a future state of affairs, some form of imagination of a hoped for future is a vital feature of hope. Maybe Selma was not forming mental pictures of the outcome of trans-plantation but imagining outcomes in other ways. Imaginations involved in hope can take many forms – detailed, fragmented, vague, visualized, or otherwise. An example Walker uses is that of people clutching and pulling the railing at the racetrack as horses enter the home stretch. She suggests that this gesture can be seen as embodied imagination. In the period leading up to transplantation, there can be imagination of a hoped-for future in the ways parents care for their child, perceive the child's condition, listen to doctors and to stories of other parents, or follow the recovery of other patients.

One can ask if the hope of David's mother would be better or stronger if she did imagine the future more clearly. In answering this question, we have to keep in mind that in reimagining a desirable and possible future for their child after transplantation, parents have to confront the loss of certain possible futures as well. The process of reimagining an uncertain future often requires recognizing the loss of some hoped-for futures one had, and the risk of losing new hopes as well. This loss can make reimagining the future painful, as it was to David's father, or unbearable, as it was to his mother. For Selma, relying on the imagination of others allowed her some time to accept this loss and to learn to value another possible future for her child.

These three ways of attending to the future, exemplified by Barbara, Margaret, and Selma, contribute to different economies of hope. With their different approaches of the future, parents spent their energy on other aspects of their situation. Parents who, like Margaret, prepared for all possible scenarios, invested energy in developing a critical stance in the process of care for their child, in order to get the best possible care. With their broad orientation via the Internet, they tried to reduce their dependence on the transplant team. They also had to spend a lot of energy on handling the emotions inspired by the upsetting information they often found. In the approaches exemplified by Barbara and Selma, parents depended more on the steps the doctors proposed, spending most of their own energy on keeping a positive frame of mind and on daily care. We saw that "living day by day" contributed to an economy of hope in which emotions about uncertain outcomes, and the loss of a future once hoped for, were regulated. This regulation of her emotions allowed David's mother to devote full attention and energy to the problems and necessary care of that moment.

What can we say about good or vulnerable aspects in these different economies of hope? At some moments in the interview, parents explained their own ways of dealing with uncertain prospects as a necessity; something they could not have done otherwise, and at other moments as an approach that in their eyes was most sensible. Both Barbara and Margaret characterized their own attitudes as more level-headed, compared to attitudes of other parents they had met. Their specific ways of inviting a good future for their child fitted in with values they held in life. Margaret emphasized her autonomy, whereas Barbara spoke about being (emotionally) strong and positive toward her daughter. Apart from these connections to values, there are vulnerabilities as well in these different patterns of hoping. Parents who confined their attention to positive aspects or to short-term problems were more vulnerable to disappointment, problems they did not prepare for, or abuse of trust. Parents who tried to control the care process and stay informed of everything that could be relevant to their situation were more vulnerable to exhaustion and friction with professionals. Ways of attending to the future were geared to the way parents entered relations with professional caregivers and vice-versa; relations were geared to specific patterns of hope.

The Social Character of Hoping

For a complete picture of economies of hope, we have to look at social contexts as well. The words, expressions, and attitudes of professionals in the transplant team were often described in detail by our respondents. They seemed to be important to the ways parents managed to construe their situation as open to good outcomes. In what follows, we outline the relational dimension of the three ways of attending to the future we have described.

Like Barbara, Melle's parents both indicated that their attention to risks was limited. However, they also indicated that the decision-making process took place in a constellation with professionals, one of whom was perceived as remarkably open and concerned about risk. Melle's father recalled: "This doctor was really considerate and open and also harsh and clear about the risks [of liver-donation]. All the same, however, as a parent you are in a certain flow with your child and you shut certain things out. [That is, you don't consider risks] because you're the parent."

The impression that risks were handled and communicated with special care was meaningful to Melle's parents, although they distinguished their own concerns in this respect from those of the team. Not risk itself, but the belief that the risks were handled by trustworthy professionals, was deemed relevant by Melle's parents. While hearing the information related by the doctor, they observed the way the doctor (and with him the team) dealt with their situation. They tried to get a view of the moral landscapes in the medical practice they had entered.

Margaret had other ways of involving professionals in her hope. In the long periods she had spent with her son in different hospitals, she had seen many professional mistakes. Her trust in professionals was placed more carefully, and she made a routine of checking different sources of information and stories. In this way she tried to control what happened to her son. The involvement of others was conditional. Some professionals found this a very difficult kind of involvement. In two reflective meetings with pediatric nurses in which their relations to parents of patients were discussed, nurses reported they felt very uncertain and less capable under her controlling eyes.[7] From their perspective, according to their economy of hope, the investment of energy and attention was not working well with the conditional way Margaret entered relations. From Margaret's perspective, however, with the experiences she had, it was the best way of realizing a future for her son.

In discussing the way David's mother invited the best possible future for her son, we already mentioned her reliance on professionals. Her hope and its investments depended completely on the relations with professionals. She not only relied on their interventions but also depended on health professionals to start imagining and valuing a possible future for her child.

This short overview shows how parents involved professionals in their specific patterns of hope. What can professionals in a transplant team do with this involvement to support a good economy of hope? We think there is not one specific way of communicating information or of counseling that works to inspire a good kind of hope in all parents. Health professionals are not the gatekeepers of hope; they cannot regulate the hopes of parents. However, they can critically assess and adjust their own involvement in the hopes of parents. To support the hopes of parents, professionals need to clarify whether they can agree with and live up to the involvement that parents assign them in their hopes. Compared to views in which professionals are pictured as gatekeepers of hope, this is a more modest professional approach. The critical reflection in this approach encompasses more, however, because it requires sensitivity toward the hoping patterns of parents, as well as self-reflection and team discussions.

---

[7] The reflection in these meetings was facilitated by the ethicists Els Maeckelberghe and Enne Feenstra. We thank them and the pediatric nurses for the opportunity to observe in these meetings.

Assessing or adjusting professional involvement in hopes of parents
entails negotiating mutual expectations. Professionals must be clear
about their professional norms and procedures, but they also need to
be sensitive to the diverging ways parents involve them in their
hopes. For critical reflection on their involvements in the hopes of
parents, it is important to recognize the values and vulnerabilities
that are present in different economies of hope, as we have pointed
out. However, assessing their involvements in hopes of parents also
requires self-reflection. In the hopes of parents, professional values
and vulnerabilities are addressed as well. David's mother tapped the
support and comfort-giving that for many professionals is a valuable
part of their work. The way Barbara or Melle's parents involved
professionals was flattering, underscoring their medical authority
and resulting in a smooth and (in health care, highly valued) efficient
cooperation. Margaret, however, made clear that some of the
involvements professionals get to have in the hopes of parents are
more difficult to deal with. Many nurses felt less capable in her
critical presence. It can be tempting to see ways of hoping that build
on professional values as better than the hopes that address professional limits or vulnerabilities as well. However, the more difficult
involvements of professionals in hopes of patients, parents, or family
can be seen as a good opportunity for critical self-reflection and
discussion of professional and team values.

The time leading up to liver transplantation of a child is a period
of transition, in which parents enter a new moral landscape with
unfamiliar risks and uncertainties. Hope is a central quality when it
comes to facing the challenges in this period. We discussed the
usefulness of different conceptions of hope to come to an understanding of our research material. In the interpretation of interviews
about this period, hope can only be understood and appreciated if
its dynamic tendencies are taken into account. Margaret Walker
(2006, 47) explains this tendency as the tendency "to attend to or be
attuned to what is hoped for in a way that tilts us or propels us toward
making it so." While adjusting and readjusting to the condition of
their child and the new practice they entered, parents actively regulated their intake of information and the awareness of information
given. They guarded and re-created their hoping space in different

ways, attended to the future in different ways, and, accordingly, entered into relations with professionals in different ways. The stories of parents showed that professionals cannot be the gatekeepers of their hope, as is suggested in some accounts of hope in health care. The information, behavior, and attitudes of professionals were important to parents to inspire trust; however, professionals did not control the risk awareness of parents or determine their hopes. Professionals can support the hopes of parents by caring about their own involvement in these hopes.

9

Consent as a Grant of Authority

A Care Ethics Reading of Informed Consent

Joan C. Tronto

The medical intervention is scheduled. The doctor visits the patient and explains again the procedure. She draws a picture of what she is going to do. She mentions the risks entailed in the procedure. She asks, "Have I answered all of your questions?" The patient nods. The doctor hands the patient a form to sign. "Could you sign this form, then? It indicates that we have discussed the procedure and you have consented to it."

This ritual of consent is performed thousands of times every day in hospitals, doctor's offices, and other medical settings. Yet what does this ritual really mean? As Ruth Faden and Tom Beauchamp (1986) argue, there are two elements to the traditional way to view consent. It is both an exercise of the *patient's* autonomy and an *institutional arrangement* whereby the medical actors can demonstrate that they had authority to act (Cates 2001). These two elements are separated into an ethical concern, focused on the individual patient, and a legal concern, focused on the institution. But suppose, as a naturalized ethics might suggest we should, we try to put these two pieces together? For the most part, discussions of consent focus more on the concern for patient autonomy than on the ways in which they authorize actions. While consent has made health care providers more sensitive to the dangers of paternalism, if we focus on both aspects of consent, we will see something else. Because consent does not, in fact, show respect for patients' autonomy, and because it masks other ethical problems within health care that need to be acknowledged and addressed, I propose that we rethink what consent means from the standpoint of an ethics of care.[1]

By an ethics of care approach to bioethics, I mean one that takes relationships as fundamental to the description of bioethical problems.[2] Almost all medical care is necessary care, that is, care that one could not provide for oneself (Waerness 1990). In such settings, there is always a *power imbalance* between the care providers and the care receivers. The contrast between how principled and care ethics deals with this power imbalance forms a central part of the argument of this chapter. An ethics of care also requires that we pay attention to the *context* of moral activities. Thus, we will consider what aspects of bioethics are "backgrounded" (Plumwood 1993) by the framing of consent as an act of autonomy.

We can take this consent scenario and use it to explore two different ways to explain its significance. On the one hand, we can view this scene as an exercise of the patient's autonomy, as a contractual agreement. On the other hand, we can view the scene as a grant of authority. What happens when we stop thinking of consent as an

---

[1] Few theorists of care have considered the nature of consent; an exception is Cates and Lauritzen 2001. There are some profound differences between my view of the care ethic and the one presented in that volume; nonetheless, I have learned a great deal from reading Cates 2001.

[2] There is a voluminous literature by now about the nature of an ethic of care. Although there are also differences in approach, most theorists of care share a view that their work is opposed to a kind of principles-based moral thinking. See, among others, Held 2006; Sevenhuijsen 1998; Tronto 1993. For an exception, see Engster 2007. For a metaethical justification for eschewing principles, see M. Walker 1998.

Interestingly, the contrast between an ethic of care and most principled bioethics is not even the difference between respect for relationships versus respect for the individual. As an academic outsider in the field of bioethics, I find it curious that "respect for the person" is so quickly transformed into respect for the *person's autonomy*. Thus, in the Belmont Report, the heading for the principle is "respect for the person," but the text that follows states, "Respect for persons incorporates at least two ethical convictions: first, that individuals should be treated as autonomous agents, and second, that persons with diminished autonomy are entitled to protection. The principle of respect for persons thus divides into two separate moral requirements: the requirement to acknowledge autonomy, and the requirement to protect those with diminished autonomy" (*National Commission for the Protection of Human Subjects of Biomedical and Behavioral Research* 1979, 5). That dignity might be an alternative way to understand consent, and the issues taken up in this chapter, cannot be explored fully here. For some readings of dignity as a more fundamental principle in health care ethics, see, among others, Häyry 2004; Marmot 2004.

exercise of a right to autonomy and put it instead in a more integrated framework of the responsibilities brought about by a grant of authority?

CONSENT AS AUTONOMY: THE PROBLEMS

There are several problems with using autonomy as the most basic ethical category by which to view the relationship of patient and doctor. In the first place, autonomy is a notoriously slippery concept. Although its formal meaning, the capacity to make decisions for oneself, is straightforward, what this phrase signifies, in any context, is highly debatable (see, e.g., Gylling 2004; McKenzie and Stoljar 2000; O'Neill 2003). In the second place, when the act of consent stands in for autonomy, it distorts the reality of medical care. After all, informed consent does not usually happen at the beginning of a medical situation. A patient has arrived, described symptoms, and probably undergone tests. A doctor or group of doctors and health professionals (perhaps radiologists, phlebotomists, lab technicians) have applied their professional skills and judgments and constructed a diagnosis and a course of treatment. Much has already occurred before this consent ritual takes place. Why, then, is the moment of consent so important?

Its importance cannot be attributed to being a "turning point" in medical practice, because patients almost always agree to the procedures for which their consent is being sought. As Epstein observes, a large number of empirical studies show that when people give their consent, they are *not* acting according to the standards we might set for autonomous decision making. As Epstein (2006, 342) summarizes this literature,

Over 70 studies performed in a variety of clinical settings indicated that legally and institutionally valid consents and refusals had frequently failed to reflect genuinely autonomous decision making. ... Low socio-economic status, poor education, old age, lengthy hospital stays, stress, language barriers, and misinterpretation of probabilistic data were found in these studies to be associated with such outcomes.

Partly as a response to such criticisms, a discussion now grows to talk about consent as "shared decision making." But not only is this discussion vague (Schneider 2007); it also presumes that those who are not genuinely autonomous in granting consent will somehow be equal to the task of participating in shared decision making. But something more fundamental is going on in this attempt to strengthen consent, and it will help if we begin by naming this issue properly: it is about the power inherent in the care-giving position in conditions of necessary care and of trying to think about the problematic nature of such care. The problem with the view of consent-as-autonomy as a solution to the problem of unequal power is that it lacks a realistic view of the place of power in the medical setting.

Whenever unequal power is involved in human relationships, it raises the eons-old concern: what can compel the powerful to act in the interests of the weaker parties, rather than in their own interests? Plato himself used the analogy of the way in which the physician's interests are subordinated to those of the patient in *The Republic*. Eva Kittay (1999) has talked about the responsibilities of caregivers to their "charges." It is in this context that we can wonder, What is the ethical status and significance of this ordinary and familiar scene of informed consent? From an autonomy-based standpoint, the focus is on the cared-for person's autonomy. From another standpoint, informed consent is important because it prevents abuse on the part of the caregiver (O'Neill 2003). In both of these perspectives, there is a power imbalance between the care provider and the person cared for. Both view consent in terms of checking the power of the more powerful party in an asymmetric power relationship. The care provider holds, in a sense, the upper hand. If the care provider withholds or provides inadequate care, the consequences for the patient may be dire indeed. In both cases, consent bears the burden of trying to offset any harm that may come to the patient from this unequal power.

This connection between informed consent and the correction of a power imbalance follows a familiar route in contemporary liberal thinking. Insofar as rights are "trumps," to possess a right, that is, to compel another to perform a corresponding duty, is a kind of power. By turning informed consent into a "right," patients have recourse if physicians abuse their power, thereby setting a power-imbalance back, to some extent, in their favor. O'Neill observes that the capacity to revoke consent must also continue throughout the medical care. If the empirical evidence suggests that consent rarely functions as a real choice, it does seem to provide a protection against the most egregious abuses. In this regard, even if it is a fiction, it is a useful fiction, because it makes clear to patients how to stop abuse. Thus, when patients enter a hospital in New York State, they are given a copy of the state's legislated Patient's Bill of Rights, which includes one's right to "receive all the information that you need to give informed consent for any proposed procedure or treatment. This information shall include the possible risks and benefits of the procedure or treatment" (New York State 1989).

The problem with this approach is that, though it begins with a recognition of the unequal power of physicians vis-à-vis patients, the "rights" trump in the patient's hands is not so strong a tool. First, as Howard Brody (1992) observed, were they so inclined, doctors could manipulate information about the medical situation vis-à-vis their patients to obtain the results that they wished for.[3] Second, the asymmetry of doctor-patient is very deep, so that the power cannot be rebalanced by giving the patient a "right." Among the fundamental causes of this imbalance are not only that the patient is not fully informed but that the patient is ill. Illness makes one disoriented in one's own body. It brings with it a whole set of emotional and intellectual challenges to one's sense of self. These drains on patients are not shared by the doctor, and so this extra burden on patients cannot be undone. Furthermore, the doctor and patient are situated differently with respect to this illness. For even the most compassionate of doctors, treating this patient's disease is one part of the doctor's *work*; for the patient, on the other hand, *this* disease is literally one's *life*. When faced with such an imbalance, how can one begin to think about consent as setting this balance right?

BEYOND CONSENT AS AUTONOMY

Many other feminist scholars have noted the problems with autonomy as the starting point for medical ethics. For them, too, the

---

[3] Indeed, Michael Henry (2006, 322) describes the move toward patients as consumers as an attempt to right this power imbalance: "Patients have turned to other sources and taken more responsibility upon themselves because of evidence or fear that their physician is giving them incomplete information. ... Patient use of the internet has grown largely because of the need for, and availability of, online information."

power imbalances of doctor and patient are more severe when we add in the ways in which sexist and gendered assumptions continue to operate in society to the disadvantage of women. One way in which feminist scholars have tried to solve the problem of the limits of autonomy is to construct the category of relational autonomy. Carolyn McLeod and Susan Sherwin (2000, 260) explain this perspective:

> Whereas traditional accounts concern themselves only with judging the ability of the individual to act autonomously in the situation at hand, relational autonomy asks us to take into account the impact of social and political structures, especially sexism and other forms of oppression, on the lives and opportunities of individuals. … In particular, a relational view of autonomy encourages us to understand that the best way of responding to oppression's restrictive influence on an individual's ability to act autonomously is to change the oppressive conditions of her life, not to try to make her better adapt to (or simply to manage to "overcome") those conditions privately.

Although a conception of relational autonomy marks a breakthrough in thinking about autonomy, it does not tell us which "oppressive conditions" might be relevant in thinking about autonomy in a situation in which an individual is being asked to consent. As Epstein has noted, gender differences in compliance are one reason for being suspicious of the degree of autonomy in consent (see also Hamberg et al. 2002). But knowing this fact does not yet help us to determine *how* we might better construct the consent process so that people are genuinely agreeing, and how that consent might affect the ongoing relationship between health care provider and patient.

A further refinement and solution may be found in bringing the two sides of consent together. In order to understand how this account might work differently, we need to take a closer look at the relationship of consent, power, and authority.[4]

A CHANGE IN OUR VIEW OF CONSENT

If we wish to change how we view consent, it might be instructive to retrace how consent became such a central notion in modern

---

[4] Epstein (2006) considers consent as a form of "autonomous authorisation." In some ways I find Epstein's argument persuasive in its critique of consent but, as is clear in this chapter, I have a different view about the meaning of authority and its role.

thought. As part of the social contract tradition, consent precedes and gives rise to "autonomy."

For early social contract theorists, consent signified a surrender. For Thomas Hobbes (1994), consent to the surrender of one's "right of nature" is the rational alternative to the unbearable predicament of the state of nature. In the political theory of John Locke (1992), we encounter a less stark account of why we should leave the state of nature. But Locke also agrees that given the "inconveniences" of the state of nature, we should be willing to surrender something (here, our power to enforce the laws of nature) in order to create a state and the conditions for a secure way of life (and property). From the standpoint of Hobbes and Locke, the analogy with medical consent is a trade-off; the patient's consent permits a physical incursion on the body in order to achieve another good that comes from this incursion. Rousseau (1987) found that this trade-off was an absurdity; in making such a deal, he writes, "They all ran for their chains." The solution of both Rousseau and Kant (2003) to this trade-off was to view the acceptance of the state as an act of autonomy: If we mean by autonomy the capacity to rule ourselves, then imposing rules on ourselves leaves us free at the same time it gives us rules. So consent becomes a way of self-rule. For Rousseau and Kant, then, when I consent to a medical procedure, I am surrendering my capacity to remain free from this action against my body. I am doing so, though, because I have persuaded myself that this action will, in the long run, be better for me (and, for Rousseau, if one makes an error in judgment, then the state has the power "merely to force one to be free").

If we think of consent-as-surrender, we can see consent as a loss of power. In strict terms of power, we can also say that patients lose their power, depending upon how we think about power. "Power over," the power to coerce, was defined by Robert Dahl (1957, 202–3) as "A has power over B to the extent that he can get B to do something that B would not otherwise do." In a regular consent situation in a hospital, there is no state of nature, but an existing regime of power toward which patients learn to defer (Brody 1992). The individual comes into a set of existing institutions that have a deep context, though that context may be an unfamiliar one for the patient. The new context is constructed to boost as much as possible the doctor's authority and to reduce as much as possible the patient's own sense of context. Clothing, space, time, everything is organized around the hospital's routines. Epstein's findings, that patients acquiesce, are not surprising in this setting.

Consent-as-autonomy differs from consent-as-surrender; consent-as-autonomy assumes that there is no trade-off. One consents because it is best for oneself. Thus, consent is a final outward manifestation of an internal calculus. No relationship of power has changed. As the feminist thinker Wendy Brown (1988) concludes, consent never changes power; it simply legitimizes it. But in raising the question of what power is legitimate, we must switch registers and begin to discuss not only power but also authority.

Suppose that we think of consent not as autonomy, and not as surrender, but as a grant of authority. To do so, we need also change our conception of power. In contrast to Dahl's notion of power as "power over," other thinkers, including Hannah Arendt (1970), describe power as arising out of our collective ability to accomplish a common end; this kind of power is often labeled as "power to." Authority can similarly be defined in two ways, then: when authority is the legitimate exercise of power over, it legitimates domination (cf. Gerth and Mills 1949), but when authority is the exercise of power to, it has a meaning closer to a conception of public trust, which Arendt argues was the original Latin meaning of the term.

To change our thinking about consent from consent-as-autonomy (i.e., an internal check about what is best for me) to consent-as-authority (i.e., should I enter into and legitimate this power relationship?) transforms consent. Such consent-as-authority, connected to power as a "power to" do something, is not a surrender, but the creation of something new, a relationship of authority. Authority is thus by its very nature relational. As a result, to think of consent as a grant of authority is to raise a different set of questions than the internal calculus captured by consent-as-autonomy.

In the first place, authority does not create specific duties, it creates responsibilities. For Thomas Hobbes (1994), "authority" was the actions authorized by consent, carried about by an agent who then possessed the "authority" to act upon this consent. For Hobbes, this grant of authority was analytically true; one could never then question the wisdom of a sovereign's action because the sovereign was acting for oneself, and to question the sovereign's action was to question one's own actions, which Hobbes thought an absurdity. Nevertheless, ever since Locke (1992) pointed out that Hobbes's notion that a grant of authority would undermine the very purpose for creating social order in the first place, most thinkers are willing to acknowledge some limits to authority. As a result, we can think of authority as a kind of trust, and a responsibility.

On what basis might people give either kind of power to authorities? The logic of the former case implies that we might grant authority to those whose power threatens us. But in a medical setting, it makes more sense to think of the authority granted to those more powerful as granted on behalf of a "power to" achieve the end of improving one's health. In such a case, their agency is granted to them on the basis of a perceived competence.

Yet how does one know who are the proper "authorities?" How are people able to judge the competence of the authorities around them? Especially if they have a special competence that is not widely available, how might it be measured? Frequently, as with universities and many other professions, the profession itself assumes responsibility to make certain that no one exercises its authority inappropriately. Limiting authority is rarely left to the less powerful person in the relationship of care that an authority relationship establishes.

If we are concerned with the abuse of authority, it is interesting to note that different forms of authority bring different limits, and the more clear the limits, the less likely that there will be abuse. So, in classic constitutions of the seventeenth and eighteenth centuries, many limits on authority were built into the system of governance in order to prevent abuses of authority (Huntington 1968). On the other hand, in medical care, where much of the ongoing practice is a result of rather snap decisions of diagnosis made by single doctors, it is difficult to know how to set the limits to the doctors' authority. Here, perhaps, does consent enter the picture again.

I have argued that we can think of consent as a method for respecting the patient's autonomy but that we can alternatively think of consent as a grant of authority to the doctor(s). An important advantage of this description is that it widens the conception of responsibility and the context of the act of consent, both for doctors and for patients.

RELATIONSHIPS BETWEEN PATIENTS AND DOCTORS: TRUST AND BENEFICENCE

If we think of consent as a grant of authority rather than as a protection of our autonomy, we see the modes for dealings between health care providers and patients differently. Authority and responsibility raise a different set of conceptual questions, morally and politically, than do rights and duties. Consent-as-autonomy requires that a patient's *rights* be adequately respected. Thus, at the moment at which consent is granted, patients need to be capable of making a judgment. They need to be apprised, as in the "Patient's Bill of Rights," of their options. They have a right to all the information that they need to make their decision transparent. The doctor has a duty to respect that patient sufficiently to seek consent before performing an action, and the doctor fulfills his or her duties by acting according to the agreement (though doctors sometimes must also go beyond those procedures for which consent has been granted).

These are important safeguards for patients. Nevertheless, the view of what is required at the moment of consent looks different from the standpoint of consent-as-a-grant-of-authority. From this perspective, the act of consent is an acknowledgment of the doctor's responsibility to treat the patient. It is, as are all responsibilities, the result of not only an agreement but also a relationship. Thus, consent is an acknowledgment of the existence of such a relationship as well as an assignment of responsibilities within it. Because the patient expects that the doctor will act not only according to the agreed upon terms but also in the patient's best interest, it creates trust.

A striking aspect of these two perspectives is the temporal one. The act of consent bears a resemblance to a contract; however, the agreement represents a one-time action on the part of the patient, whereas it grants authority to the physician that extends both earlier and later in time. This is an important difference; it conjures entirely different views of the relationship between doctor and patient. On the other hand, a grant of authority is an act of trust; the assumption made by the grantor is that the person entrusted will act in ways that are consistent with the reason one consented and granted authority in the first place. Annette Baier (1986), for example, defined trust as a "reliance on others' competence and willingness to look after, rather than harm, the things one cares about which are entrusted to their care." Trust is based upon some way of knowing that the one relied upon will be competent and willing to care about the things entrusted to their care. It thus rests upon experience of some sort and makes a projection into the future about the reliability of the entrusted one. In this way, trust and authority are different from contractual consent. Contracts are generally not made about an uncertain and indefinite future but are based upon the rational calculus of exchange at the moment. Asking patients to consent to medical procedures implies that they are making a judgment about medical treatment similar to one made about any other option in a market – hence, the ubiquitous notion of patients as consumers. But patients are not simply consumers. As Brody observes, any doctor who wished to manipulate information in order to produce a consent outcome can figure out how to do it. The real limitation of this model of patient as consumer, though, is that more is involved in making a medical judgment than possessing information. Even with a lot of information, patients cannot adequately make medical judgments. They do not necessarily know how to weigh the information before them. As a result, the more appropriate model is not between equals making a contract but between a trustee and her charge. Brody describes this kind of interaction not as "consenting the patient" but as the "conversation model" in which patients express their concerns but do not necessarily try to substitute their judgments for the physician's. Brody's use of this language for sharing power is interesting; one important element of authority, surely, is the sharing of a common language (Hearne 1987).

All of these points suggest this difference: consent-as-authority-and-trust speaks to a substantive account of what the consent process is doing, whereas consent-as-autonomy speaks to a procedural account of consent; by consenting, *by the act itself*, autonomy has been respected. Trust is a substantive concern that points toward the content of health care itself (Dworkin 2003). In this way, trust and authority also express a wider sense of responsibility than does consent; indeed, from a legal perspective, one benefit of consent agreements is that they limit responsibility.

If consent is a sufficient condition for respecting the patient's autonomy, then as soon as the consent form is signed, the problem of whether the individual has exercised his or her autonomy is resolved. So what if patients would later say that this was not what they intended to do? If they have signed the form, then they have consented and exercised their autonomy. For many reasons, both personal (such as the difficulty of illness, the complexity of emotions that it produces, etc.) and political (such as the ways in which racist, classist, sexist and other sorts of assumptions still seem to play into the making of health care decisions), although consent-as-autonomy may fulfill the formal requirements of autonomy, it does not often fulfill the broader requirements of what feminists call relational autonomy, that is, recognizing the ways in which context restricts autonomy (Mackenzie and Stoljar 2000).

FOREGROUNDING THE BACKGROUND CONDITIONS OF POWER AND JUSTICE

Within the model of consent-as-authority, autonomy does not require that we attribute to individual actors complete transparency or sovereign capacities of decision making. What autonomy requires is not a complete agreement with the "deal" being offered, but a renewal of an expression of trust in the care that one has received.

From this perspective, of course, the doctor is seen as deserving of the patient's trust. The patient assumes that the doctor takes his or her commitment to the patient as the starting point for treatment. While this may seem to be fundamental to what it means to practice medicine, we should note that the situation in which the patient is trusting is not only the skills and professionalism of the individual physician. In a way, patients are never going to be adequate to the task of making this evaluation. Still, patients can be well cared for by beneficent doctors who do not view them paternalistically.[5] After all,

---

[5] Among the early and constant critiques of any form of consent is that if one eliminates trust, one eliminates not only paternalism but also beneficence. Consider, for example, "The emergence of a 'language of rights,' however, 'abruptly turned the focus in a different direction,' that is, away from a fiduciary relation and toward informed consent – that is, to a discourse focused more on autonomy, entitlement, and rights than on beneficence" (Sokolowski 2001, 46). The claim that I am making here is that a fiduciary relationship is not incompatible with informed consent; one can consent to the relationship by granting authority to the trustee.

as *professionals*, doctors owe responsibilities beyond those to their patients to treat them with beneficence. As professionals, they are also obligated to practice their profession with skill and in keeping with the standards of care that exist within the profession.

In this way, too, the image of the patient as a consumer is inadequate. The model of sovereign choice presumes that patients are able to make decisions as if they were simply the consumers of health in the way that they are consumers of washing machines. Because of the incompleteness of information and the patients' vulnerability, it remains important to make certain that doctors treat them not only as consumers, for whom "the customer is always right" is a sensible idea. The care in health care is not a dyad between doctor and patient, as important as that relationship is. When we realize that there is always a broader set of relationships also implicated in health care, then consent-as-authority allows us to see how such a larger context needs to return to its relationship to the individual patient.[6] In this way, thinking of consent as a grant of authority changes the relationship of doctor and patient from one of mutually consenting parties to one in which the fiduciary responsibility of the doctor toward the patient is acknowledged through the grant of authority. Thus, consent is not only about the principle of respect for the patient's autonomy but also about the principle of beneficence. Insofar as patient autonomy needs to be understood more broadly and in relational terms, questions beyond the scope of the doctor-patient relationship also seem to enter the picture.

Once we go beyond the assumption that consent means that the patient has acted autonomously simply by consenting, we must revisit

[6] Roger Dworkin (2003, 237) makes a similar argument: "What we need is a system that allows each person to receive as much benefit as possible from health care providers' expertise while assuring that professionals do not impose their power in areas beyond their expertise. This article will address that challenge, and make some tentative suggestions about designing that system. It will suggest that we reject the dominance of patient autonomy, abandon the exclusive, fiduciary nature of the doctor-patient relationship, and substitute a system in which professionals owe legally enforceable obligations to behave toward importantly affected individuals with respect for their well-being. Such a system would be more in keeping with the reasons a society has professionals and accords them special powers and privileges than is the present state of affairs. It would also be more consonant with the realities both of modern medicine and modern health care delivery and financing than is the current situation."

the question about the meaning of autonomy. Autonomy is linked with trust only if assumptions about the equalizing of power through the act of consent are true. Otherwise, we cannot assume that this exercise of autonomy is tantamount to an expression of trust. If autonomy means that patients would substantively, in accordance with their own concepts of trust, consent, then the scope of the doctor's responsibility now goes further. Now doctors must make certain not only that the patients have been given relevant information but also that they have a solid grounding on which to make the decisions before them. If one does not simply assume that every consent is an exercise of autonomy, then one must ask, To what extent is this patient *capable* of making a judgment that has not been influenced by outside factors? In this way, consent concerns not only the principle of respect for the individual's rationality as a way to understand autonomy, or only the principle of beneficence expressed through the individual's grant of trust in the physician. In this way, consent also reaches to the principle of justice, according to which the physicians must genuinely consider whether systemic forms of discrimination, substandard treatment, exclusion, and so on color too profoundly the patient's capacity to make a judgment.[7]

As McLeod and Sherwin's thinking implies, institutional injustices also raise profound questions about the meaningfulness of consent. If we look beyond the individual doctor-patient dyad, then we will need to recognize that larger questions such as social justice also affect this grant of authority. If we view consent as a grant of authority, it also allows us to bring back to the center of medical ethics the problem of justice. That health care currently suffers from the reality and the perception of being unjustly distributed is clear. It seems that it might also affect the granting of consent or the choice of treatment options. Once again, the power-balancing act that consent is made to do prevents us from seeing some of these other important dimensions of the problems in the health care system.

---

[7] A group of Swedish researchers discovered, for instance, that "low trust in the health-care system is associated with poor self-rated health" (Mohseni and Lindstrom 2007). If those who are least well served by the health care system are least trusting of the health care system, then what effect will this situation have on the capacity of those individuals to make good and well-informed decisions about their own health care?

We need to recall here that to grant authority, consenters make a judgment about trust, and about the legitimate exercise of power. In this way, consent is not solely about an individual instance or situation but is also about the larger system within which it rests. This way of looking at consent-as-authority has, by now, considerably broadened the range of consideration – and, indeed, actors – in the act of consent. But in spelling out these implications, this rethinking of consent takes us to another point as well: the principle of justice.

After all, insofar as trust in a doctor is also a reflection of the doctor's place within and among health care professionals and a health care system, then we have to ask the question: why should one trust the health care system? Two issues arise.

Full Disclosure

Increasingly, medical journals require a disclosure of the author's or authors' interest in the research and issues reported in the article. For example, if the research on a particular drug's effectiveness was funded by the drug's manufacturer, readers might use this knowledge to make a different judgment about the content of the article. So, too, consent-as-authority requires that doctors divulge their interests. Patients also deserve access not only to "information" but to the information necessary to transform what they know into a considered judgment. The doctors would need to say something like this to patients: "I am going to prescribe that you take drug x. Pharmaceutical company Y gave me some samples of drug x (and took me out to dinner, and paid for my greens fees on a golfing trip), but I am not prescribing it to you because of any financial or personal interest in drug x. I am prescribing it because, in my opinion, it is the best drug for your condition." Or, imagine this statement: "We would like to do a coronary catheterization this afternoon. In full disclosure, I need to also tell you that our hospital is authorized to perform catheterizations but not to repair any damaged heart muscles that we might see. If we see further damage, we will refer you to another hospital. When we have done this procedure another 400 times, we will be able to perform more complex procedures here as well." Under such a condition, what can we expect patients to do? I expect that patients will likely still accede to the authority of doctors and still conceive of their activity as a kind of power being exercised over them. But it may also make clear what is at stake in the procedure. It may provide more accurate informed consent. And it may, as informed consent has in the first place, force doctors to think more carefully about how they provide care to patients.

Justice

When patients grant authority to their health care providers, a key background condition for them to consider is the overall fairness and justice of the health care system. How can one place trust in an unjust system? How can one decide to trust one's own health care providers if there is a structural background condition of injustice? Consider, for example, the fact that, in the United States, a hospital's financial choices may affect the quality of the care one receives after a heart attack. Gina Kolata (2007), reporter for the *New York Times*, wrote:

Studies reveal, for example, that people have only about an hour to get their arteries open during a heart attack if they are to avoid permanent heart damage. Yet, recent surveys find, fewer than 10 percent get to a hospital that fast, sometimes because they are reluctant to acknowledge what is happening. And most who reach the hospital quickly do not receive the optimal treatment – *many American hospitals are not fully equipped to provide it but are reluctant to give up heart patients because they are so profitable.* (emphasis added)

If we think of consent as a grant of authority to the system of care, then the background of injustice comes into play in two ways. First, people who face unjust health care provision are likely to have to make more difficult decisions about their own health care and whether to grant authority (through consent) to their health care providers. African Americans, for example, are more dubious about do-not-resuscitate orders (Shepardson et al. 1999).

Finally, we can speculate about how changing consent to a grant of authority helps us to break out of the model of seeing health care only as a set of individual medical interventions into a social system. Beyond the act of consent in a particular medical setting, what is it that we authorize when we take the current form of health care for granted? The question of justice in the health care system reappears when we begin to consider what consenting, and legitimating, the health care system means. "The higher the levels of inequality – the more rungs on the economic scale, the greater the distance between the richest and the poorest – the worse the nation's health" (Morone and Jacobs 2005, 6). What many health care researchers have shown is that social inequality worsens a nation's health. Individuals currently have trust in their own doctors but have low levels of trust in the health care system as a whole (Hall 2005; Thom et al. 2004; Gilson 2003; Fox 1991). What does this unwillingness to extend trust past the individual case signify? Among other things, it signifies that the individual case ranks above the institution as a whole and that everyone believes that they are able to "get away" with adequate care and so on, even if it is not going to be adequate for everyone. This attitude creates a vicious circle in which those with greater resources are then able to pursue their own private interests, exacerbating the injustice and therefore distrust for the system as a whole.

Health care systems, not only individual doctors and hospitals, require that people have trust in them in order for them to work. If individuals believe that only they can protect themselves, then they will act in ways that are self- and not other-regarding. The vicious circle of privatizing and individualizing care (Tronto 2006) will continue. To legitimate a health care system that is embedded in an unequal society means legitimating a health care system that will produce less desirable outcomes regardless of the spending on health. While this concern is not the concern of individuals engaged in an act of informed consent, it does provide an important part of the background to this picture: not everyone finds herself in the situation of being able to make such decisions. Granting authority in such a system may also require citizens to think more broadly about health care and their responsibilities for living in a healthy society.

In this chapter I have suggested some alternative readings of the ritual of consent. Consent cannot really be seen, in a meaningful way, as respect for the autonomy of patients. The empirical evidence suggests that this is not what happens. If, however, we think of consent as a grant of authority to this doctor, who is part of a system of health care, then we begin to see how individuals – doctors, patients, and others – bear greater responsibility for creating a health care system that, in addition to respecting individual autonomy, takes seriously its commitment as well to beneficence and justice.

1 O

Professional Loving Care and the Bearable Heaviness of Being

Annelies van Heijst

A central thesis of this chapter is that to naturalize bioethics, one must adopt the perspective of the ethics of care. Doing so not only would question basic presuppositions of medicine and nursing but would also better orient bioethics to vulnerability (and therefore carnality), thereby offering a more relational, situated understanding of what health care is all about.

Theoretically and on a practical level, the ethics of care already influences present-day bioethics, at least in the Netherlands, where I live. At the University Medical Center of Groningen, the director of the Center for the Ethics of Care is Marian Verkerk, one of the Dutch pioneers of the ethics of care. In other hospitals, but also in nursing homes and institutes for mentally handicapped people, psychiatric patients, and children, there are many professionals who sympathize with the ethics of care. They view it as a contribution to their work, because of its person-oriented, practical, situation-specific approach. Economic and managerial thinking has a heavy impact on the health care system here as well: in the 1990s the implementation of managed care rationalized the way of working, and in the beginning of the third millennium, although Dutch health care is still partly financed by public means, the principle of the marketplace was introduced.[1] In this chapter, however, the focus is on ethics.

---

[1] Consider the influential Porter and Teisberg (2006), who advocate a solely *economic* strategy of "value-based competition on results."

In Western history, two paradigms have governed institutional health care. The first took shape in monastic contexts, from the beginning of the Middle Ages until the middle of the nineteenth century, as religiously motivated women and men took themselves to be *mending bodies in order to save souls* (Risse 1999, 69–289; Wall 2004; van Heijst 2008). Because this type of care was based on a religious split between body and soul, it ultimately aimed at the eternal flourishing of spiritual beings whose real life would begin only in heaven. In the last quarter of the nineteenth century, a second paradigm emerged due to the secularization of society and the rise of medical and nursing professionalism: the aim of health care was now understood as that of *restoring health and prolonging life*. This paradigm continues to govern much of health care today. The value of postponing death still seems self-evident to many of our contemporaries, who consider it the touchstone of good care. Because of rapidly expanding medical capabilities, however, questions arise with regard to the quality of life. It is one thing to prolong life, but what if medical and technological excellence results in a period of extraordinary misery and grief for the patient?

There are reasons to plead for a next paradigm shift, which would define the final goal of professional care as the *professional relief of suffering in accordance with the patient's own good*. The progression to this paradigm will occur only if, on a cultural and symbolic level, we succeed in making friends with the human conditions of transience and mortality. Although this seems a rather sad thing to do, it would not leave patients without solace, because humans have the capacity of establishing comforting relationships and it is possible for professionals to relate to those who are in pain.

NATURAL VALUES IN HEALTH CARE?

Several reasons can be listed to support this paradigm shift and to destabilize the seemingly natural value of postponing death and mending bodies. First, there is the aforementioned expansion of medical knowledge and technological capability, which paradoxically may lead to the prolongation of a life – but one of utter despair. Perhaps there is too much of a Dutch outlook in my observation, but in the Netherlands questions arise concerning severely handicapped infants who are operated on repeatedly and hardly ever live at home, or gravely demented people who are sustained with drips and tubes, or terminally ill cancer patients whose last months are nothing but a cascading chain of therapeutic events. The underlying moral question is whether *life as such* will suffice as an ultimate value. Do treatments of this kind suit the patients' own good, or are they forms of sophisticated cruelty?

A second reason for reevaluating the presumed natural values of prolonging life and restoring health is the contemporary pluralism in Western societies and the corresponding absence of commonly shared conceptions of the good. Doctors and nurses can no longer take it for granted that they know what is best for patients. They cannot presume to know what a particular patient considers as his or her own good. It may be to live a little longer, but it may just as easily be to die peacefully. Because respect for autonomy is a central value in current medical ethics, professionals must take into account the patient's conception of the good, in sickness and in death. The solution, however, is more complicated than avoiding paternalism and stimulating autonomous decision making in the health care system. What we need are new ways of finding out what really benefits those who are weak, ill, or infirm, in their particular situation. Several authors have suggested that this can be determined only in interpretative, and therefore relational, ways (Welie 1998, 159–201; Olthuis 2007, 133–56).

A third reason for reconsidering the values of prolonging life and restoring health has to do with the type of professionalism within the present health care system. Advances in biomedical technology provide almost unlimited possibilities, and cultural expectations regarding medicine are high. This tempts professionals to do all they can – even to force diagnostic and therapeutic interventions upon people who have little or no chance to recover and cannot defend themselves against these intrusions. The concentration on saving lives sometimes renders professionals oblivious to the needs of patients who cannot be healed.

One morning in 2007, for example, an elderly Dutch patient was told by his specialist that there was nothing the doctors could do to cure him. He would be transferred to a nursing home, where he would soon die. That afternoon the specialist returned to the patient's ward, walked past him as if he were not there, and addressed himself to the patient in the next bed, who presumably would recover. The terminally ill patient, devastated by this treatment, commented: "The doctor simply overlooked me, because *I* represent *his* failure."

A more positive example is the nurse in another Dutch hospital in 2007 caring for an elderly man, lamed because of a stroke, who had just undergone surgery. When he regained consciousness, he was surprised to see her sitting there waiting for him to open his eyes. She said, "I knew how afraid you were, and now I can reassure you it is all fixed and finished." The patient spoke of this incident with tears in his eyes. To him, the nurse's being there was the essence of excellent care.

A fourth reason for reassessing central values that inform the course of action in the health care system is the rise of a technocratic and functionalistic type of medical and nursing professionalism. There are various objectifying tendencies in nursing and medicine, not only at the administrative level but also within the practices themselves. Evidence-based medicine and evidence-based nursing are expressions of this trend, as is the rise of so-called best practices. If these approaches lead to an unlimited faith in figures and statistics – and this seems to be happening – they also undermine clinical interpretative practices, such as talking with the patient, close watching, and physical examination. The tendency to objectification could reinforce a contemporary scientific and secular split between body and mind. Professionals concentrate their interventions on the impaired parts of the patient but are indifferent to the pain and suffering of the patient as a whole. Highly specialized and objectified interventionism might even make professionals think that how the patient feels is not their business, because that goes beyond the specific nursing or medical intervention that is their only concern.

Instead of such a thin conception of professionalism, I advocate a thicker one. We need a conception that is critical of distancing trends in medicine and nursing, dares to relate to patients and their suffering, and is attuned to patients' particular conceptions of a good life and a good death. In short, we need a conception that is infused with professional loving care.

PROFESSIONAL LOVING CARE

The concept of professional loving care (PLC) is akin to tender loving care, the gentle and practical touch that makes humans and things flourish in daily life. PLC, however, can be found in the interaction between health care workers and the people they care for. In a deliberate transgression of fixed moral boundaries, PLC reintroduces the word *love* into the public domain. Its source is not theoretical but is found in the actual affection and respect that exists between health care workers and their patients. Patients say they are fond of this doctor or that nurse, that they like and respect them, and even sometimes that they will never forget them. Health care professionals in turn state that they really *love* their patients, maybe not all of their patients all the time, but some of them, every now and then.[2] PLC is a type of love that is carried out in the context of institutional organizations and within the domain of paid labor. The concept is affiliated to Aristotle's notion of friendship between people who are unequal, to the Christian idea of agape or neighborly love, and to Michael Ignatieff's idea of "solidarity with strangers" (*Nicomachean Ethics* 1158b–1130; Vaceck 1994, 157–98; Ignatieff 1986).

PLC manifests itself in four ways. First, it is historically located, institutionally and legally rooted in social solidarity with the weakest members of society. Viewed in this light, the health care sector itself might be interpreted as an expression of PLC. Next, it can be found in health professionals' willingness to perform a kind of work that is not morally neutral and should not too quickly be equated with other forms of paid labor in capitalist society. The moral quality lies in the readiness of health care workers to be present to those who need them no matter who these other people are. Third, PLC is visible in skilled and competent professionalism that comprises much more than good intentions and requires much effort in learning what to do and how to do it. Actually doing this job as a skilled professional would, I suggest, is a materialization of loving care. Fourth, PLC becomes apparent in the professional's personal dedication, reaching

---

[2] This is the case in the Netherlands, but as I understand it other professionals use a similar idiom.

out to general others in distress but being concretized, again and again, in others who happen to need help. When professionals do not distance themselves but use their relational skills, they can reach out to their fellow creatures in ways that mean a lot to them, even when they are not able to heal and cure them.

If we are going to naturalize bioethics by infusing it with the ethics of care, we will find ourselves attending to the themes of carnality and relationality. Instead of importing new sets of principles, virtues, or utilitarian standards, the ethics of care introduced a distinct perspective that puts care situations in a new light. Its core notions are the revaluation of caring relationships and the personal and emotional implications of that; the recognition of vulnerability and the corporal dependencies that accompany it; and the acknowledgment of the particularistic nature of situations in which care is given. From this, it follows that an ethics of care is critical of individualized notions of autonomy, overly muscular conceptions of human beings, and generalizing approaches that abstract away from precisely those details, medical or nonmedical, that appear to be relevant to patients and their loved ones.

In my view, however, the ethics of care should expand its scope by putting more weight on the concepts of vulnerability – more specifically, *carnality* – and of relationship. A deeper awareness of carnality is needed, in which the transient nature of humans is fully acknowledged. In addition, professionals can and should practice their nursing and medical interventions in a relational and contextual manner, instead of in a merely instrumental and objectified way. Such an approach would have consequences for medical training and for the standards of professionalization.

FEMINIST INTERPRETATIONS OF NATURE

When we naturalize ethics, there is a theoretical challenge that should be resolved first, given the feminist roots of the ethics of care. The challenge concerns the concept of nature or *naturalizing* itself. Why naturalize ethics anyway? Feminist theory was, and still is, critical of links between ethics and nature, or morality and the body, because the body of women has been identified with "woman's nature" and "woman's place," whatever that might be.

Throughout two millennia of Western thinking, women have been identified with the body and nature, seen as equivalent to their procreative and caring abilities, not acknowledged to be fully rational, and denied social equality with men. Contemporary feminists from Simone de Beauvoir (1952) on have strenuously resisted this natural and bodily determinism, so when pioneering thinkers within the ethics of care – Carol Gilligan (1982), Nel Noddings (1984), and Sara Ruddick (1989), among others – introduced a gender-specific moral discourse in which women's moral voices and mothering occupied a central place, they were soon subjected to the charge of gender essentialism. They allegedly poured too much "nature" and "body" into their ethics, and were upbraided for sentimentalizing care.[3] As a result of these charges, Noddings, Ruddick, and other gender-sensitive ethicists were silenced within the mainstream of the ethics of care, at least in the European tradition. This did no justice to their innovative work in gender, physicality, and moral theory.

Nevertheless, the sticky question remains whether one should call for any type of naturalized ethics within a feminist frame of reference. In *Moral Understandings*, Margaret Urban Walker uses the word "nature" in the previously mentioned negative meaning when she describes how women and blacks have been condemned to social servitude because of their feminine or black nature. According to Walker (1998, 171), powerful groups use a strategy of "naturalizing identities" to suggest that some people are by their natures destined for servitude. It was nature that gave them their servile type of body or skin color, and therefore their subjugation was inescapable. Walker rejects the move to this kind of naturalizing, whereby natural facts are characterized as things that exist independently of human opinions, attitudes, or practices, and morality relegates people to the roles they are somehow assigned by nature.

There is, however, a positive feminist interpretation of ethical naturalism. From this viewpoint, naturalism can be conceived of as the capacity for moral expression of a norm-hungry social species whose members need to synchronize attitudes and actions. In my opinion, the ethics of care is in line with this kind of naturalism (van

---

[3] Joan Tronto has rightfully objected to this interpretation of Gilligan. See Larrabee 1993.

Heijst 1995, 82–92). For one thing, the ethics of care was understood right from the start as relying on contextual knowledge and in that way is socially situated and highly particularistic. For another, health care situations are in one way or another always rooted in the natural fact of human flesh. (The Latin word *carne* means flesh.) Traditionally, carnality evokes connotations of sinfulness, sexuality, and lack of control, but I would like to expand these connotations to cover other areas of human existence such as sickness and death. Human carnality, socially interpreted and culturally modified as it is, often lies at the very core of care situations.

HANDICAPPED BODIES IN SOCIAL CONTEXTS

For people who are physically or mentally handicapped, the flesh seems a self-evident signifier. In their cases, however, is it the social and cultural context that determines which, and how, problems surface? In *Bodies in Revolt: Gender, Disability and a Workplace Ethic of Care*, Ruth O'Brien attacks the view that pits handicapped people with special needs in the workplace against normal people without any needs. She also criticizes the dualism between care giving, as something belonging to the private realm, and work, as belonging to the public sphere. Everyone has needs that should be met in the workplace, O'Brien (2005, 32) argues, and therefore "every individual should be viewed as having or potentially having a disability." Real justice in the workplace will be realized, she believes, only if these common human needs are met. This could happen if employment provisions were used to place employers in the position of becoming caregivers. Noting that people with disabilities have considerable political influence, she summons them to start and lead a workplace reform. She concludes that a new legal (and ethical) concept of equality is needed – one that can include differences between people, especially with respect to their disabilities and physical and mental needs. The right thing to do is not to maintain existing standards and exclude the disabled, she claims, but to modify the demands of the workplace so that a woman breastfeeding and a man with heart disease can find their place. Such a transformation would liberate those American workers who must work under alienating and self-disciplining circumstances.

O'Brien correctly reminds us of the repressed neediness of human existence. She is right when criticizing the standard of "normal healthy" people, humans without dependencies and limitations, without any need for care or special attention. This muscular standard reveals the current Western alienation from our material condition. However, we should not characterize all dependencies as disabilities, as O'Brien suggests. Instead of declaring all people handicapped, we would do better to learn to welcome fragility and brokenness as a part of what it is to be human. After all, what kind of subject matter *is* carnality? We tend to think carnality is the sum of objective physical data, because all people are more or less alike. There are, however, reasons to question this presupposition.

CARNALITY IN MEDICAL PRACTICE

The feminist philosopher and physician Annemarie Mol (2002) undermines the fixed opposition between disease, as the presumably objective side of medicine, and illness, as the interpretative category of not feeling well to be dealt with psychologically and sociologically. *Disease*, according to Mol, is itself the interpretative outcome of an ongoing interaction between what patients tell and show, what doctors hear and say, and what can be seen with the help of technical instruments.

Mol (2006) conducted two ethnographic analyses in professional contexts, observing medical responses to atherosclerosis (a deterioration of the walls of blood vessels) and nursing responses to diabetes. She discovered that the biotechnical data of scans, blood research, and microscopic tissue research, when presented apart from the patient's history and the doctor's or nurse's clinical examination, were unreliable indicators for the patient's condition. Postmortem research determined that some deceased patients had very bad vessels but never complained, whereas others complained constantly although their vessels were in a better condition. "Real," then, is the mix of what patients report, what doctors conclude, and what instruments show. Mol (2006, 182) therefore opposes the current "scientific" tendencies in medicine and nursing (best practices, evidence-based medicine and nursing) that rely on so-called objective, rationalized data and scorn the "messiness" of clinical practice.

If disease turns out not to be a "natural" category ready to be captured in objective biomedical data, it must be reconsidered as the outcome of a practice that is enacted by patients, clinical professionals, and all kinds of medical instruments. Medical *practices*, not figures and statistics, give meaning to impaired bodies. Mol (2006, 6) believes that today's professionals tend to rely too much on figures, statistics, and technological instruments and that young professionals are not trained enough to use their eyes, hands, and common sense. She argues that the good at stake in medicine should be doubted and diversified, because people vary in what they consider to be good in daily life.

Mol therefore advocates a shift from the present *who politics* in health care (is the doctor the one to decide, or the patient?) to a *policy of what* (what good is at stake for this particular patient and how can it be served?). Values are not given in the medical order of things, or hidden in the human body, or statistically obtainable, or based solely on the autonomous decision making of the patient. The shift toward a "policy of what," Mol (2006, 172) predicts, would lead to an open-ended debate of a political nature on what to do in health care.

CULTURAL IDEAS OF CARNALITY

By now we may conclude that human carnality is not "there" in an uninterpreted, raw form but rather is the outcome of social, juridical, and medical practices, as O'Brien and Mol suggest. Cultural and symbolical ideas, however, play a role as well, as it is not just individual humans who find it difficult to give meaning to situations of physical and mental deterioration. Western culture as such struggles with suffering and transience, ambiguity and doubt. Individuals draw on cultural symbolic frameworks both religious and philosophical when giving meaning to what happens to them, to their hopes and fears (see C. Taylor 2004).

In her intriguing essay *L'oubli de l'air* (The forgetting of air), Luce Irigaray states that our androcentric culture has expanded at the expense of the massive refutation of the material nature of women and men. According to Irigaray, humans should become aware that they, like everything that surrounds them, consist of the four elements: water, earth, wind, and fire. Irigaray (1983, 31–32) speaks of "ce don de ce dont en quoi il est," which means "this gift out of which living creatures exist." At the beginning of our lives, we received the material substance that determined who we would become, and indeed we could become a human being only because we were conceived and grew in our mother's body.[4] Irigaray's revaluation of the materiality of mankind is thus an antidote against the notion of modernity that humans could and should *master* their life, sickness, and death.

Another French philosopher, Michel Onfray, reflects in a similar materialist manner. At a time when his oeuvre was already a passionate plea for a materialist and hedonist approach of human existence, his wife Marie-Claude was diagnosed with breast cancer. This made him reconceptualize the idea of a good life, turning him against the Christian heritage, which installs a negative a priori against the body and is suspicious of the happy, cheerful, and proud body. These deeply rooted religious elements, he argues, hinder people from dealing with suffering when, inevitably, they must confront it.

Philosophers are seismographs of their time, but artists are as well. Roel d'Haese's sculpture *Song of Evil* represents a horseman who is not impressive and authoritative, as men in statues usually are, but terrified and repellent. Although his stomach is ripped open, the gestures of this quasi hero signify that he is afraid to confront his own suffering. With this sculpture, d'Haese condemns the attitude of denying suffering and death, which he thought was "the barbarity of modernity."[5] The work of d'Haese's contemporary, the British painter Francis Bacon, is rife with a parallel intuition. Bacon painted numerous suffering and decaying bodies, human flesh that is losing its shape and degenerating into blood, semen, urine, and excrement.

Current awareness of human transience was also prominently expressed in two art exhibits in the fall of 2006, one in Louvain, Belgium, and the other in Düsseldorf, Germany, both of which focused on human beings as suffering bundles of flesh. The artworks interrogated the Western ideology of human life and the human body as an object for design and styling, laying bare the hidden and

---

4 There are parallels here with Kittay 1999.
5 For a picture of the statue, see Maréchal and de Jong 2000. D'Haese's explanation of the statue is in the museum, on the pedestal of the work of art.

dark side of carnal reality. Both exhibitions, like the oeuvres of d'Haese and Bacon, displayed a range of people in pain, being tortured, or in solitude and utter despair.

These philosophical and artistic expressions can be interpreted as exemplifications of a contemporary *memento mori*. The ethical impact is limited, however, because they do not show how people could come to terms with their transience. Irigaray keeps silent on the issue of how one can deal with one's material condition, and the artistic works are even grimmer, as they suggest that there is little consolation or hope left.

Although there are no easy solutions in dealing with finitude and suffering, there is a way out, or rather a modest path. On a cultural and symbolic level, we might develop a kind of plural and secularized *ars moriendi*, the trained ability to live in the constant awareness that one will die. In the Middle Ages, *ars moriendi* was the Christian contemplation of decay, whereby the believer continually bore in mind that in the midst of life we are in death. The consoling part of this Christian message was the religious promise of an eternal life, but that consolation is not particularly evident any more. Today's pluralistic society asks for a route that is accessible to various philosophies of life, nonreligious and religious alike.

Perhaps, however, a deeper awareness of vulnerability would only burden the individual. Is there any gain in such a painful awareness of decay and death? Or would it be more convenient to persist in denial and live as if the struggle against illness and death could be won? To address this question, I turn to a real-life case study.

RELATIONALITY IN PROFESSIONAL PRACTICE

At a conference for health care workers in 2006, Marja Morskieft told this story.

I was thirty-two and had just given birth to my third baby. Since I had lost my first baby during a traumatic delivery, this delivery was "high risk": the operation room had been reserved and pouches of blood had been kept ready. It was quite an effort to deliver the thick young boy, but I did it. Our son lived! It was such a relief to my husband and me. Within a few minutes, however, things went very wrong. I lost half of my blood and began to lose consciousness.

One week later, I went home, but had to stay in bed. All of a sudden, everything around me began to rotate, and things seemed to be out of proportion. I saw the ceiling hanging down in strange curves. I understood neither my perceptions, nor my impaired body, nor my exhaustion. Later on, we found out this had been an attack of multiple sclerosis, but at that time we did not know. I was readmitted to the hospital. I felt miserable because my newborn son stayed far from me in the baby ward. The maternity ward was very hot, the windows could not be opened, there was no air conditioning and we lay on plastic mattresses. I was swimming on the bed. Supervised by an experienced nurse, a giggling medical student pulled and pricked me. Then, I slipped off the bed. For the first time in my life I had fainted.

When I regained consciousness, I started to cry and could not stop. The head nurse came to see me. She snapped that I should not imagine I was the only woman who had lived through hard labor and an after bleeding. Then she stalked away, leaving me in utter despair.

After a while an elderly nurse approached me. She sat down on the bed and said, "Just cry. That is not extraordinary after all you have gone through." Then, in the middle of the day and contrary to hospital routine, she proposed to do "some nice washing." At that point, I was a signboard of human misery, covered with blood, sweat, and tears, too dirty to touch. How nice it felt, to be washed with cool water and a soft but determined hand! Not only did I feel cleaner, I was also consoled. She restored my dignity; I will never forget her.

What does the story reveal, read from the viewpoint of asymmetry in power relations, carnality, and relationality? How is PLC revealed in the case? The patient's lack of physical power is obvious and omnipresent. It makes her extremely dependent on the professionals and defines her situation. How could it happen that this patient, who had been through so much already, was pricked by a giggling (nervous, perhaps not very dedicated) medical student? The most likely answer is that the nurse who supervised the medical student saw the patient merely as one of the many patients in the maternity ward who happened to need a blood transfusion and was therefore a prime candidate for the medical student to practice on. It was generalizing and thoughtless; the nurse could have known better, because the patient's history was known in the hospital.

The second question regards the head nurse. Some people in the workshop, nurses themselves, responded to the case by condemning the head nurse's conduct as "unprofessional" because she was rude to a patient. This kind of argument does not satisfy, however. The nurse's rank reveals that she was an acknowledged professional who was granted responsibility by the hospital, and the incident occurred in the open without her being fired. She must have been thinking she was just doing her job. Apparently, her professional code of conduct contained no elements that prohibit nurses from addressing patients in such a way.

When the three paradigms with which I began this article serve as our touchstones, we can see that the nurse was not relating to the patient or to the patient's suffering. She referred to a global scheme of recovery: the patient had survived, she would manage, and therefore she should not complain. Perhaps the nurse would have reacted differently had she known about the multiple sclerosis, because this was an objective threat to the patient's heath. To my mind, however, that is irrelevant. If we allow the third paradigm to guide our thinking, we can see that it is not the diagnosis of multiple sclerosis per se but rather the grief this particular woman expressed that is decisive here.

This patient's story makes us reconsider what "the real thing" is in professional nursing. Apparently, it has something to do with knowing how to put a needle in an arm, but it also has to do with creating a trusting atmosphere in which a patient can cry and make herself understood. Although the nurse could not change the medical condition of the patient, she completely altered the way the patient experienced her situation. "She restored my dignity," the patient testified, and therefore she will never forget her.

We have seen how nurses can do it. Can PLC also take place in the interaction between a doctor and a patient? We return once more to Michel and Marie-Claude Onfray , meeting them in the consulting room of the oncologist, where her diagnosis will be discussed.

As a professional, Dr. J. M. Ollivier reverberated "radical asepsis," as a person, he radiated simplicity. According to Onfray, the doctor had a beautiful, calm, serious and warm voice that showed no attempt to please. During the entire first visit the doctor was occupied with things, almost consumed by them, but meanwhile he kept an eye on the patient. The papers, radiographic photos, and figures informed him about her, and he knew what was in them.

The doctor hardly met the eyes of the patient. He concentrated on *things*, such as a piece of paper with the diagnostic results, a computer screen, a card on which he noted down the patient's answers. He looked at his fingers and his pen. Occasionally, he threw a short but intense glace at his patient, very short so that he would not lose his concentration. When the doctor told Marie-Claude that the tumor was malignant and explained which treatments were possible, she immediately reacted by saying she wanted a radical mastectomy, but the doctor encouraged her to take some time and reflect on it before making a decision. (Onfray 2003, 19–20; author's translation)

As in the case on the maternity ward, Doctor Ollivier's professional intervention has a relational quality, though it is not at all a sentimental one. According to Onfray, the doctor's entire way of addressing Marie-Claude and dealing with her medical condition *modifies* her suffering: though she is in distress, she is not left alone. There is someone she can turn to. And even though he never touches her and barely looks at her, his medical attention is nevertheless loving. He is fully present to her and she to him, and by that connection he eases her grief and fear.

QUALITIES OF PROFESSIONAL LOVING CARE

The elderly nurse and Doctor Ollivier are professionally and personally gifted people. Their qualities will flourish best within a health care system that recognizes the relief of suffering as its ultimate goal, rather than focusing primarily on restoring health and prolonging life. On the one hand, it should not be forgotten that excellent care still is a matter of *best persons*: both Dr. Ollivier and the elderly nurse are estimable human beings. On the other hand, we should not overpersonalize care. Their presence resulted from the *institutional* existence of a health care system that trained and paid them, allows them to do their work properly, and offers important standards of good care. Devoted professionals can carry out PLC only within the confines of institutionalized professionalism.

What are the qualities of PLC? First, there is the reliability of the institution to which people in distress can turn and where they know they will find qualified professionals who are ready to help them. A second quality is the harmonious meshing of professional competences and personal dedication. This happens when a health care worker approaches the patient as both a generalized and a concrete other: as a representative of the category "patients" for whom the professional is responsible and as this particular man or woman. The third quality consists of openness to the suffering of this individual's hurt and a readiness to share, at that time and in that place, a small part of the patient's life. Finally, PLC calls for a redefinition of the final goal of health care: wisdom in dealing with what cannot be cured or solved. Knowing how to endure the grief of permanent loss is not a matter of rationality alone but is closely linked to emotional and spiritual maturity.

TRAINING PROFESSIONALS IN PLC

What are the implications of PLC for the education and training of professionals? What should be taught and practiced? Given that PLC is not exclusively centered on healing and recovery, there are parallels with palliative care (see Verkerk and Hartoungh 2003). It would be good to broaden the notion of palliation to underscore its relevance not only for end-of-life care but for good care in general.

Also important is not demolishing the motivation with which health care workers enter their training: a sincere desire to mean something for people in need. Sometimes medical students and nurse-trainees have other motivations, such as obtaining a part-time job (which is more easily achieved in the health care sector); sometimes it is technology that fascinates them. Yet, many young women and men who choose these professions wish sincerely to help others. Schools of medicine and nursing should encourage this, but, all too often, young doctors, nurses, and paramedics in my country are taught not to get personally involved. They are told to play it safe, which leads to a correct but rather formal way of dealing with patients.[6] Being taught to maintain their distance from patients destroys the initial motivation that could have been vital for their work, if only it had been reflected upon and modified appropriately to their future tasks. In addition to cultivating the existing motivation, professional training should pay attention to the moral value of personal engagement, which contributes to the decency and goodness of the society. Young professionals should experience social

---

[6] For two best-selling recent novels, written by medical students from their own experience, see Bulnes 2004 and Hermans 2006.

recognition, in the form of recognition by the school that teaches them, for the work they are going to carry out.

A further task should be to balance human-directedness with technological means, and the technical skills needed to handle it, both of which are vital to present-day medicine and nursing. Machines and technology easily attract the attention of health care workers, at times causing patients to feel overlooked. Striking a balance between these two kinds of skill should be part of the training, so that patients do not feel subjected to the machines they are put in, or under, or on. Neither should professionals give the impression that the complicated machine is very interesting, while the patient is not.

Another type of balancing is needed between figures and data, which today's medicine and nursing cannot do without, and interpreting what the professional sees, hears, feels, and observes. Relying only on objective data might make the professional feel more secure, but it will not further the best possible care for individual patients. Young professionals should be trained to observe and communicate their findings (with patients and colleagues) and should be encouraged to use both their professional knowledge and their common sense.

Young professionals should also be taught that there is no such thing as one-size-fits-all good care. The goodness of the care depends on how well it is tailored to each particular patient. If professionals learn how to relate particularistically, in an attentive and responsive way, they will find out how to serve best the needs of every single patient. This sounds like it would require an immense effort, but in actual practice it will turn out to be not that difficult, because many patients, especially seriously ill ones, are not very demanding.

Meeting the needs of patients in this way also requires teamwork. If students learn the value of establishing relationships within health care, they could be trained to organize care in a way that maximizes the bonding between professionals and patients. Chemistry in human contact is ambiguous: it may work out well, but it can also spoil the interaction. If problems arise, experienced teams know to reshuffle their tasks so that confrontations are avoided. Young professionals must be taught the importance of this, as it is their duty to care for all their patients and not favor – or neglect – any of them.

A moral and spiritual aspect of training concerns how young professionals are taught to think of themselves. It would be as well if health care were no longer presented to young doctors and nurses as the heroic mastering of human nature and conquering of death but as a modest way of serving vulnerable human beings. Though it goes against the grain of our culture, young professionals must be reminded of their physical limitations, and they should learn that acceptance of finitude and decay is not a defeat. It would help if they could draw here on a cultural repertoire of images, stories, songs, and rituals that are at ease with the transient nature of the human condition.

A last crucial theme in a curriculum of PLC would be to highlight the significance of relating to humans who are in pain, and practice the capability of being there even if one is unable to solve the problem. There are two intertwined skills here: discerning what is going on and knowing how to respond. A new scheme of reference must be introduced to the students, who usually come in with the assumption that their work lies with those who can be healed and cured. They need to learn how they can mean something for patients on another level – an insight that can be put into practice through concrete cases.

PLC demands a reconceptualization of the standards of health care professionalism and its institutional and structural components. Apart from the problems that follow from the paradigm of restoring health and fighting death, there are other threats to PLC. In particular we should think here of the current institutional tendency to avoid uncertainties within the health care system, such as a "total control" management style and the efforts that are made to prevent lawsuits by exercising procedural correctness (Dubet 2002). That tendency should be challenged, as contemporary health care runs the risk of becoming the kind of total institution that Erving Goffman (1961) and Michel Foucault (1975) warned against: anonymous regimes in which no one can be held responsible, but all kinds of things happen that harm people who are caught up in those institutions and can neither free nor defend themselves. When procedural correctness takes precedence over loving care, human uniqueness will be destroyed and the weakest members of society will be sacrificed to the contemporary and secular mode of professional safety.

A naturalized bioethics, in the guise of the ethics of care, would endorse standards of professional health care that are informed by the fact of our carnality and the possibility of our relationality. Although it is impossible to avoid the pain and sorrow of carnal existence, the establishment of relationships of loving care is an appropriate response to misery, for patients can experience the comfort of the other's committed concern. Professionals have a mission here. They cannot cure all patients or prevent them from dying. But they can mean something for them by relating to them, which is a modest but truly humane way of dealing with the bearable heaviness of being.

11

Ideal Theory Bioethics and the Exclusion of People with Severe Cognitive Disabilities

Eva Feder Kittay

> What distinguishes ideal theory is the reliance on idealization to the exclusion, or at least marginalization, of the actual. . . . [I]deal theory either tacitly represents the actual as a simple deviation from the ideal, not worth theorizing in its own right, or claims that starting from the ideal is at least the best way of realizing it.
>
> – Charles W. Mills, " 'Ideal Theory' As Ideology"

Onora O'Neill (1987, 41, 42) writes that idealization "can easily lead to falsehood." She points out that idealizations, particularly idealizations of persons, are especially problematic in the arena of practical reasoning. The difficulty is that "if the world is to be adapted to fit the conclusions of practical reasoning, and these assume certain idealizations, the world rather than the reasoning may be judged at fault. More concretely, agents and institutions who fail to measure up to supposed ideals may be blamed for the misfit." In this chapter I suggest that, at times, the omissions and problematic conclusions that result from idealizations are truly *moral* lapses in the practice of ethics itself. The theories under consideration are typical of a brand of philosophical bioethics that depends heavily on idealizations and hypothetical examples. In the name of simplification, hypotheticals and hyperboles, employing empirically inadequate descriptions drawn from stereotypes, are used to explore and illuminate intuitions. The effects of the idealizing assumptions on the outcomes, however, are rarely examined.

Of particular concern here is a sort of philosophical appropriation of people with disabilities, and particularly those with severe cognitive impairments. The exclusion of this group from the protection of "moral personhood" comes to seem inevitable, unavoidable, and fully justified only because these philosophers neglect important maxims of responsible inquiry, maxims drawn from "best practices" in ethical inquiry and ethical practices. The intent is not to malign any group of individuals. The arguments are often in the service of otherwise admirable ethical ideals, but the consequence of the lapses in responsible modes of inquiry are sufficiently serious to need comment.

PROBLEMATIC INCLUSION AND EFFECTIVE EXCLUSION FROM THE MORAL COMMUNITY

As O'Neill points out, when an ethical theory idealizes persons, the misfit can have important repercussions. Idealizations exclude both by ignoring the existence of those who are too far afield from the idealization and by including in problematic ways those who fall far short of the idealization.

We see this especially clearly when those people who are usually invisible do make an appearance in the theoretical work. Their presence is primarily used to underscore a point, to seal an argument, or to provide a contrast between those within and those outside the scope of the theory. In their role as placeholders rather than participants, as instruments of an argument rather than the subject of discussion, they are invariably misrepresented and reduced to stereotypes. Thus, while people with "normal" characteristics and capacities enter the theoretical stage as idealized versions of themselves, usually featuring selves with all and only desirable characteristics, the others bear all the weight of that which in our human existence is "abjected."[1] Women have long complained about their absence or stereotyped presence in such theories. People of color have joined in the protest, as have people of oppressed gender identities. But the exclusion of people

---

[1] The concept of abjection originated with Julia Kristeva (1982, 1): "There looms, within abjection, one of those violent, dark revolts of being, directed against a threat that seems to emanate from an exorbitant outside or inside, ejected beyond the scope of the possible, the tolerable, the thinkable."

with disabilities, especially those with cognitive disabilities, has until very recently gone without comment.

I illustrate the problematical inclusion of this group in idealized theorizing within bioethics. The work of philosophers Peter Singer and Jeff McMahan illustrate a philosophical strain in biomedical ethics that relies especially heavily on ideal theories of justice, especially utilitarianism. Much biomedical ethics and bioethics are practice based. This more practice-based bioethics encourages clinical experience, actual case studies, and participation in medical rounds. Bioethics is frequently practiced in a multidisciplinary setting that includes scholars of academic specialties other than philosophy, medical practitioners, patients, and families. Such bioethics dips into ideal theory when it looks to theory to determine ethical norms. Some bioethics is closer to care ethics insofar as it deduces norms from the practices themselves. But it is the top-down, theory-driven idealized approaches of philosophers such as Singer and McMahan that has gained them acceptance by philosophers who otherwise have been reluctant to acknowledge "applied" areas of philosophy such as biomedical ethics.

Singer and McMahan are the major proponents of the view that I wish to examine because it has serious implications for people with severe mental disabilities.[2] The view is that the category "human being" is not a morally significant one, and that moral personhood ought to be assigned on the basis of cognitive capacities as determined on a transgenic spectrum – that is, the comparison may be made across species. The case they make for our obligations to nonhuman animals is tied to the possibility of making such comparisons, and making them intelligible. Therefore, their arguments depend heavily on the presence or absence of the capacity philosophers have presumed to be the central requirement for personhood, the capacity for rationality. Out of deference to their past capacities or in anticipation of those that will develop, the status of personhood might be accorded to those who will acquire these capacities and those who may have had them at some point but lost them through accident or disease. The hard case, then, is that of those who never have possessed and never will acquire the requisite cognitive capacities.

---

[2] Others who are well-known proponents of variations of this view include James Rachels (1990), Tom Regan (1983), and Michael Tooley (1984).

Peter Singer focuses on infants who are severely disabled, especially those with severe mental retardation (not those who are beyond the stage of infancy however), while Jeff McMahan considers the congenitally severely mentally retarded (CSMR) of any age. The examples in their works are meant to establish that our moral preference toward our own species is unwarranted. The point is hammered in by questioning the extension of that preference to those humans who lack the requisite moral capacities for personhood and denying that status to animals that supposedly demonstrate higher mental functioning than the impaired humans.

In his book *The Ethics of Killing*, McMahan (2003) makes the argument that it is less bad to kill a CSMR person than to kill "one of us." In the most provoking of Singer's books, *Should the Baby Live?* he and his coauthor, Helga Kuhse, state quite baldly that "we think that some infants with severe disabilities should be killed" (Singer and Kuhse 1985).

Both authors set forth their arguments so that the conclusion seems inescapable that some nonhuman animals deserve better treatment than they now get and that some humans deserve treatment on par with animals. I do not dispute the soundness of the moral conviction shared by Singer, McMahan, and others that our treatment of animals, especially those who are our close cousins on the evolutionary scale, is ethically unjustifiable. The moral disenfranchisement of human beings born with severe mental retardation is, however, no less morally repugnant than the moral disenfranchisement of any other group of fellow human beings, whether it serves as a premise or as an outcome of a philosophical argument, and whether or not that argument is used in the service of another morally worthy proposition.

But the arguments that lead Singer and McMahan to their conclusions are not free from prejudicial input. The bias enters through the idealized presumptions that establish the premises and guide the line of argument. Furthermore, by declaring themselves to be engaging only in pure argumentation, they free themselves from the need to be constrained by empirical realities, namely, the actual lives of people with severe cognitive disabilities who are not party to the discussions, and the fact that some of these speculations can have disastrous implications for those lives. The problematic use of idealizations can be found in:

1. Ontologies deployed in both sets of writings
2. Detachment of the theory from empirical data
3. Willingness to "go where the argument leads," even when the moral implications of the conclusions are repulsive
4. Use of hypothetical examples that are imported into the theory without considering the methodological distortions inherent in such thought experiments

The use of such moral theorizing fails to meet the standards of what I would suggest are found in the "best practices" of ethical inquiry, practices that are attentive to an ethics of philosophizing.

Singer's Arguments

Singer's arguments are familiar. He avers that there is no justification for privileging those who belong to a certain group for no other reason than that they belong to that group. Justifying differential treatment based on group membership has, claims Singer, the same logical form as the defense of racism, sexism, and other forms of discrimination we reject. Arguments that privilege humans simply because they belong to the group of humans is speciesism and is as much a prejudice to be overcome as racism. Instead, if humans have some privileged status morally, it is by virtue of their possession of attributes that turn out to have moral relevance. If beings other than humans possess these attributes, then they too have the same moral standing. Those humans who do not possess these attributes do not share this moral standing. Human animals who do *not* have those attributes have no moral priority over nonhuman animals. For example, when considering whose organs to harvest for the purposes of organ transplants, Singer argues that to take the life of a brain-dead individual or an infant who is so severely impaired that cognitive functioning would be very minimal is morally preferable to killing a perfectly healthy primate or pig for the purpose of harvesting its organs.[3]

---

[3] In fact, Singer believes this is true of infants with Down syndrome as well, and their cognitive functioning is generally not minimal. They are usually classified as having

To make his argument in its latest version, Singer (1994) invokes a provocative example. In *Rethinking Life and Death* he asks us to think about a "special institution" for the retarded that is found in the Netherlands. Here mentally retarded individuals are confined but live a life without many of the constraints to which residents of such institutions normally are subject. They are free to wander about, free to form associations with one another, even free to engage in sexual activity, and have and raise children when they result from sexual encounters. None of the residents have language, but they indicate their desires and wants with grunts and gestures. From Singer's description, it appears that they have no physical problems, other than their cognitive deficits. They communicate perfectly well with one another. These residents, he tells us, raise their children, pick leaders, get elderly females to help with raising the little ones. Close to the end of the description he notes that when one of the residents kills another, the death is not treated as would be the death of a nonresident, and the killer is not thought to have done the same sort of injury. This "special institution" for the retarded, it turns out, is not for people at all but for chimpanzees. From the description we are meant to think that the behavior of the chimps is adequate to a description of a group of retarded persons and so conclude that both populations share the same morally relevant attributes determining their moral standing.

Singer's use of this elaborated image of the "special institution" illustrates well the features we pointed to earlier. A hypothetical example, one that is not tethered to any actual circumstance, is used establish an argument that has results we would otherwise find unpalatable, namely that there is no moral difference between humans with mental retardation and chimpanzees. According to the social ontology underlying the example, persons are distinguished by the possession of certain cognitive capacities that make killing them more serious than killing nonpersons. There is little reflection on how the simplifications and representations demanded by a hypothetical of this sort create serious distortions of the reality of people with cognitive impairments, the notion of community, and

mild to moderate retardation. But I put the point this way to put forward what many may think is the stronger argument.

the relationships we bear to people and to nonhuman animals. Finally, his use of the example makes it clear that he is willing to go where the argument leads, even when the results are strongly counterintuitive and would adversely affect the population of human beings under discussion.

Jeff McMahan's Arguments

Jeff McMahan (1996) argues in "Cognitive Disability, Misfortune, and Justice" that those with congenital severe cognitive impairments fall below the threshold of capacities needed for personhood and thus are not subject to the claims of justice. In *The Ethics of Killing: Problems at the Margins of Life*, he sets out to determine when and why killing is wrong. McMahan (2003, vii) is especially interested in cases where those concerned are ones "whose metaphysical or moral status ... is uncertain or controversial." In contrast to "them," there are "us." But who are "we"? McMahan answers by determining what "we" are, when we come into existence, and when we cease to exist.

McMahan develops a complex metaphysics derived from the work of Derek Parfit. Here, the self we are at any one time is only contingently related to the selves that preceded and that might succeed our present self. To the extent that we can recall previous selves and can anticipate future ones, we are more closely connected to these selves. The more continuity we have to our previous selves and our future selves, the more we can think of our own interests at this moment as tied to the interests of the past and future selves. If we have little continuity with a future self, then our current interests have little in common with the interests of that future self. Being able to have that continuity requires, for McMahan, a set of psychological capacities, the ones that characterize us, rationality and other higher-order cognitive capacities. This metaphysics is then based on the idealization of an "us" – "we" persons who have rationality and higher-order cognitive capacities – and the "us" is exclusive of all who lack these capacities. Infants and, arguably, those who are congenitally severely mentally retarded (CSMR) lack these. The lack of capacities means that they lack the interests of folks like us, that is to say, persons. In particular, they lack the same sort of interest in not being killed as persons. Note that "congenital" is often added to this list of adjectives characterizing the individuals in question, so as to exempt those who have at some point in their lives been sufficiently cognitively able to fall under the philosophical use of the term "person." This narrows the category of individuals whom these discussions concern. However, because the concept of person these philosophers favor involves a continuity of mental life that is often disrupted by severe injury to the centers of cognitive activity, it is arguable that the individual in question is no longer the "same person," and so it becomes mysterious why they ought to have a different moral status from those who were born with the cognitive deficits that they believe disqualify human individuals from personhood.

The CSMR are not persons on at least two counts. First, they fall outside the descriptive bounds of personhood as traditionally philosophically defined. Second, they fail to be persons on metaphysical grounds, which similarly require psychological capacities that they appear to lack. That they are not persons also leads to the conclusion that we ought to treat CSMR as we treat animals. Although this does not comport with common beliefs, McMahan eventually concludes that we have to bite the bullet and accept that those with the same cognitive functioning and psychological capacities should be given the same moral status regardless of their species. This means treating many animals better than we do now and treating some humans worse than we do now. To support the need to accept this counterintuitive conclusion, he makes the following appeal in this remarkable passage:

It is arguable ... that a[n] ... effect of our partiality for members of our own species is a tendency to decreased sensitivity to lives and well-being of those sentient beings that are not members of our species.

One can discern an analogous phenomenon in the case of nationalism ... [where] the sense of solidarity among members ... motivates them. ... But the powerful sense of collective identity within a nation is often achieved by contrasting an idealized conception of the national character with caricatures of other nations, whose members are regarded as less important or worthy or in many cases, are dehumanized and despised as inferior or even odious. ... In places such as Yugoslavia and its former provinces – the result is often brutality and atrocity on an enormous scale. ...

I believe our treatment of the severely retarded and our treatment of animals follows a similar pattern. While our sense of kinship with the severely retarded moves us to treat them with great solicitude, our perception of animals as radically "other" numbs our sensitivity to them. ... We are not ... aggressively hostile, ... we are simply indifferent. But the indifference ... when conjoined with motives of self-interest ... involve[s] both killing and the infliction of suffering on a truly massive scale. ... When one compares the relatively small number of severely retarded human beings who benefit from our solicitude with the vast number of animals who suffer at our hands, it is impossible to avoid the conclusion that the good effects of our species-based partiality are greatly outweighed by the bad. (McMahon 2003, 221–22)

Here McMahan uses the results from a theory whose idealizations are embedded in a metaphysics of the person and persists in following the argument to whatever unpalatable conclusion it may lead. Where it leads is to the "impossible to avoid" conclusion that we pamper the cognitively incompetent at the expense of the well-being of nonhuman animals.

McMahan's indignation at the coddling of individuals merely because they bear the relation of same-species membership to "us" is palpable. Yet, his own portrayals of the severely mentally retarded are mere "caricatures" of the "other," viewed "as less important or worthy," "dehumanized," and, if not "despised as inferior," at least regarded as inferior. Elsewhere I also argue that the analogy is inapt, but I leave that point for the purposes of this chapter. (For a fuller elaboration of this argument, see Kittay 2005.)

The moral dangers of drawing lines among human beings, even in the worthy cause of advancing the well-being of animals, are not hypothetical. As Nozick (1983) warned in his review of Reagan's *Animal Rights*, it is less likely to bring about better treatment of animals than much worse treatment of humans. Furthermore, cultivating moral sensitivity to the suffering of animals is no guarantee that the same sensitivity will extend to the nonperson humans, as we learn from the history of Nazism.

The law for the protection of animals was passed by the Nazis on November 24, 1933, very shortly after the National Socialists took power. It was a law "designed to prevent cruelty and indifference of man towards animals and to awaken and develop sympathy and understanding for animals as one of the highest moral values of a people" (T. Taylor 1949). The law called on Germans to not regard animals in terms of mere utility. Experimentation involving animals had to avoid causing them pain, injury, or infection, except in very special circumstances, and special authorization was required for the use of animals for experimental or medical purposes. As we learned from the Nuremberg Trials, the same doctors who rendered certain humans as beyond moral protection were filled with noble moral sentiments toward animals. They could not only experiment on but neglect these precautions in the case of those who were outside the bounds of moral consideration. Sensitivity to the suffering of non-human animals did nothing to foster sensitivity to the suffering of human nonpersons.

THE ETHICS OF PHILOSOPHIZING AND THE BEST PRACTICES OF ETHICAL THINKING

The exclusion of the mentally retarded from the community of human persons and its moral consequences result from some highly questionable ways of theorizing. Such theorizing rides roughshod over empirical realities and descriptive adequacy, takes the values of a privileged group as the principal values worthy of endorsing, and fails to consider the consequences of one's theorizing on those whom the theory deems outside the purview of its principal considerations.

In light of these faults, I want to articulate four maxims that are not heeded in this philosophizing, maxims too easily ignored when we are no longer tethered by the actuality of practices. Two (epistemic responsibility and accountability) are maxims of responsibility; the others (epistemic modesty and humility) are maxims of humility.

Epistemic Responsibility: Know the Subject That You Are Using to Make a Philosophical Point

Let us consider the thought experiment set up by Singer: that of a community of cognitively subpar humans that turns out to be a description of a community of chimpanzees. From the description, we are meant to think that the behavior of the chimps is adequate to a description of a group of retarded persons, and so conclude that both populations share the same morally relevant attributes determining their moral standing. However, the description is suspect because human impairments are multiple and the sorts of deficits in a population of retarded persons would vary considerably. Yet these residents are pretty much alike – function at much the same level – in large measure because they are chimps without the sort of deficits of the severely cognitively impaired human. To borrow from Tolstoy, "All unimpaired humans are alike; all humans with severe impairments are impaired in their own special way." We can retain some characteristically human capacities and lose others. What is lost and what is retained determines how much of the scope of human existence we can take in. Therefore, it is most unlikely that one could have a community of humans who all have the same cognitive impairments, all functioning at the same level, and all able to function as a human community without the assistance of humans without such impairments. If they could, then they would be capable of the moral capacities of other humans and the last somewhat shocking claim that killing among them would be of no moral consequence would be inconsistent with the premises of the thought experiment. What the example indicates is that the author has a very little knowledge of people with the sorts of impairments he is presumably speaking about. Now this is a thought experiment, and so it can surely include counterfactual elements. What is counterfactual, however, is exactly what is at stake in the example – that is, whether chimps are functionally indistinct from mentally retarded humans. So it cannot be effective in proving that very point without begging the question. As Singer is an astute philosopher, it is probably more likely that he erred in the empirical claims embedded in the example than in the form of argumentation. Moreover, the example depends on the reader's ignorance of what mental retardation in humans looks like.

The sense that it is unnecessary to acquaint oneself sufficiently with the empirical realities of mental retardation is still more evident in the work of McMahan. McMahan (1996, 5, 8) defines the severely mentally retarded (in a note he excludes the mildly and moderately retarded and those with subsequent brain injury) as human beings "who not only lack self-consciousness but are almost entirely unresponsive to their environment and to other people"; he elaborates, "The profoundly cognitively impaired are incapable ... of deep personal and social relations, creativity and achievement, the attainment of the highest forms of knowledge, aesthetic pleasures, and so on."

This is seriously misinformed. Most severely retarded people can speak at least a few words and can be and are involved in activities and relationships. Even profoundly mentally retarded individuals are far from being unresponsive to their environment and to other people. My daughter, Sesha, was diagnosed as severely to profoundly retarded. She is enormously responsive, forming deep personal relationships with her family and her long-standing caregivers and friendly relations with her therapists and teachers, more distant relatives, and our friends. Although she will tend to be shy with strangers, certain strangers are quite able to engage her. I have written quite a bit about her love of music, especially but not exclusively classical symphonic music, with the master of this form, Beethoven, being on the top of her list. So much for the assertion that persons with severe mental retardation cannot experience aesthetic pleasures!

Since I wrote the article in which I counter McMahan's claims and arguments, I experienced one of the most profound learning experiences of my life. My daughter now lives in a group home with five other people who are all considered to be severely mentally retarded, and have been so since birth. Two of her housemates lost their fathers within the period of a month. One, a young woman diagnosed with Brett's syndrome, would be found sitting with tears streaming down her face after she was told that her father was extremely ill and would die. In the case of the other, a young man who invariably greets me with a huge smile, I myself witnessed the howling, wailing grief minutes after his mother and sister informed him of the death of his father. He waited until they left before he began his heart-wrenching sobbing. They most likely left not knowing what he had understood and learned of his response only when they later spoke to the staff. It is not unreasonable to suppose, in the case of this young man, that he held back his grief to spare his mother and sister. We are speaking here of the capacity to understand the very abstract concept of death, the death of a beloved person. So much for cavalier claims that the severely retarded cannot form profound attachments.

McMahan has other characterizations of the CSMR. In the *Ethics of Killing*, he sometimes speaks of their having psychological capacities equivalent to that of a chimp or, in other places, to that of a dog.

I am not going to rehearse the things that Sesha can or cannot do and what a dog can or cannot do. Such comparisons are otiose and odious. They are also senseless, for nowhere do we learn what it means to say that a human individual has *the same level* of psychological capability as a nonhuman animal. What Sesha can do, she does as a human would do them, though frequently imperfectly. But it is humanly imperfect, not canine perfect. However, even with all that Sesha cannot do and seems not to be able to comprehend, her response to music and her sensitivity to people is remarkably intact – or more correctly, quite simply remarkable. What a discordant set of abilities and disabilities she exhibits! This unevenness, a feature of many severely and profoundly retarded persons, is evident in neither the transgenic comparisons of McMahan nor those of Singer. Such unevenness is not a feature of the animals with whom McMahan and Singer equate them.

Epistemic Modesty: Know What You Don't Know

What cognitive capacities Sesha possesses I simply do not know, nor do others. And it is hubris to presume. Every so often, I am shocked to find out that Sesha has understood something or is capable of something I did not expect. Although she has consistently been exposed to some of the most progressive teaching available and her gains have been modest, the surprises keep coming. And, as I related, other people with similar diagnoses keep surprising me and their caregivers. These surprises can only keep coming when their treatment is based not on the limitations we know they have but on our understanding that *our* knowledge is limited. If my daughter's housemates had not been told of their fathers' death, on the premise that they could not possibly understand the concept of death, we never would have known that they could. Matt's response to his father's death was like that of any son who learns of a much beloved father's death. The grief expressed was as full and as profound as any I have seen or experienced.

Humility: Resist the Arrogant Imposition of Your Own Values

Humility in the face of our ignorance of what others know and do not know must extend to humility in the face of our uncertainty of what people care about as well. This means that we need to be alert to the possibility that the values we hold dear blinker us and allow us to presume that these values *must* have the same importance for others. To a certain extent such projection, in the face of our ignorance of what another finds salient, may be a gesture of solidarity. To stay with the example at hand, we know that the death of a parent is a momentous occasion in our own lives, and we think that it may be no less so in the lives of people with severe mental retardation. So we conclude that we should at least expose an individual to the fact, and do so in a sensitive manner. In so doing, we refuse to distance the individual with mental retardation as an Other who bears scant resemblance to ourselves.

But when we pay little heed to what others have to say about what they believe to be important, create hierarchies in which our own values always trump those of another, or unreflectively rely on such hierarchies when we appeal to "what is evident" or what is "surely" the case, then we act out of hubris.[4] While we cannot help but make appeal to our own values and perspectives, we need to pay close attention to the role these are playing and not presume our logical argumentation is untouched by the importation of such values.

When philosophers hold that contemplation is the highest human endeavor or that logical inquiry is the crown jewel of the human mind, they either fail to perceive a major source of that value – namely, that of a philosophical temperament – or fall prey to a hubris, which takes what philosophers hold dear to be what all *should* hold *equally* dear. Such projection is disrespectful of the lives of others, or of other conceptions of the good, and is contrary to any liberal principles that maintain the plurality of goods.

Violation of this principle is found in both Singer's and McMahan's work, each overemphasizing the importance of cognitive capacities and depending on the self-evident nature of claims that are not at all self-evident. It is found in McMahan's presumption, one shared widely among philosophers, that a life without developed cognitive skills is always and inherently an inferior life. McMahan extends this presumption to the life of animals, arguing that they have less good in their lives than we have because they have reduced

---

[4] This is fairly close to what Iris Young (1990) calls "cultural imperialism," which she takes to be one "face of oppression."

cognitive capacities. By closing off the horizons of those whose life is not centered on cognitive capacities, we help make a self-fulfilling prophecy of the claim that such a life is a lesser life.

Accountability: Attend to the Consequences of Your Philosophizing

It is ethically irresponsible to fail to consider the real-world consequences of one's philosophical position, especially for those who are not – and cannot be, in a crucial sense – a party to the debate. Where there is a danger that some will be harmed if policies based on a theory are put in place, the philosopher must be ready to acknowledge responsibility for these harms or, better still, reconsider the theoretical options. Clearly philosophers often engage in this sort of reflection; it is part of the practice of philosophizing that keeps it responsive to the actuality of what is being discussed. The method of reflective equilibrium, for example, aims to reconcile philosophical theorizing and common moral intuitions in part because of the possible negative consequences of abandoning common moral intuitions in favor of philosophical theory. McMahan appears cognizant of the potential harm of treating the CSMR as animals and so is not unaware of the negative consequences of his theoretical conclusions. He weighs these consequences against the improvement in the treatment of animals and, taking into account mitigating factors that allow us to treat CSMR somewhat better than animals, concludes that he is satisfied with the outcome. But this version of "reflective equilibrium" seems very inadequate.

How can he seriously suppose that sentences such as "Allowing severely retarded human beings to die, and perhaps even killing them, are correspondingly somewhat less serious matters than we have believed," are responsible statements, especially given the history of murder and abuse of this highly vulnerable population? Imagine McMahan as the parent of such a child who finds himself without the financial means to save his child because some legislator was responsive to McMahan-type arguments. Could he find this acceptable? If he cannot, can he really allow his own results to stand?

McMahan acknowledges that the line between those who are persons and those who are not is somewhat arbitrary, and that we might want to draw the line so as to offer ourselves maximum protection, but asserts that his argument implicitly acknowledges that there is no difference between the CSMR and animals. It seems to me that what is arbitrary is not the line between humans with mental retardation and nonhuman animals but, rather, making cognitive capacity the criterion for personhood.

We have seen clearly in the Nazi experience – and not only in the case of Nazis – how quickly dissolved are the lines people draw between humans who are like us and those who are not, how easily those on the right side of the line pass to the wrong side. We also know that what is a severe impairment and a mild impairment, what is a disability and what is not, is frequently determined by the way the persons with impairments are viewed.

McMahan has responded to some of my criticism by saying that he did not intend the term CSMR to refer to people such as my daughter or her housemates; that he was using the term "stipulatively," a liberty philosophers often take. That is, the CSMR are just those people who have just the characteristics he attributes to them – the acronym is merely shorthand for just that description. This he believes lets him off the hook for the first principle. But if it does, it merely adds weight to the charge that he violates the fourth principle. To claim that a diagnostic term such as "congenital severe mental retardation" can be used stipulatively is to ignore the fact of its circulation in diagnostic, treatment, and policy contexts; thus, it is to ignore the consequences of the philosophical argument on all those who bear that label. A defense that McMahan uses the term "congenitally severely mentally retarded" stipulatively could only be acceptable if he were aware of the empirical fact that the term had a clinical use and had carefully distinguished his use from the conventional one. This is not what the text reveals. But even if he had done so, his "stipulative definition" employs all the stereotypes of people who are in fact labeled "severely mentally retarded" although these, like negative stereotypes in general, are based on ignorance, misrepresentations, and prejudice. It is as if I argued for conclusions that supported adverse policies to deal with people who are avaricious, loud, pushy, too smart for anyone's good. For convenience, I *stipulate* that I will call those who fit the description, "Jews." Now, suppose that a policy maker, influenced by my arguments, then imposes severe restrictions on actual Jews. Can I beg out of any responsibility for this anti-Semitism on the grounds that my use of the term "Jew" was merely stipulative?

Works as apparently rigorous and authoritative as McMahan's or as seemingly cogent, accessible, and widely read as Singer's have serious destructive possibilities, even when their motive is the worthy one of improving our treatment of animals.

ETHICAL "BEST PRACTICES"

Where, one might ask, do these particular maxims of humility and responsibility come from? I would suggest that, first, they can be traced to certain values within the practice of philosophy itself, even though much philosophizing ignores them. Second, they can be seen in the practices that constitute our ethical life: they are among those "best practices" that allow us to live together harmoniously. In a naturalized ethics such as care ethics, for example, it is relatively easy to identify each of these maxims in the "best practices" of giving care.

Consider the first maxim, *epistemic responsibility*. Philosophy, by many accounts, is concerned with truth. The truth cannot be served if philosophers do not acquaint themselves with the basic facts about the subject under consideration. As I have indicated, both Singer and McMahan fail to do so in their discussions of individuals with mental retardation. One might ask, Why is such a clear violation of a philosophical value tolerated? Here a pernicious effect of idealization displays itself. Empirical realities give way to idealized descriptions and "stipulative definitions," in order to construct a theory that then can be "applied" to the real world. But these idealizations and stipulative definitions may well construct a theory that is not applicable, or not applicable to that part of the real world that it purports to cover.

Consider, in contrast, the way in which a naturalized care ethics is theorized. The practice of caring requires attention to the actual condition of the individuals who need care. Broad generalizations and presumptions – such as, "The severely mentally retarded cannot have aesthetic experiences" – cannot be the basis of good care, because the principle source of joy for many people with severe cognitive impairments derives from aesthetic experiences such as music. A person intent on giving good care must reject stereotypes and be attentive to what and how the person in front of her responds.

(Certainly this is no less true of health care situations, although practical pressures result in a considerable relaxation of this demand of care.) A care ethic thus expresses the central values of attentiveness and responsiveness to actual conditions and, with that, the responsibility to make oneself knowledgeable about the facts on the ground. That is to say, it reflects the value of epistemic responsibility of the sort that I discuss in the previous section under that heading.

Not only do we need to be responsible and insure that our philosophizing does not ignore salient empirical realities that are known, but we have to be humble in the face of that which is as yet unknown (the third maxim, humility). It seems hardly necessary to remind philosophers of what Socrates taught, that the greatest wisdom is to know what one does not know. Yet idealized theorizing, with its tendency to prefer clear lines of definition and opposition, makes it easy to forget to keep a focus on knowing what we do not know.

Humility in the face of ignorance also reflects a value, one might say a necessary virtue, in the practice of caring. When we presume to know what we do not know, we are likely to fail in truly meeting the needs of the one for whom we care. In the practice of medical care, such hubris can easily cost lives.

With respect to the third maxim, we can point out that liberalism is a dominant philosophical position, central to which is the recognition of a plurality of goods. This elevates to a central precept of contemporary philosophy the stricture against the arrogance of imposing one's own values as the true and only ones. Reasonable value pluralism (as distinguished from value relativism, where anything goes) is, if you will, the received view. But philosophers frequently violate it by presuming the overriding value of reason.

An antidote for such presumption is found in the very practice of care. Many who need care are not in a position to exercise their rational functioning (to whatever degree they possess it). Yet for the person who does good care, the value of, and respect owed, the person is never in doubt. The very act of care (when it is good care and not merely the perfunctory carrying out of assigned duties) attests to the value we place on the person's life and well-being whether or not he is capable of rational deliberation. Caring for one who is seriously dependent on our ministrations can, however, tempt one to presume to know what is good for another and what is of value. It can tempt us to think that we can (or even should) impose our own view on the other. However, such caring, I maintain, is not respectful caring, caring that respects another's agency. Thus, I believe, best practices of care equally demand that we do not presume that what we value is the only thing that is valuable.[5]

Finally, there is the issue of accountability, the final maxim. The need for accountability is inherent in any practice, for without it, one cannot guarantee a consistency of standards. This is evident in practices of care. Parents are held accountable for their children's harmful actions when these were foreseeable and preventable. In medical practice, physicians similarly must be held accountable for foreseeable consequences. Any ethic of care must include the importance of being accountable for what we do.

Yet, philosophical practice has been strangely inattentive to the importance of accountability. In this, philosophers appear to take their cue from theoretical science, in which practitioners claim that their only concern is the truth and that if others use their discoveries in a harmful fashion, that is not the scientist's fault.

There may be a conceit in philosophy that philosophy is of interest only to other philosophers, and thus philosophers need not worry about accountability. Again, consider the widespread move to idealization in philosophy. If one is doing ideal theory, one is not writing about philosophy that can apply in a straightforward way to the world, and to presume that it can be, so the argument goes, is to misconstrue the philosophical project. A related conceit is that philosophy is so abstruse, so prone to misunderstanding and multiple interpretations, that the philosopher ought not to be held to account for misreadings and misapplications. Socrates, after all, was unjustly held to account for his teachings, with disastrous consequences.

---

[5] Arrogance in the practices of medicine and health care are often easy to detect but can also enter into the practices in ways that are not easily seen. When it does, it is deemed paternalistic and currently is not considered to be the standard of (good) care. For two excellent accounts of how medical care is undermined by the imposition the physician's own values, see Ellen Feder (2002), who discusses the interaction between parents of intersexed children and their physicians; and Ann Fadiman (1998) for an account of a collision of values between a Hmong family and well-meaning physicians and the disastrous results for the child.

Yet people who write about ethics often do want their work to have an impact outside the confines of academic philosophy. Clearly, it would seem, this is true about applied and practical ethics such as bioethics. The kind of writing that is the focus of my criticisms is a sort of hybrid between the theoretical and the applied. While it is like bioethics that is strongly tied to clinical practice, its authors take up issues that are of immediate relevance: euthanasia, the infanticide of neonates, abortion, prenatal testing, the rights of animals. Yet they develop their positions on such topics by deducing their conclusions from theories that are full of idealizations. This hybridity can be quite pernicious when the levels of discourse are not clearly delineated and when the central concepts and conceptions are only loosely related to the facts on the ground.

Biomedical writings, whether of the philosophical sort or the more practice-based sort, do have a reach beyond the academic community. And those of us who engage in this work must understand ourselves to be engaged in a practice that holds people accountable for the foreseeable consequences of their writings. By remaining attuned to the practices themselves, I suggest, we are better equipped to accept such responsibility, even when we reach out to ideal theory for guiding norms. Still, it is better to do bioethics on the model of a care ethics, which finds the guiding norms within the practice itself.

Epilogue

Naturalized Bioethics in Practice

Marian Verkerk and Hilde Lindemann

As the chapters in this collection show, naturalizing bioethics is a dynamic business: it requires us to move continually from theory to practice and back again. Theory is overhauled, adjusted, and fine-tuned in the light of practice and practice in the light of theory, and justification rests on the norms that have been tested and found good in critical and self-reflexive deployments of this process. The essays gathered here offer many examples of how bioethicists might build better theory by understanding individuals in context, attending to the web of relationships in which we all live, appreciating the reality of power, and – a not unimportant point to which we will return – situating themselves within their own work. But what does all this mean for bioethicists in clinical settings? In this epilogue, written specifically for bioethicists working in health care institutions, we set out an agenda for a naturalized bioethics in practice.

The agenda can be thought of as a call for three closely interconnected kinds of change. First, bioethicists will have to alter how they engage in – and teach clinicians to engage in – moral deliberation. Second, because working conditions greatly affect how well health care professionals can exercise their moral agency, bioethicists may need to initiate changes in those conditions. Third, bioethicists will have to change how they understand their own role in the clinical setting. We take up each of these in turn.

MORAL DELIBERATION

Over the past two centuries or so, moral philosophy has largely aimed at finding the right method for producing "clear and decisive precepts or counsels" (Sidgwick 1981, 199). If we take the dynamic nature of morality seriously, however, philosophy must aim at something else. Rather than set out on a misguided quest for a single correct method for moral deliberation, philosophers do well to embrace bottom-up methods, such as hermeneutics, casuistry, and reflective equilibrium, that are open and responsive to change. But they also need to describe the continuing process of reflection and moral action that values plurality, dissent, and controversy. This is a departure from traditional ethics.

The Dutch philosopher Wibren van der Burg (1999) makes a relevant distinction in this respect between a so-called product model and a process model of morality. A product model focuses on morality as a set of normative propositions, such as rules or principles, that guide human interactions. A process model focuses on the interactions themselves. It conceives of morality as a living thing, a continual interpersonal process of holding ourselves and others to account for what we value, negotiating responsibilities, making ourselves morally intelligible, and constructing and reconstructing our moral views of how best to go on together (M. Walker 1998). This is a model of participatory ethics, in which all actors are involved in a collaborative mode of deliberation.

On a dynamic view of morality, moral deliberation is primarily aimed at making sense of these complicated moral interactions and is only secondarily concerned with problem solving. It calls attention to the essentially interpersonal nature of morality and moral thinking. Finally, it engages the moral imagination and other moral faculties.

From the perspective of a naturalized bioethics, one good reason why moral deliberation must attend to the interpersonal nature of morality is that health care professionals provide care in highly organized and complex surroundings, where they interact not only with patients but also with other professionals. Doctors, nurses, other members of a health care team, hospital or nursing home administrators, and patients all participate in practices of giving and receiving good care. And, because good care is a matter not only of

doing things in the right way but doing the right things, among these
health care practices are practices of moral responsibility, where each
participant has her or his own role to play. These practices can be
"mapped," as it were, into a geography of responsibility (M. Walker
1998). In such a geography, we can read how and upon whom
responsibilities fall, and how shared understandings flow with regard
to who is to see to and account for arrangements, outcomes, or tasks.

To map their responsibilities, professionals must first realize that
their practice contains multiple perspectives and positions. This
means that they must be aware of their own professional norms and
values and be able to express them to their colleagues, their patients,
and the patients' families. Once they have a good sense of who they
and the other players are, they can do a better job, morally speaking,
of working together with these other actors to make decisions about
ethically troublesome cases.

This is where the bioethicist comes in. To enhance the ability of
professionals to engage in this kind of moral reflection, bioethicists
can offer them a framework for mapping their responsibilities
(Verkerk et al. 2004). The bioethicist proceeds in three stages. First,
she helps professionals develop a heightened moral sensitivity to the
vulnerabilities, values, and responsibilities they encounter in their
work, by showing them that they can identify and develop their own
point of view from which to make decisions about the best way of
proceeding. In this stage, the bioethicist presents a case that circles
around a puzzling moral situation, perhaps some incident from the
professionals' own experience that produced unease – for example,
heart-valve replacement surgery for an uncooperative heroin addict
in the care of several professionals with differing views of what should
be done. The bioethicist asks the professionals to write down their
reaction to the case, reflecting only on how it seems to *them*.

In the second stage, the bioethicist asks the professionals to reflect
together. To facilitate this conversation, the bioethicist introduces a
heuristic we have dubbed the reflection square (see Figure 1). The
bioethicist begins by discussing the four dimensions of professionalism that are represented by the quadrants of the reflection square.
The top two quadrants are tightly interconnected in that the professional's actions can be explained in terms of her values and beliefs,
and vice versa. The Social Norms quadrant refers to culturally

Agent's Core Values and Beliefs	Agent's Actions
Social Norms	Consequences

FIGURE 1. The Reflection Square

prevalent norms: professional codes, laws, common moral beliefs, what "we" do but "they" do not. The Consequences quadrant refers to the effect of social norms on people's lives, which are closely connected to power relations – for example, there are consequences for racial minorities of living in a racist society. Next, the bioethicist asks one of the professionals to report her reactions to the case that was presented in stage 1. She writes down the response in the appropriate quadrant and asks the professional how the response coheres with the considerations of the other three quadrants. The aim of stage 2 is to show the professional how to think of his *identity* in terms of the reflection square. He critically examines his own views as they are embodied in his values and past actions, but because he is always defined in relation to others, he cannot know himself fully without setting his values and actions against the social under-standings that guide what others do and the consequences of those understandings for those with whom he interacts. Once he has a better sense of his professional identity, the bioethicist asks him to retell the case as he now sees it, dropping elements from the original telling that seem irrelevant, foregrounding (or making visible for the first time) considerations that were previously underplayed. In doing this, he represents not only how he now understands the case but who he understands himself to be. The bioethicist then turns to another professional and takes him all around the reflection square, repeating the exercise until she is satisfied that the case has been thoroughly discussed.

In stage 3, the professionals learn to map responsibilities. Once they are reflectively aware of their own beliefs and how these may differ from the beliefs of others, they are ready to reflect on their place in the broader picture and to decide, together with the others, on the best way to resolve disagreements and problems. The point of this phase is to teach professionals how to establish, reestablish, or maintain their professional integrity in working with other professionals to respond to their patients' needs. The bioethicist asks one of the professionals to consider what his own professional responsibilities would be in the case he reflected on in stage 2. Then she shows him how other people's identities and wider social forces put pressure on his integrity: as a surgeon, for example, he thinks the patient should receive the heart valve, but the hospital pressures him to save money and the wider society pressures him not to take too seriously a patient who is a drug addict, perhaps with a criminal record. In stage 2, the other professionals too will have worked their way around the reflection square and discovered that they all have somewhat different moral identities. So the members of the group must now negotiate with the others to come to an integrity-preserving understanding of what each in particular is responsible for, and to whom.

The bioethicist facilitates this by setting them the task of arriving at a group consensus about the resolution of the case. In this process, the professionals will find they must reflect *critically* about who they take themselves to be: one of them might find he was not taking the problem of follow-up care seriously enough, while another comes to see that he had an overinflated sense of his own moral authority. They thereby become more intelligible both to themselves and to their colleagues. The end result of this mapping is that the professional can reliably account to the others for who he is and what he stands for. So, for example, the professionals trying to decide about the problematic heart-valve replacement might decide that the surgery is more cost-effective than repeated visits to the emergency service would be, and that every effort must be made to see to it that follow-up care includes a drug rehabilitation program. Perfect consensus may elude the group, yet even if disagreement persists, the group members may discover that they have come to understand *why* they disagree.

The bioethicist's role in ethics education, then, can be seen as one of helping professionals to improve their moral competence, where "competence" is a matter of seeing what is morally relevant in a given situation; knowing the particular point of view from which one sees it; understanding that others involved in the situation may see it differently; and, together with those others, responding well to what is there to be seen. The bioethicist emphasizes these skills for a number of reasons. First, in many clinical situations, practitioners may have difficulty in recognizing that what they are dealing with has moral dimensions. Team members can work together for years without noticing that their differences of opinion are grounded in different perceptions of their professional identities, and that these in turn are shaped by plural and sometimes conflicting values. Over those years, however, the professionals doubtless experienced many frustrations and not a few turf battles, resulting in less competent care for their patients. Becoming aware of the moral dimensions of their work results in a heightened sense of how they shape and sustain not only their own professions but the professions of those with whom they work.

Second, in teaching busy professionals how to increase their moral competence, the bioethicist also provides them with a rare opportunity to reflect on their practice. Without this reflection, professionals can become alienated from themselves, uncertain whether they are acting out of their own best professional judgment or simply according to hospital policy or office routine.

Third, many people do not fully appreciate the moral importance of knowing the viewpoints of others in addition to their own. The exercise here described gives them the opportunity of listening to others' ways of organizing the moral landscape, noting how those ways differ from their own, and constructing, with those others, some good-seeming way to go on. This reinforces the idea, central to a naturalized bioethics, that morality is something we do together.

Finally, these skills can be honed by any competent moral agent; they do not require the technical knowledge of a specialist in ethics.

Yet enhancing the ability to see, narrate, and respond takes patience and practice. In giving professionals the opportunity to practice these skills, the bioethicist helps them to build on what they – what all of us – already know. The importance of this becomes more apparent in our discussion of the change in the bioethicist's self-understanding that a naturalized bioethics demands.

CHANGING PRACTICE

The change in how the bioethicist teaches moral deliberation is a good start, but a naturalized bioethics is not content to focus solely on reasoning and rationality: it also attends to the material conditions that must obtain for certain sorts of reasoning to occur at all. In *Balance and Refinement*, the philosopher Michael DePaul criticizes the dominance of an overly intellectualist moral epistemology. People sometimes fail to see certain things or make unwarranted moral judgments, he argues, not because they do not know how to reason well, but because they have missed out on formative *experiences*. He compares our faculty of moral judgment to our faculty for making complex perceptual discriminations and offers this example. Raised in a suburban setting where he had not spent much time around horses, he could not see how his equestrienne wife could tell whether a horse was cantering on the left lead or on the right lead. The problem was not that he did not understand the concept of a lead, nor was there anything wrong with his eyesight. All that was wrong was that he was unable to "see" what he needed to in order to apply the concept. It took considerable experience of watching horses, in addition to understanding the concept, before he got to the point where he could see whether the canter was on the left lead or the right (DePaul 1993, 203). So too, he argues, with moral "seeing." A well-developed faculty of moral judgment and understanding rests on certain formative experiences.

That is why residents learn to discuss moral issues to any real purpose only once they are in the clinic. It is not until then that they are able to see certain morally salient aspects of what it is to be a doctor. Most medical students start out by espousing the traditional medical values of fidelity, trust, doing good, and so on. Once they begin their clinical training, however, they learn – not by what their attending physicians say but by what they do – to adopt a more technical view of medical practice. Tacitly they are taught not only by their attendings but by the institutional forces and social pressures to which the attendings themselves are vulnerable, to view patient care as reductionistic and additive: the more procedures the patient receives, the better, or at least, the more technologically proficient the doctor is, the better. They learn to see that what really counts is objectivity, detachment, compartmentalization, and distrust – of emotions, patients, insurance companies, administrators, and the state. They learn this way of understanding who they are because, despite what bioethicists teach them about the ethics of their profession, their formative experiences in the clinic show them a different set of values.

If clinical ethicists really want to develop professionals' moral sensitivity and sensibility, then, they must do more than teach them careful moral reasoning. They must also pay attention to the way the work environment shapes practitioners' sense of what is important. And because clinical bioethicists do not as a rule rank very high in a health care institution's power hierarchy, this means that they must recruit the active involvement of highly placed physicians to create the conditions in which more adequate moral identities and self-understandings are possible.

Bioethicists might also be influential in changing practice in other health care settings. Aides in a nursing home, for example, might value their customary coffee break every morning even though this means they must bathe and dress all the residents before 10:30. The residents complain that they are awakened too early and that their morning care is rushed. On the other hand, the aides are badly underpaid and many of them are immigrants from a culture in which elders are cared for at home, so they regard nursing home placement as a sign that the resident is unworthy of family care. In this situation, the bioethicist might help the aides, the nursing home administrator, and perhaps the residents or their family members to discuss how the morning care routine could be changed so the aides receive the break they need without inconveniencing the residents in their charge. Changing the time of the coffee break in this way might help the nursing aides appreciate more fully the moral worth of the residents in their care.

CHANGING THE BIOETHICIST'S
SELF-UNDERSTANDING

Finally, a naturalized bioethics calls on the bioethicist to rethink her own professional identity. The power hierarchy within health care institutions dictates that professionals take precedence over non-professionals and that, among the professionals, medical specialists take the highest precedence of all. Bioethicists see themselves as professionals, so it is quite tempting for them to think of themselves as another kind of medical specialist: when someone has a kidney problem, you call in a nephrologist; when someone has an ethical problem, you call in a bioethicist.

This sort of thinking has led a number of clinical ethicists in the United States to sport a white coat while "rounding" and, as of this writing, a task force of the American Society of Bioethics and Humanities has been charged with drafting a code of ethics for ethics consultants, modeled on the codes of medical subspecialties (the rationale offered is that if the ethicist is asked to do something ethically unsavory, she can save her job by pointing to the code).

This view of the bioethicist as ethics expert is, we argue, misguided. It assumes that morality is primarily a "timeless, contextless, pure core of moral knowledge" (M. Walker 1998, 9) whose mastery gives the ethicist special cognitive authority. As this collection has demonstrated repeatedly, however, morality is not like that. If we think of it instead as a socially embodied practice through which we express ourselves and negotiate responsibility for the things we find worthy of care, we can see plainly enough that the clinical ethicist cannot cure a moral quandary by the expert application of a spot of moral knowledge. If that is what health care professionals expect them to do, it is no wonder that bioethicists so often have to struggle for respect within health care institutions.

A better way for bioethicists to understand themselves is to think of themselves as scholars who make and maintain moral spaces in health care settings (M. Walker 1993). They are scholars because maintaining these spaces requires a knowledge of ethical – and metaethical – theory, as well as knowledge of the bioethics literature. But their role is not to deploy expertise; rather, they are to afford professionals the opportunity to reflect on what they do and, when the need arises, to initiate changes in clinical practice. The ethics education in which bioethicists engage is, on this conception, aimed at helping professionals to use this space to best advantage.

Because morality is not a pure core of moral knowledge, then, bioethicists cannot be ethics experts. For the same reason, they cannot adopt a transhistorical, transcultural, disembodied moral perspective. The ideal of abstract impartiality that has characterized traditional ethics must be abandoned as not only unattainable but dangerous: as feminist ethicists have argued, it is all too easy for those who aspire to that ideal to import the prejudices and pre-occupations of their own social group into their theorizing under the guise of a false universality. But just as naturalizing requires the bioethicist to pay attention to others' race, class, gender, and the like, so too it requires her to attend to her own. She too is always only one among other socially located moral agents deliberating together about what is best to do. If, from her perspective, she sees morally important considerations that others have missed, the others could very likely return the compliment. In this sense, morality is genuinely democratic: there is no humanly accessible vantage point that assures the authority of anyone's moral judgments, including the profes-sional ethicist's. This means that the bioethicist, like everyone else, can speak only from her own knowledge and experience.

As we have suggested, all of the changes required by a naturalized bioethics are interrelated. If the bioethicist cannot be an ethics expert, she cannot use her teaching to convey expertise: instead, ethics education becomes a matter of refining competencies her "pupils" already possess. If morality is not as intellectualist as has traditionally been assumed, the bioethicist may have to work toward changing the material conditions that put pressure on clinicians' economy of values. If moral deliberation requires collaboration with others, the bioethicist must see herself as only one among those others. In the end, our agenda for a naturalized bioethics in practice amounts to a reorientation to bioethicists' clinical colleagues, their patients and families, and themselves. It is perhaps a modest adjustment, but it is aimed at an immodest end: to change, decisively and thoroughly, the way bioethics is done.

Bibliography

Andrews, M., and M. Talbot. 2000. *All the world and her husband: Women in twentieth-century consumer culture*. London: Cassell.

Anscombe, G. E. M. 1957. *Intention*. Oxford: Blackwell.

Arendt, Hannah. 1970. *On violence*. New York: Harcourt.

Ashcroft, Richard E. 2003. Constructing empirical bioethics: Foucauldian reflections on the empirical turn in bioethics research. *Health Care Analysis* 11 (1): 3–13.

Bacon, L., et al. 2005. Size acceptance and intuitive eating improve health for obese, female chronic dieters. *Journal of the American Dietetic Association* 105 (6): 929–36.

Baicker, K., K. S. Buckles, and A. Chandra. 2006. Geographic variation in the appropriate use of cesarean delivery. *Health Affairs* (Web exclusive), August 8, W355–W367.

Bandura, A. 1998. Personal and collective efficacy in human adaptation and change. In *Advances in psychological science*, ed. J. G. Adair, D. Bélanger, and K. L. Dion. New York: Psychology Press.

Barad, Karen. 2007. *Meeting the universe halfway: Quantum physics and the entanglement of matter and meaning*. Durham: Duke University Press.

Bauman, Richard. 1986. *Story, performance, and event: Contextual studies of oral narrative*. Cambridge studies in oral and literate culture. Cambridge: Cambridge University Press.

Beck, U. 1992. *Risk society: Towards a new modernity*. London: Sage.

Benjamin, Walter. 1968. *Illuminations*. New York: Harcourt.

Berenson, A. 2007. Cancer drug representatives spelled out the way to profit. *New York Times*, June 12. http://www.nytimes.com/2007/06/12/business/12cancerside.html, accessed May 12, 2008.

Berghs, G., and E. Spanjaards. 1988. De normale zwangerschap: Bevalling en beleid (The normal pregnancy: Birth and policy). Ph.D. dissertation, Catholic University, Nijmegen.

Betrán, A. P., et al. 2007. Rates of caesarean section: Analysis of global, regional and national estimates. *Paediatric and Perinatal Epidemiology* 21: 98–113.

Beauchamp, Tom L. 1984. On eliminating the distinction between applied ethics and ethical theory. *Monist* 67: 514–31.

Beauchamp, Tom L., and James F. Childress. 2001. *Principles of biomedical ethics*. 5th ed. New York: Oxford University Press.

Beauvoir, Simone de. 1952. *The second sex*. Ed. and trans. H. M. Parshley. New York: Knopf.

Blackburn, Simon. 1998. *Ruling passions: A theory of practical reasoning*. Oxford: Clarendon Press.

Bourdieu, Pierre. 1990a. *The logic of practice*. Trans. Richard Nice. Cambridge: Polity Press.

Bourdieu, Pierre. 1990b. *In other words: Essays towards a reflexive sociology*. Trans. Matthew Adamson. Stanford: Stanford University Press.

Bourdieu, Pierre. 1993. *Sociology in question*. Trans. Richard Nice. London: Sage.

Bowden, Peta. 1997. *Caring: Gender-sensitive ethics*. New York: Routledge.

Brody, Howard. 1987. *Stories of sickness*. New Haven: Yale University Press.

Brody, Howard. 1992. *The healer's power*. New Haven: Yale University Press.

Brown, Roger. 1986. *Social psychology*. 2nd ed. New York: Free Press.

Brown, Wendy. 1988. *Manhood and politics: A feminist reading in political theory*. Totowa, N.J.: Rowman & Littlefield.

Buchanan, Allen. 1996. Choosing who will be disabled: Genetic intervention and the morality of inclusion. *Social Philosophy and Policy* 13: 18–46.

Bull, Thomas H. 1998. *On the edge of deaf culture: Hearing children/deaf parents*. Alexandria, Va.: Deaf Family Research Press.

Bulnes, Miguel. 2004. *Zorg* (Care). Amsterdam: Vassallucci.

Bump, R. C. 2002. Advising prospective mothers about the maternal morbidity of vaginal childbirth. *American Journal of Obstetrics and Gynecology* 187: 823.

Burg, W. van der. 1999. Two models of law and morality. *Associations* 3 (1): 61–82. Translated into German as "Zwei Modelle von Recht und Moral," in *Ethik und Gesetzgebung: Probleme – Lösungsversuche – Konzepte*, ed. A. Bondolfi and S. Grotefeld. Stuttgart: Kohlhammer, 2000.

Callahan, Daniel. 1993. *The troubled dream of life: Living with mortality*. New York: Simon & Schuster.

Campbell, R. G., and A. S. Babrow. 2004. The role of empathy in responses to persuasive risk communication: Overcoming resistance to HIV prevention messages. *Journal of Health Communication* 16 (2): 159–82.

Campbell, Richmond, and Bruce Hunter, eds. 2000. *Moral epistemology naturalized*. Calgary: University of Calgary Press.

Caplan, Arthur L. 1983. Can applied ethics be effective in health care and should it strive to be? *Ethics* 93: 311–19.

Cassell, Eric. 1982. The nature of suffering and the goals of medicine. *New England Journal of Medicine* 306 (11): 639–45.

Cates, Diana Fritz. 2001. Caring for girls and women who are considering abortion: Rethinking informed consent. In *Medicine and the ethics of care*, ed. Diane Fritz Cates and Paul Lauritzen. Washington, D.C.: Georgetown University Press.

Cates, Diana Fritz, and Paul Lauritzen, eds. 2001. *Medicine and the ethics of care*. Washington, D.C.: Georgetown University Press.

Cavell, Stanley. 1981. *Pursuits of happiness: The Hollywood comedy of remarriage*. Cambridge, Mass.: Harvard University Press.

Chadwick, Ruth, et al., eds. 2007. *The bioethics reader: Editors' choice*. Oxford: Blackwell.

Chambers, Ross. 1984. *Story and situation: Narrative seduction and the power of fiction*. Vol. 12 of *Theory and history of literature*. Minneapolis: University of Minnesota Press.

Couser, G. Thomas. 1997. *Recovering bodies: Illness, disability, and lifewriting*. Madison: University of Wisconsin Press.

Covello, V. T., et al. 2001. Risk communication, the West Nile virus epidemic, and bioterrorism: Responding to the communication challenges posed by the international or unintentional release of a pathogen in an urban setting. *Journal of Urban Health: Bulletin of the New York Academy of Medicine* 78 (2): 382–91.

Dahl, Robert A. 1957. The concept of power. *Behavioral Science* 2 (2): 202–10.

Dancy, Jonathan. 2004. *Ethics without principles*. Oxford: Clarendon Press.

Daniels, Norman. 1979. Wide reflective equilibrium and theory acceptance in ethics. *Journal of Philosophy* 76: 256–82.

Davis, Dena S. 1997. Genetic dilemmas and the child's right to an open future. *Hastings Center Report* 27: 7–15.

Day, J. P. 1970. The anatomy of hope and fear. *Mind* 79 (315): 369–84.

Day, J. P. 1998. More about hope and fear. *Ethical Theory and Moral Practice* 1 (1): 121–23.

Declercq, E. R., C. Sakala, M. P. Corry, and S. Applebaum. 2006. *Listening to mothers 2: Report of the second national U.S. survey of women's childbearing experiences*. New York: Childbirth Connection.

Deigh, John. 1983. Shame and self-esteem: A critique. *Ethics: An International Journal of Social, Political, and Legal Philosophy* 93 (2): 225–45.

DeLancey, J. O. L. 2000. Identifying and managing anal sphincter injury. *Obstetric and Gynecology Management* 2000: 18–29.

DePaul, Michael. 1993. *Balance and refinement: Beyond coherence methods of moral inquiry*. New York: Routledge.

Devine, J. B., D. R. Ostegard, and K. L. Noblett. 1999. Long term complications of second stage labor. *Contemporary OB/GYN* 1999: 119–26.

De Vries, Raymond G. 2005. *A pleasing birth: Midwifery and maternity care in the Netherlands*. Philadelphia: Temple University Press.

De Vries, Raymond G., R. Dingwall, and K. Orfali. In press. The moral organization of the professions: Bioethics in the United States and France. *Current Sociology* 56.

De Vries, Raymond G., Leigh Turner, Kristina Orfali, and Charles Bosk, eds. 2007. *The view from here: Bioethics and the social sciences*. Oxford: Blackwell.

De Vries, Raymond G., S. Wrede, E. R. van Teijlingen, and C. Benoit, eds. 2001. *Birth by design: Pregnancy, maternity care, and midwifery in North America and Europe*. New York: Routledge.

de Waal, Frans. 1996. *Good natured: The origins of rights and wrong in humans and other animals*. Cambridge, Mass.: Harvard University Press.

Doris, John. 2002. *Lack of character: Personality and moral behavior*. Cambridge: Cambridge University Press.

Drabble, Margaret. 2006. *The sea lady*. London: Penguin.

Dresser, Rebecca. 1995. Dworkin on dementia: Elegant theory, questionable policy. *Hastings Center Report* 25 (6): 32–38.

Dubet, François. 2002. *Le déclin de l'institution* (The decline of the institution). Paris: Seuil.

Dupré, John. 1993. *The disorder of things: Metaphysical foundations of the disunity of science*. Cambridge, Mass.: Harvard University Press.

Durose, C. L., et al. 2004. Knowledge of dietary restrictions and the medical consequences of noncompliance by patients on hemodialysis are not predictive of dietary compliance. *Journal of the American Dietetic Association* 104 (1): 35–41.

Dyson, Freeman. 2007. Our biotech future. *New York Review of Books* 54 (12): 4–8.

Dworkin, Roger B. 2003. Getting what we should from doctors: Rethinking patient autonomy and the doctor-patient relationship. *Health Matrix: Journal of Law-Medicine* 13: 235–96.

Dworkin, Ronald. 1993. *Life's dominion: An argument about abortion, euthanasia, and individual freedom*. New York: Alfred A. Knopf.

Elder, K., et al. 2007. African Americans' decisions not to evacuate New Orleans before Hurricane Katrina: A qualitative study. *American Journal of Public Health* 97 (suppl. 1): S124–29.

Elliott, Carl. 2001. Throwing the watchdog a bone. *Hastings Center Report* 31 (2): 9–12.

Engster, Daniel. 2007. *The heart of justice*. New York: Oxford University Press.

Epstein, M. 2006. Why effective consent presupposes autonomous authorisation: A counterorthodox argument. *Journal of Medical Ethics* 32 (6): 342–45.

Epstein, R. M., et al. 1998. Awkward moments in patient-physician communication about HIV risk. *Annals of Internal Medicine* 128 (6): 435–42.

Faden, Ruth R., and Tom L. Beauchamp. 1986. *A history and theory of informed consent*. New York: Oxford University Press.

Fadiman, Anne. 1998. *The spirit catches you and you fall down*. New York: Farrar, Straus & Giroux.

Farmer, Paul, and Nicole Gastineau Campos. 2007. Rethinking medical ethics: A view from below. In *The bioethics reader: Editors' choice*, ed. Ruth Chadwick, Helga Kuhse, Willem Landman, Udo Schüklenk, and Peter Singer. Oxford: Blackwell.

Feder, Ellen K. 2002. Doctor's orders: Parents and intersexed children. In *The subject of care: Feminist perspectives on dependency*, ed. Eva Feder Kittay and Ellen K. Feder. Lanham, Md.: Rowman & Littlefield.

Fels, Anna. 2005. *Necessary dreams: Ambition in women's changing lives*. New York: Random House.

Fischhoff, B. 1989. Helping the public make health risk decisions. In *Effective risk communication: The role and responsibility of government and non-government organizations*, ed. V. T. Covello, D. B. McCallum, M. T. Pavlova, and Task Force on Environmental Cancer and Heart and Lung Disease (U.S.). New York: Plenum.

Fitzgerald, F. T. 1994. The tyranny of health. *New England Journal of Medicine* 331 (3): 196–98.

Flanagan, Owen, Hagop Sarkissian, and David Wong. 2008. Naturalizing ethics. In *Moral psychology*, vol. 1: *The evolution of morality: Adaptations and innateness*, ed. Walter Sinnott-Armstrong. Cambridge, Mass.: MIT Press.

Fludernik, Monika. 1996. *Towards a "natural" narratology*. New York: Routledge.

Forster, E. M. 1985. *Aspects of the novel*. San Diego: Harcourt Brace Jovanovich.

Foucault, Michel. 1975. *The birth of the clinic: An archeology of medical perception*. New York: Vintage.

Fox, Daniel M. 1991. The politics of trust in American health care. In *Ethics, trust, and the professions: Philosophical and cultural aspects*, ed. E. D. Pellegrino, R. M. Veatch, and J. P. Langan. Washington, D.C.: Georgetown University Press.

Frank, Arthur W. 1995. *The wounded storyteller: Body, illness, and ethics*. Chicago: University of Chicago Press.

Frankfurt, Harry. 1988a. Identification and externality. In *The importance of what we care about*. Cambridge: Cambridge University Press.

Frankfurt, Harry. 1988b. Freedom of the will and the concept of a person. In *The importance of what we care about*. Cambridge: Cambridge University Press.

Fritel, X., et al. 2005. Mode of delivery and severe stress incontinence. A cross-sectional study among 2625 perimenopausal women. *BJOG: An International Journal of Obstetrics and Gynaecology* 112: 1646–51.

Gawande, Atul. 2002. Whose body is it anyway? In *Complications: A surgeon's notes on an imperfect science*. New York: Henry Holt.

Gerth, H. H., and C. Wright Mills, eds. 1949. *From Max Weber: Essays in sociology*. Oxford: Oxford University Press.

Gibbard, Allan. 1990. *Wise choices, apt feelings: A theory of normative judgment*. Cambridge, Mass.: Harvard University Press.

Gilligan, Carol. 1982. *In a different voice: Psychological theory and women's development*. Cambridge, Mass.: Harvard University Press.

Gilson, Lucy. 2003. Trust and the development of health care as a social institution. *Social Science and Medicine* 56 (7): 1453.

Glik, D. C. 2007. Risk communication for public health emergencies. *Annual Review of Public Health* 28: 33–54.

Glover, Jonathan. 2000. *Humanity: A moral history of the twentieth century.* New Haven: Yale University Press.

Goffman, Erving. 1961. *Asylums: Essays on the social situation of psychiatric patients and other inmates.* New York: Anchor.

Goffman, Erving, Charles C. Lemert, and Ann Branaman. 1997. *The Goffman reader.* Cambridge, Mass.: Blackwell.

Goldberg, R. P., et al. 2005. Delivery mode is a major environmental determinant of stress urinary incontinence: Results of the Evanston-Northwestern Twin Sisters Study. *American Journal of Obstetrics and Gynecology* 193: 2149–53.

Gopnik, Alison. 1993. How we know our minds: The illusion of first-person knowledge of intentionality. *Behavioral and Brain Sciences* 16 (1): 1–14.

Groopman, Jerome. 2005. *The anatomy of hope: How you can find strength in the face of illness.* London: Simon & Schuster.

Gutting, Gary. 2005. Review of Brian Leiter, *The future for philosophy. Notre Dame Philosophical Reviews*, December 14. http://ndpr.nd.edu/review.cfm?id=5161, accessed December 23, 2005.

Gylling, Heta Aleksandra. 2004. Autonomy revisited. *Cambridge Quarterly of Healthcare Ethics* 13: 41–46.

Habiba, M., et al. 2006. Caesarean section on request: A comparison of obstetricians' attitudes in eight European countries. *BJOG* 113: 647–66.

Haimes, Erica. 2007. What can the social sciences contribute to the study of ethics? Theoretical, empirical and substantive considerations. In *The bioethics reader: Editors' choice*, ed. Ruth Chadwick et al. Oxford: Blackwell.

Hall, Mark A. 2005. The importance of trust for ethics, law, and public policy. *Cambridge Quarterly of Healthcare Ethics* 14: 156–67.

Halpern, Jodi. 1995. Can practice guidelines include patient values? *Journal of Law, Medicine and Ethics* 23 (Spring): 75–81.

Halpern, Jodi. 2001. *From detached concern to empathy: Humanizing medical practice.* Oxford: Oxford University Press.

Halpern, Jodi. 2007. Empathy and patient-physician conflicts. *Journal of General Internal Medicine* 22 (5): 696–700.

Halpern, Jodi. Unpublished. When fear undermines autonomy: Concretized emotions and deliberative incapacity.

Hamberg, Katarina, Gunilla Risberg, Eva E. Johansson, and Göran Westman. 2002. Gender bias in physicians' management of neck pain: A study of the answers in a Swedish national examination. *Journal of Women's Health and Gender-Based Medicine* 11 (7): 653–66.

Hamilton, B, E., J. A. Martin, and S. J. Ventura. 2007. Births: Preliminary data for 2005. *National Vital Statistics Reports* 55, no. 11. Hyattsville, Md.: National Center for Health Statistics.

Handa, V. L., T. A. Harris, and D. R. Ostegard. 1996. Protecting the pelvic floor: Obstetric management to prevent incontinence and pelvic organ prolapse. *Obstetrics and Gynecology* 88: 470–78.

Hannah, M. E. 2004. Planned elective cesarean section: A reasonable choice for some women? *Canadian Medical Association Journal* 170 (5): 813–14.

Hannah, M. E., et al. 2000. Planned caesarean section versus planned vaginal birth for breech presentation at term: A randomised multicentre trial. *Lancet* 356: 1375–83.

Haraway, Donna. 1988. Situated knowledges: The science question in feminism as a site of discourse on the privilege of partial perspective. *Feminist Studies* 14 (3): 575–99

Haraway, Donna. 1989. The biopolitics of postmodern bodies: Determinations of self in immune system discourse. *differences* 1 (1): 3–43.

Haraway, Donna. 1991. *Simians, cyborgs, and women: The reinvention of nature.* New York: Routledge.

Hare, R. M. 1981. *Moral thinking: Its levels, method, and point.* Oxford: Oxford University Press.

Harer, W. B., Jr. 2000. Patient choice cesarean. *ACOG Clinical Review* 5 (2): 12–16.

Harremoës, P., et al. 2002. *The precautionary principle in the 20th century: Late lessons from early warnings.* London: Earthscan.

Harris, Jennifer. 1995. *The cultural meaning of deafness.* Aldershot: Avebury.

Harris, John. 1995. Should we attempt to eradicate disability? *Public Understanding of Science* 4: 233–42.

Harris, John. 2000. Is there a coherent social conception of disability? *Journal of Medical Ethics* 26: 95–100.

Harris, John. 2003. Consent and end of life decisions. *Journal of Medical Ethics* 29 (1): 10–15.

Hart, P. L. 2005. Women's perceptions of coronary heart disease: An integrative review. *Journal of Cardiovascular Nursing* 20 (3): 170–76.

Haskell, Thomas L. 1998. *Objectivity is not neutrality: Explanatory schemes in history.* Baltimore: Johns Hopkins University Press.

Haynes, R. B., et al. 2002. Helping patients follow prescribed treatment: Clinical applications. *Journal of the American Medical Association* 288 (22): 2880–83.

Häyry, Matti. 2004. Another look at dignity. *Cambridge Quarterly of Healthcare Ethics* 13 (1): 7–14.

Hearne, Vicki. 1987. *Adam's task: Calling animals by name.* New York: Knopf.

Held, Virginia. 2006. *The ethics of care: Personal, political, and global.* New York: Oxford University Press.

Henry, Michael S. 2006. Uncertainty, responsibility, and the evolution of the physician/patient relationship. *Journal of Medical Ethics* 32: 3.

Hermans, Anne. 2006. *De co-assistent* (The co-assistant). Amsterdam: Podium.

Higgins, Paul C. 1980. *Outsiders in a hearing world: A sociology of deafness.* London: Sage.

Hobbes, Thomas. 1994. *Leviathan.* Ed. Edwin Curley. Indianapolis: Hackett.

Hockenberry, John. 1995. *Moving violations: War zones, wheelchairs, and declarations of independence.* New York: Hyperion.

Holtgrave, D. R., et al. 1995. Encouraging risk reduction: A decision-making approach to message design. In *Designing health messages: Approaches from communication theory and public health practice*, ed. E. Maibach and R. Parrott. Thousand Oaks, Calif.: Sage.

Horne, R. 2006. Compliance, adherence, and concordance: Implications for asthma treatment. *Chest* 130 (suppl. 1): 65S–72S.

Hunt, L. M., and K. B. de Voogd. 2005. Clinical myths of the cultural "other": Implications for Latino patient care. *Academic Medicine* 80 (10): 918–24.

Hunter, Kathryn Montgomery. 1990. Overview. *Second Opinion* 15: 64–67.

Huntington, Samuel P. 1968. *Political order in changing societies*. New Haven: Yale University Press.

Hursthouse, Rosalind. 1999. *On virtue ethics*. New York: Oxford University Press.

Hyde, M., and D. Power. 2006. Some ethical dimensions of cochlear implantation for deaf children and their families. *Journal of Deaf Studies and Deaf Education* 11 (1): 102–11.

Ignatieff, Michael. 1986. *The needs of strangers*. London: Picador.

Irigaray, Luce. 1983. *L'oubli de l'air* (The forgetting of air). Paris: Minuit.

Jaeger, C., O. Renn, E. Rosa, and T. Webler. 2001. *Risk, uncertainty, and rational action*. London: Earthscan.

Jaggar, Alison. 2000. Ethics naturalized: Feminism's contribution to moral epistemology. *Metaphilosophy* 31 (5): 452–68.

Jaworska, Agnieszka. 2007. Caring and internality. *Philosophy and Phenomenological Research* 74 (3): 529–568.

Jaworska, Agnieszka. Unpublished. Moral psychology in practice: Lessons from Alzheimer's disease and the "terrible twos."

Johnson, K. C., and B.-A. Daviss. 2005. Outcomes of planned home births with certified professional midwives: Large prospective study in North America. *British Medical Journal* 330: 1416.

Jordan, Catherine, Susan Gust, and Naomi Scheman. 2005. The trustworthiness of research: The paradigm of community-based research. *Metropolitan Universities Journal* 16 (1): 39–57.

Kant, Immanuel. 2003. *Perpetual peace and other essays*. Indianapolis: Hackett.

Keller, Evelyn Fox. 1985. *Reflections on gender and science*. New Haven: Yale University Press.

Kitcher, Philip. 2005. The hall of mirrors. Romanell Lecture. *Proceedings and Addresses of the American Philosophical Association* 79 (2): 67–84.

Kittay, Eva Feder. 1999. *Love's labor: Essays on women, equality, and dependency*. New York: Routledge.

Kittay, Eva Feder. 2005. On the margins of moral personhood. *Ethics* 116 (1): 100–131.

Klein, M. 1995. Studying episiotomy: When beliefs conflict with science. *Journal of Family Practice* 41 (5): 483–88.

Knuist, M., M. Eskes, and D. Van Alten. 1987. De pH van het ateriele navelstrengbloed van pasgeborenen bij door vroedvrouwen geleide bevallingen (The pH of umbilical cord blood of newborns at midwife-accompanied births). *Nederlands Tijdschrift voor Geneeskunde* (Dutch journal of medicine) 131 (9): 362–64.

Kolata, Gina. 2007. Six killers: Heart disease; Lessons of heart disease, learned and ignored. *New York Times*, April 8.

Kreps, G. L., et al. 2005. Emergency/risk communication to promote public health and respond to biological threats. In *Global public health communication: Challenges, perspectives, and strategies*, ed M. Haider. Sudbury, Mass.: Jones and Bartlett.

Kristeva, Julia. 1982. *Powers of horror: An essay on abjection* Trans. Leon S. Roudiez. New York: Columbia University Press.

Kukla, Rebecca. 2005. Conscientious autonomy: Displacing decisions in healthcare. *Hastings Center Report* 35 (2): 34–44.

Ladd, P., and M. John. 1991. *Deaf people as a minority group: The political process*. Course D251, Issues in Deafness. Milton Keynes: Open University Press.

Lane, H. 1992. *The mask of benevolence: Disabling the deaf community*. New York: Knopf.

Lane, H., and B. Bahan. 1998. Ethics of cochlear implantation in young children: A review and reply from a Deaf-World perspective. *Archives of Otolaryngology – Head and Neck Surgery* 119 (4): 297–313.

Larrabee, Mary Jeanne, ed. 1993. *An ethic of care: Feminist and interdisciplinary perspectives*. New York: Routledge.

Latour, Bruno. 1979. *Laboratory life: The social construction of scientific facts*. Beverly Hills: Sage.

Leeman, L. M., and L. A. Plante. 2006. Patient-choice vaginal delivery? *Annals of Family Medicine* 4: 265–68.

Leeuw, F. De, and A. Verhoeven. 2006. Tijd voor bezinniing (Time to think again). *Medisch Contact* (Medical contact) 61 (43): 1700–1703.

Lefler, L. L., and K. N. Bondy. 2004. Women's delay in seeking treatment with myocardial infarction: A meta-synthesis. *Journal of Cardiovascular Nursing* 19 (4): 251–68.

Lenman, James. 2006. Moral naturalism. *The Stanford encyclopedia of philosophy* (Fall 2006 edition), ed. Edward N. Zalta. http://plato.stanford.edu/archives/fall2006/entries/naturalism-moral/, accessed December 15, 2007.

Lerner, Barron H. 2006. *When illness goes public: Celebrity patients and how we look at medicine*. Baltimore: Johns Hopkins University Press.

Leventhal, H., et al. 2008. Health psychology: The search for pathways between behavior and health. *Annual Review of Psychology* 59 (1): 477–505.

Liaschenko, Joan, and Debra DeBruin. 2003. The role of nurses in ensuring the responsible conduct of clinical trials. *Minnesota Medicine* 86 (10): 35–36.

Lievaart, M., and P. A. de Jong. 1982. Neonatal morbidity in deliveries conducted by midwives and gynecologists: A study of the system of obstetric care prevailing in the Netherlands. *American Journal of Obstetrics and Gynecology* 144: 376–86.

Linton, Simi. 2005. *My body politic*. Ann Arbor: University of Michigan Press.

Little, Margaret. 1998. Cosmetic surgery, suspect norms, and the ethics of complicity. In *Enhancing human traits: Ethical and social implications*, ed. Erik Parens. Washington, D.C.: Georgetown University Press.

Locke, John. 1992. *Two treatises of government*. Ed. M. Goldie. Rutland, Vt.: Tuttle.

Lupton, D., ed. 1999. *Risk and sociocultural theory: New directions and perspectives*. Cambridge: Cambridge University Press.

MacIntyre, Alasdair C. 1984. *After virtue: A study in moral theory*. 2nd ed. Notre Dame, Ind.: University of Notre Dame Press.

MacIntyre, Alasdair. 1999. Interview. In *Key philosophers in conversation: The Cogito interviews*, ed. A. Pyle. London: Routledge.

Mackenzie, Catriona, and Natalie Stoljar, eds. 2000. *Relational autonomy: Feminist perspectives on autonomy, agency, and the social self*. Oxford: Oxford University Press.

Maréchal, Els, and Leen de Jong. 2000. *The Royal Museum of Fine Arts Antwerp*. Ghent and Amsterdam: Ludion.

Marmot, Michael. 2004. Dignity and inequality. *Lancet* 364 (9439): 1019–21.

Martin, Wallace. 1986. *Recent theories of narrative*. Ithaca: Cornell University Press.

May, Larry, Marilyn Friedman, and Andy Clark, eds. 1996. *Mind and morals: Essays on ethics and cognitive science*. Cambridge, Mass.: MIT Press.

McComas, K. A. 2006. Defining moments in risk communication research: 1996–2005. *Journal of Health Communication* 11 (1): 75–91.

McGeer, Victoria. 2004. The art of good hope. *Annals of the American Academy of Political and Social Science* 592: 100–127.

McKinley, J. B., and L. D. Marceau. 2002. The end of the golden age of doctoring. *International Journal of Health Services* 32 (2): 379–416.

McLeod, Carolyn, and Susan Sherwin. 2000. Relational autonomy, self-trust, and health care for patients who are oppressed. In *Relational autonomy: Feminist perspectives on autonomy, agency, and the social self*, ed. Catriona Mackenzie and Natalie Stoljar. New York: Oxford University Press.

McMahan, Jeff. 1996. Cognitive disability, misfortune, and justice. *Philosophy and Public Affairs* 25 (1): 3–34.

McMahan, Jeff. 2003. *The ethics of killing: Problems at the margins of life*. Oxford: Oxford University Press.

Middleton, A. V., J. V. Hewison, and R. V. Mueller. 2001. Prenatal diagnosis for deafness: What is the potential demand? *Journal of Genetic Counseling* 10: 121–31.

Miles, Steven H. 1990. The case: A story found and lost. *Second Opinion* 15: 55–59.

Miles, Steven H., and Kathryn Montgomery Hunter. 1990a. Case stories: A series. *Second Opinion* 15: 54.

Miles, Steven H., and Kathryn Montgomery Hunter. 1990b. Commentary. *Second Opinion* 15: 60–63.

Mill, John Stuart. 1978. *On liberty*. Indianapolis: Hackett.

Miller, Alexander. 2003. *An introduction to contemporary metaethics*. Cambridge: Polity Press.

Miller, D. A. 1981. *Narrative and its discontents: Problems of closure in the traditional novel*. Princeton, N.J.: Princeton University Press.

Mills, Charles W. 1997. *The racial contract*. Ithaca: Cornell University Press.

Mills, Charles W. 2005. "Ideal theory" as ideology. *Hypatia* 20 (3): 165.

Mohseni, Mohabbat, and Martin Lindstrom. 2007. Social capital, trust in the health-care system and self-rated health: The role of access to health care in a population-based study. *Social Science and Medicine* 64 (7): 1373–83.

Mol, Annemarie. 2002. *The body multiple: Ontology in medical practice*. Durham, N.C: Duke University Press.

Mol, Annemarie. 2006. *De logica van het zorgen: Actieve patiënten en de grenzen van het kiezen* (The logic of caring: Active patients on the verge of choice). Amsterdam: Van Gennep.

Morone, James A., and Lawrence R. Jacobs. 2005. Introduction. In *Healthy, wealthy, and fair: Health care and the good society*, ed. James A. Morone and Lawrence R. Jacobs. New York: Oxford.

Morrill, A. C., and C. D. Chinn. 2004. The obesity epidemic in the United States. *Journal of Public Health Policy* 25 (3–4): 353–66.

Mundy, Lisa. 2002. A world of their own. *Washington Post Magazine*, March 31.

Musschenga, A. W. 2005. Empirical ethics, context-sensitivity, and contextualism. *Journal of Medicine and Philosophy* 30 (5): 467–90.

Myerhoff, Barbara G. 1978. *Number our days*. New York: Dutton.

Narayan, Uma. 1997. *Dislocating cultures: Identities, traditions, and Third-World feminism*. New York: Routledge.

National Commission for the Protection of Human Subjects of Biomedical and Behavioral Research. 1979. *Belmont report: Ethical principles and guidelines for the protection of human subjects of research*. Washington, D.C.: Department of Health Education and Welfare.

Nelson, Hilde Lindemann. 2001. *Damaged identities, narrative repair*. Ithaca: Cornell University Press.

Nelson, Hilde Lindemann. 2002. What child is this? *Hastings Center Report* 32 (6): 29–38.

Nelson, Hilde Lindemann, ed. 1997. *Stories and their limits: Narrative approaches to bioethics*. New York: Routledge.

Nelson, James Lindemann. 2000a. Moral teachings from unexpected quarters: Lessons for bioethics from the social sciences and managed care. *Hastings Center Report* 30 (1): 12–17.

Nelson, James Lindemann. 2000b. Prenatal diagnosis, personal identity, and disability. *Kennedy Institute of Ethics Journal* 10: 213–28.

New York State. 1989. Patient's Bill of Rights. 10 NYCRR, 405.7,405.7(a) (1),405.7(c).

Nichols, Shaun. 2004. *Sentimental rules: On the natural foundations of moral judgment*. New York: Oxford University Press.

Noddings, Nel. 1984. *Caring: A feminine approach to ethics and moral education*. Berkeley and Los Angeles: University of California Press.

Nozick, Robert. 1983. About mammals and people. *New York Times Book Review*, November 27, 11.

Nygaard, I., and D. P. Cruikshank. 2003. Should all women be offered elective cesarean delivery? *Obstetrics and Gynecology* 102: 217–19.

O'Boyle, A. L., G. D. Davis, and B. C. Calhoun. 2002. Informed consent and birth: Protecting the pelvic floor and ourselves. *American Journal of Obstetrics and Gynecology* 187: 981–83.

O'Brien, Ruth. 2005. *Bodies in revolt: Gender, disability and a workplace ethic of care*. London: Routledge.

Olthuis, Gert. 2007. *Who cares? An ethical study of the moral attitude of professionals in palliative care*. Enschede: Printpartners.

O'Neill, Onora. 1987. Abstraction, idealization and ideology in ethics. In *Moral philosophy and contemporary problems*, ed. J. D. G. Evans. Cambridge: Cambridge University Press.

O'Neill, Onora. 2003. Some limits of informed consent. *Journal of Medical Ethics* 29: 4–7.

Onfray, Michel. 1991. *L'art de jouir* (The art of enjoying). Paris: Bernard Grasset.

Onfray, Michel 2003. *Féeries anatomiques: Généalogie du corps faustien* (Anatomical fairyhood: Genealogy of the Faustian body). Paris: Grasset.

Onfray, Michel. 2005. *Traité d'athéologie: Physique de la métaphysique* (Treaty of atheology: Physiognomy of metaphysics). Paris: Grasset & Fasquelle.

Ong, Walter J. 1982. *Orality and literacy: The technologizing of the word*. London: Methuen.

Ory, M. G., et al. 2002. The Behavior Change Consortium: Setting the stage for a new century of health behavior-change research. *Health Education Research* 17 (5): 500–11.

Padden, C., and T. Humphries. 2005. *Inside deaf culture*. Cambridge, Mass.: Harvard University Press.

Pateman, Carole. 1988. *The sexual contract*. Stanford: Stanford University Press.

Payer, L. 1988. *Medicine and culture: Varieties of treatment in the United States, England, West Germany, and France*. New York: H. Holt.

Pel, M., and P. E. Treffers. 1983. The reliability of the result of the umbilical cord pH. *Journal of Perinatal Medicine* 11: 169–74.

Pickering, Andrew. 1995. *The mangle of practice: Time, agency, and science*. Chicago: University of Chicago Press.

Plumwood, Val. 1993. *Feminism and the mastery of nature*. New York: Routledge.

Porter, Michael E., and Elizabeth Teisberg. 2006. *Redefining health care: Creating value-based competition on results*. Boston: Harvard Business School Press.

Pratt, Mary Louise. 1977. *Toward a speech act theory of literary discourse*. Bloomington: Indiana University Press.

Preston, P. 2001. *Mother father deaf: Living between sound and silence*. Cambridge, Mass.: Harvard University Press.

Prince, Gerald. 2003. *A dictionary of narratology*. Rev. ed. Lincoln: University of Nebraska Press.

Proulx, M., et al. 2007. Social context, the struggle with uncertainty, and subjective risk as meaning-rich constructs for explaining HBP non-compliance. *Patient Education and Counseling* 68 (1): 98–106.

Ptacek, J. T., and T. L. Eberhardt. 1996. Breaking bad news: A review of the literature. *Journal of the American Medical Association* 276 (6): 496–502.

Ptacek, J. T., and J. J. Ptacek. 2001. Patients' perceptions of receiving bad news about cancer. *Journal of Clinical Oncology* 19 (21): 4160–64.

Quine, W. V. O. 1969. Epistemology naturalized. In *Ontological relativity and other essays*. New York: Columbia University Press.

Rabinowitz, Peter J. 1998. *Before reading: Narrative conventions and the politics of interpretation; The theory and interpretation of narrative*. Columbus: Ohio State University Press.

Rachels, James. 1990. *Created from animals: The moral implications of Darwinism*. New York: Oxford University Press.

Rawls, John. 1971. *A theory of justice*. Cambridge, Mass.: Harvard University Press.

Rée, J. 1999. *I see a voice: Language, deafness and the senses – a philosophical history*. London: HarperCollins.

Regan, M., and J. Liaschenko. 2007. In the mind of the beholder: Hypothesized effect of intrapartum nurses' cognitive frames of childbirth cesarean section rates. *Qualitative Health Research* 17 (5): 612–24.

Regan, Tom. 1983. *The case for animal rights*. Berkeley and Los Angeles: University of California Press.

Risse, Guenter B. 1999. *Mending bodies, saving souls: A history of hospitals*. New York: Oxford University Press.

Roter, D. L., et al. 2006. The expression of emotion through nonverbal behavior in medical visits: Mechanisms and outcomes. *Journal of General Internal Medicine* 21 (suppl. 1): S28–34.

Rouse, Joseph. 2002. *How scientific practices matter: Reclaiming philosophical naturalism*. Chicago: University of Chicago Press.

Rousseau, Jean Jacques. 1987. *The basic political writings*. Trans. D. A. Cress. Indianapolis: Hackett.

Ruddick, Sara. 1989. *Maternal thinking: Toward a politics of peace*. Boston: Beacon.

Ruddick, William. 1999. Hope and deception. *Bioethics* 13 (3–4): 343–57.

Ruyters, Domeniek. 2006. Van vlees en bloed: Manifestaties in Düsseldorf en Leuven over het lijden (Of flesh and blood: Exhibits in Düsseldorf and Leuven concerning suffering). *de Volkskrant, Kunstbijlage* (The people's paper, arts pages), October 12, 12–13.

Sager, Morten. 2006. *Pluripotent circulations: Putting actor-network theory to work on stem cells in the USA, prior to 2001*. Gothenburg: Acta Universitatis Gothoburgensis.

Sanders, L. 2003. Diagnosis: Back pain – mottled vertebrae – anxiety. *New York Times Magazine*, October 19, 29–30.

Savulescu. Julian. 2001. Procreative beneficence: Why we should select the best children. *Bioethics* 15: 413–26.

Savulescu, Julian. 2007. In defence of procreative beneficence. *Journal of Medical Ethics* 33: 284–288.

Schechtman, Marya. 1996. *The constitution of selves*. Ithaca: Cornell University Press.

Scheman, Naomi. 1993a. Anger and the politics of naming. In *Engenderings: Constructions of knowledge, authority, and privilege*. New York: Routledge.

Scheman, Naomi. 1993b. The body politic and the impolitic body. In *Engenderings: Constructions of knowledge, authority, and privilege*. New York: Routledge.

Scheman, Naomi. 1997. Queering the center by centering the queer: Reflections on transsexuals and secular Jews. In *Feminists rethink the self*, ed. Diana Tietjens Meyers. Boulder, Colo.: Westview Press.

Schneider, Carl. 1998. *The practice of autonomy: Patients, doctors, and medical decisions*. New York: Oxford.

Schneider, Carl. 2007. Void for vagueness. *Hastings Center Report* 37 (1): 10–11.

Schneiderman, L., et al. 2003. Effects of ethics consultations on non-beneficial life-sustaining treatments in the intensive care setting: A randomized controlled trial. *Journal of the American Medical Association* 290: 1166–72.

Schoenberg, N. E., et al. 2003. Unraveling the mysteries of timing: Women's perceptions about time to treatment for cardiac symptoms. *Social Science and Medicine* 56 (2): 271–84.

Sevenhuijsen, Selma. 1998. *Citizenship and the ethics of care: Feminist considerations on justice, morality and politics*. London: Routledge.

Shepardson, Laura B., et al. 1999. Racial variation in the use of do-not-resuscitate orders. *JGIM: Journal of General Internal Medicine* 14 (1): 15–20.

Sidgwick, Henry. 1981. *The methods of ethics*. [1907.] 7th ed. Indianapolis: Hackett.

Silverman, Jennifer. 2004. One in seven quit obstetrics from 1999 to 2003: These ob/gyns say the risk of liability claims or lawsuits forced them out. *Ob Gyn News* 39 (16): 1–2.

Singer, Peter. 1994. *Rethinking life and death: The collapse of our traditional ethics*. New York: St. Martin's Press.

Singer, Peter, and Helga Kuhse. 1985. *Should the baby live? The problem of handicapped infants*. Studies in Bioethics. Oxford: Oxford University Press.

Singleton, J. L., and M. D. Tittle. 2000. Deaf parents and their hearing children. *Journal of Deaf Studies and Deaf Education* 5: 221–36.

Slovic, P. 2000. *The perception of risk*. Sterling, Va.: Earthscan.

Slovic, P., et al. 1990. Rating the risk. In *Readings in risk*, ed. T. Glickman and M. Gough. Washington, D.C.: Resources for the Future.

Smith, Barbara Herrnstein. 1981. Narrative versions, narrative theories. In *On narrative*, ed. W. J. T. Mitchell. Chicago: University of Chicago Press.

Snowbeck, C. 2004. Long, chilly wait for shots. *Pittsburgh Post-Gazette*, October 19.

Snyder, C. R. 1995. Conceptualizing, measuring, and nurturing hope. *Journal of Counseling and Development* 73 (3): 355–60.

Snyder, C. R., K. L. Rand, and D. R. Sigmon. 2002. Hope theory: A member of the positive psychology family. In *Handbook of positive psychology*, ed. C. R. Snyder and J. Lopez. Oxford: Oxford University Press.

Sokolowski, Robert. 2001. The fiduciary relationship and the nature of professions. In *Ethics, trust and the professions: Philosophical and cultural aspects*, ed. E. D. Pellegrino, R. M. Veatch, and J. P. Langan. Washington, D.C.: Georgetown University Press.

Solomon, A. 1994. Defiantly deaf *New York Times Magazine*, August 28.

Stern, S. J., et al. 2002. Attitudes of deaf and hard of hearing subjects towards genetic testing and prenatal diagnosis of hearing loss. *Journal of Medical Genetics* 39: 449–53.

Stevens, M. L. T. 2000. *Bioethics in America: Origins and cultural politics*. Baltimore: Johns Hopkins University Press.

Stolte, L., et al. 1979. Perinatale morbiditeit als maatstaf voor de verloskundige zorg (Perinatal morbidity as a criterion of obstetric care). *Nederlands Tijdschrift voor Geneeskunde* (Dutch Journal of Medicine) 123 (7): 228–31.

Strawson, Galen. 2004. Against narrativity. *Ratio* 17: 428–52.

Sultan, A. H., and S. L. Stanton. 1996. Preserving the pelvic floor and perineum during childbirth-elective cesarean? *British Journal of Obstetrics and Gynecology* 103: 731–34.

Taylor, Charles. 1989. *Sources of the self: The making of the modern identity*. Cambridge, Mass.: Harvard University Press.

Taylor, Charles. 1993. To follow a rule. In *Bourdieu: Critical perspectives*, ed. Craig Calhoun, Edward LiPuma, and Moishe Postone. Oxford: Polity Press.

Taylor, Charles. 2004. *Modern social imaginaries*. Durham, N.C.: Duke University Press.

Taylor, Telford. 1949. Trials of war criminals before the Nuremberg military tribunals under Control Council Law No. 10, October 1946–April 1949. http://www.humanitas-international.org/holocaust/drtrial4.htm.

Tervalon, M., and J. Murray-Garcia. 1998. Cultural humility versus cultural competence: A critical distinction in defining physician training outcomes in multicultural education. *Journal of Health Care for the Poor and Underserved* 9 (2): 117.

Tew, M. 1995. *Safer childbirth? A critical history of maternity care*. London: Chapman & Hall.

Thom, David H., A. Hall Mark, and L. Gregory Pawlson. 2004. Measuring patients' trust in physicians when assessing quality of care. *Health Affairs* 23 (4): 124–32.

Tooley, Michael. 1984. *Abortion and infanticide*. New York: Oxford University Press.

Traweek, Sharon. 1988. *Beam times and life times: The world of high energy physicists*. Cambridge, Mass.: Harvard University Press.

Tronto, Joan. 1993. *Moral boundaries: A political argument for an ethic of care*. New York: Routledge.

Tronto, Joan. 2006. Vicious circles of unequal care. In *Socializing care*, ed. Maurice Hamington. Lanham, Md.: Rowman & Littlefield.

Turner, Victor Witter. 1974. *Dramas, fields, and metaphors: Symbolic action in human society*. Ithaca: Cornell University Press.

Vacek, Edward Collins. 1994. *Love, human and divine: The heart of Christian ethics*. Washington, D.C.: Georgetown University Press.

Van den Berg-Helder, A. F. 1980. Neurological investigation and acid-base equilibrium in umbilical cord blood. Presented at the Symposium on Optimalization of Obstetrics, Free University, Amsterdam.

Van der Berg, Wibren. 1999. Two models of law and morality. *Associations* 3 (1): 61–82.

van Heijst, Annelies. 1995. *Longing for the fall*. Kampen and Louvain: Kok & Peeters.

van Heijst, Annelies. 2008. *Models of charitable care: Catholic nuns and children in their care, 1852–2002*. Leiden: Brill.

Veatch, Robert. 1973. Generalization of expertise: Scientific expertise and value judgments. *Hastings Center Studies* 1 (2): 29–40.

Veatch, Robert. 1997. Who should manage care? The case for patients. *Kennedy Institute of Ethics Journal* 7 (4): 391–401.

Velleman, J. David. 2000. The guise of the good. In *The possibility of practical reason*. Oxford: Oxford University Press.

Verkerk, Marian, et al. 2004. Enhancing reflection: An interpersonal exercise in ethics education. *Hastings Center Report* 34 (6): 31–38.

Verkerk, Marian, and Rudolf Hartoungh, eds. 2003. *Ethiek en palliatieve zorg* (Ethics and palliative care). Assen: Van Gorcum.

Waerness, Kari. 1990. Informal and formal care in old age: What is wrong with the new ideology in Scandinavia today? In *Gender and caring: Work and welfare in Britain and Scandinavia*, ed. C. Ungerson. London: Harvester, Wheatsheaf.

Walker, Lou Ann. 1986. *A loss for words: The story of deafness in a family*. New York: Harper & Row.

Walker, Margaret Urban. 1993. Keeping moral space open: New images of ethics consulting. *Hastings Center Report* 23: 33–40. Also in Walker 2003.

Walker, Margaret Urban. 1998. *Moral understandings: A feminist study in ethics*. New York: Routledge.

Walker, Margaret Urban. 2000. Naturalizing, normativity, and using what "we" know in ethics. *Moral epistemology naturalized, Canadian Journal of Philosophy*, suppl. 26: 75–101. Calgary: University of Calgary Press.

Walker, Margaret Urban. 2003. *Moral contexts*. Lanham, Md.: Rowman & Littlefield.

Walker, Margaret Urban. 2006. *Moral repair: Reconstructing moral relations after wrongdoing*. Cambridge: Cambridge University Press.

Walker, Margaret Urban. 2007. *Moral understandings: A feminist study in ethics*. 2nd ed. New York: Oxford University Press.

Wall, Barbara Mann. 2004. *Unlikely entrepreneurs: Catholic sisters and the hospital marketplace, 1865–1929*. Columbus: Ohio State University Press.

Watson, Gary. 2004. Free agency. In *Agency and answerability: Selected essays*. Oxford: Oxford University Press.

Welie, Jos V. M. 1998. *In the face of suffering: The philosophical-anthropological foundations of clinical ethics*. Omaha, Neb.: Creighton University Press.

Westburg, N. G., and M. H. Guindon. 2004. Hope, attitudes, emotions, and expectations in healthcare providers of services to patients infected with HIV. *AIDS and Behaviour* 8 (1): 1–8.

Williams, Patricia. 1991. *The alchemy of race and rights*. Cambridge, Mass.: Harvard University Press.

Williams, Susan H. 2005. Comment: Autonomy and the public-private distinction in bioethics and law. *Indiana Journal of Global Legal Studies* 12: 13.

Woese, Carl R. 2004. A new biology for a new century. *Microbiology and Molecular Biology Reviews* 68 (2): 173–86.

Xu, X., et al. 2007. The effects of medical liability on obstetric care supply in Michigan. *American Journal of Obstetrics and Gynecology* 198: 205e1–9.

Young, Iris. 1990. *Justice and the politics of difference*. Princeton, N.J.: Princeton University Press.

Zahn-Waxler, Carolyn, Marian Radke-Yarrow, Elizabeth Wagner, and Michael Chapman. 1992. Development of concern for others. *Developmental Psychology* 28 (1): 126–36.

Zuzelo, P. R. 2002. Gender and acute myocardial infarction symptoms. *MedSurg Nursing: The Journal of Adult Health* 11 (3): 126.

Index